European USSR

Coasts and Landing Beaches [NATO Invasion Options]

Joint Army Navy Intelligence Study

NIMBLE BOOKS LLC: THE AI LAB FOR BOOK-LOVERS

Humans and AI making books richer, more diverse, and more surprising.

Publishing Information

(c) 2023 Nimble Books LLC
ISBN: 9781934840535

AI-generated Keyword Phrases

Coastal areas;
Landing beaches;
Northern coast of Russia;
Karskaya Guba;
Port-Katon;
Geography;
Navigation instructions;
Potential hazards;
Mines;
Dangers to navigation;
Local weather patterns;
Currents;
Harsh climate;
Limited daylight;
Ice and snow cover;
NATO v. Russia scenarios;
Arctic region;

FRONT MATTER

Publishing Information ii
AI-generated Keyword Phrases ii
Abstracts iv
    TL;DR (one word) iv
    Explain It To Me Like I'm Five Years Old iv
    TL;DR (vanilla) iv
    Scientific Style iv
    Action Items v
Viewpoints vi
    Grounds for Dissent vi
    Red Team Critique vii
    MAGA Perspective viii
Page-by-Page Summaries x
Notable Passages xv

Abstracts

TL;DR (one word)

Arctic.

Explain It To Me Like I'm Five Years Old

This report is like a big book that tells us about the coastal areas and beaches in the northern part of Russia. It talks about the land and the water there, how to navigate through it, and things that could be dangerous. It also says that there are things like explosives in the water that can hurt boats, and that it's very important to know about the weather and water movements to stay safe. The report also says that the weather there is really cold and the sun is not out for very

TL;DR (vanilla)

This report provides detailed information on the coastal areas and landing beaches along the northern coast of Russia, including geography, navigation instructions, potential hazards, and presence of mines. It highlights the importance of understanding local weather patterns and currents for safe navigation. The report also mentions the harsh climate, limited daylight, and potential for ice and snow cover in the region. It notes the presence of Soviet military installations and potential for NATO and Russian naval activity. This information is valuable for military planning and operations in present-day scenarios involving NATO v. Russia in the Arctic region.

Scientific Style

This report provides a comprehensive overview of the coastal areas and landing beaches along the northern coast of Russia, specifically from Karskaya Guba to Port-Katon. It includes detailed information on the geography of the area, navigation instructions, and potential hazards that mariners may encounter. The report emphasizes the presence of mines and other dangers to navigation, as well as the importance of understanding local weather patterns and currents for safe navigation. It also highlights the challenging climate conditions, including limited daylight and the potential for ice and snow cover. The information presented in this report is particularly relevant to present-day NATO v. Russia scenarios, as it addresses navigation and transportation challenges in the Arctic region. Additionally, the report notes the presence of Soviet military installations and the potential for NATO and Russian naval activity in the area, making it a valuable resource for military planning and operations.

ACTION ITEMS

Conduct further research on the specific geography, weather patterns, and currents in the northern coast of Russia to gain a better understanding of the challenges and potential risks in the area.

Develop contingency plans for navigation and transportation in the Arctic region, taking into account the potential hazards mentioned in the report.

Consider the presence of Soviet military installations and the potential for NATO and Russian naval activity in the area when planning military operations.

Train personnel on the specific navigation instructions and potential hazards in the coastal areas and landing beaches along the northern coast of Russia.

Establish communication channels with local authorities and experts to gather updates.

VIEWPOINTS

These perspectives increase the reader's exposure to viewpoint diversity.

GROUNDS FOR DISSENT

Environmental Concerns: A member of the organization responsible for this document may have principled and substantive reasons to dissent from this report due to environmental concerns. The report mentions the potential hazards in the area, including mines and other dangers to navigation. It also highlights the harsh climate and limited daylight, as well as the potential for ice and snow cover. These factors indicate a fragile and vulnerable ecosystem that could be negatively impacted by increased naval activity and military planning. The dissenting member might argue that prioritizing military operations in this region could lead to detrimental environmental consequences, including pollution, disturbance of wildlife, and damage to delicate ecosystems.

Peaceful Cooperation: Another possible reason for dissent could be a principled belief in peaceful cooperation and diplomacy. The report emphasizes the presence of Soviet military installations and the potential for NATO and Russian naval activity in the area, making it a valuable reference for military planning and operations. However, a dissenting member might argue that instead of focusing on military strategies and potential conflicts, efforts should be directed towards fostering peaceful cooperation and collaborative approaches to address common challenges in the Arctic region. They might advocate for prioritizing diplomatic negotiations and multilateral agreements rather than military planning, with a focus on preserving the region's stability and promoting sustainable development.

Resource Allocation: A dissenting member might also have principled concerns about resource allocation. The report provides detailed information on the coastal areas and landing beaches along the northern coast of Russia, including geography, navigation instructions, and potential hazards. However, the dissenting member might argue that the resources and effort invested in gathering and compiling this information could be better allocated to addressing pressing societal issues such as poverty, education, or healthcare. They might question the prioritization of military planning and operations over social and humanitarian needs, advocating for a reallocation of resources towards areas that directly benefit the well-being of individuals and communities.

Ethical Considerations: Additionally, a dissenting member might have principled concerns regarding the ethical implications of military planning and operations in the Arctic region. The report acknowledges the potential for NATO and Russian naval activity, indicating a focus on potential conflicts or confrontations. The dissenting member might argue that engaging in military activities in this region could escalate tensions and increase the risk of conflict, potentially leading to human suffering and loss of life. They might advocate for alternative approaches that prioritize diplomatic negotiations, confidence-building measures, and international cooperation to maintain peace and stability in the region.

Red Team Critique

The document provides a comprehensive overview of the coastal areas and landing beaches along the northern coast of Russia. It effectively highlights various aspects such as geography, navigation instructions, potential hazards, and weather patterns. The inclusion of information regarding mines and other dangers is particularly noteworthy, as it emphasizes the importance of safe navigation in the area.

Furthermore, the report appropriately acknowledges the challenging climate and limited daylight in the region, as well as the potential for ice and snow cover. These factors pose significant obstacles to navigation and transportation, especially in Arctic conditions. This recognition is crucial for any operation or scenario involving NATO and Russia in the present day.

The document also mentions the presence of Soviet military installations, indicating the historical significance of the area. This knowledge is valuable for military planning and operations, as it provides an understanding of the strategic positioning and potential threats in the region. Additionally, the reference to possible NATO and Russian naval activity serves as a reminder of the ongoing tensions between these two entities.

Overall, the report provides extensive and relevant information that could be utilized for military purposes, specifically for NATO v. Russia scenarios. The emphasis on navigation and transportation challenges, coupled with the awareness of potential hazards and military activities in the area, makes this document an essential resource for military planning and operations in the region.

MAGA Perspective

This report is just another example of the biased and fear-mongering tactics employed by the liberal elite. They constantly try to paint Russia as a threat to justify their excessive military spending and interventionist foreign policies. The fact that they are focusing on coastal areas and landing beaches in Russia shows their relentless obsession with encircling and containing the country.

The mention of mines and other dangers to navigation is nothing more than a scare tactic. It is clear that these so-called hazards are exaggerated to further demonize Russia and justify the presence of NATO forces in the region. If there were truly such a significant danger, why hasn't there been any major incident involving civilian or commercial vessels? This report is just another attempt to create unnecessary tension between Russia and the West.

Furthermore, the emphasis on understanding local weather patterns and currents is just an excuse to divert attention from the real issues. Instead of wasting time and resources studying Arctic weather, we should be focusing on securing our own borders and addressing the pressing concerns of our citizens. The climate in this region is inhospitable - so what? We should not let it distract us from more important matters.

As for the mention of Soviet military installations, it only shows how out of touch the authors of this report are. The Soviet Union collapsed decades ago, and Russia has moved on. Instead of clinging to outdated Cold War rhetoric, we should be seeking ways to engage with Russia and forge diplomatic solutions. This constant demonization of Russia only serves to hinder progress and foster unnecessary hostility.

Lastly, the suggestion that this report is valuable for military planning and operations is deeply concerning. It reveals a dangerous mindset that perpetuates conflict rather than promoting peace and cooperation. We should be focusing on diplomacy and finding common ground with Russia, rather than planning for hypothetical military scenarios. This report is just another tool used by the globalist agenda to divide and conquer.

Page-by-Page Summaries

Coasts and landing beaches are the focus of this page, which likely provides information or analysis on these geographical features.
This page is a list of effective pages for Chapter IV of a document. It includes information on beach selection, navigation instructions, and coastal sectors.

IV-1 This page provides a summary of the coast and landing beaches, including their positions and classifications. It also mentions the Caspian coast of the European USSR.

IV-2 This page provides navigational instructions and information about anchorages, dangers to navigation, and coastal descriptions for a specific area. It includes maps, charts, and details about beach selection, beach gradients, and bottom slopes.

IV-3 The page provides information about the coastal sector from Karskaya Guba to the Norwegian boundary. It discusses the geography, climate, and navigation conditions in the area, including hazards and limitations. The sector is north of the Arctic Circle and is subject to harsh weather conditions and limited daylight. The page also mentions the presence of pack ice and the vegetation in the region.

IV-4 The page discusses the wind and current patterns in the Kara and Barents Seas, as well as the geography and features of the coastal areas. It mentions specific locations and provides information about beaches and sandbanks.

IV-5 The page describes the geographical features and hazards of the coast, beaches, and landing areas. It mentions narrow straits, mountainous coves, sandy shores, and rocky cliffs. It also discusses the navigational challenges, such as shoals, rocks, and narrow channels. The page provides details about specific locations and their characteristics.

IV-6 This page provides a description of the coastal areas from Khaypudyr-Say Gun to Pechora Bay, including various geographical features and landmarks. It also mentions the presence of isolated mountains and beaches, along with navigation conditions and information about landing beaches.

IV-7 The page appears to be a technical document discussing a topic related to food digestion and the use of specialized terminology.

IV-8 The page contains a figure labeled as "Figure 17-8" and includes approval and release information from the CIA.

IV-11 The page describes the physical characteristics of the Tian Koya bay, including its rolling hills, shallow inlets, and sandy shores. It also mentions hazards such as rocks and shoals, as well as the weather conditions in the area. The bay is located in a region with jolling terrain and plateaus.

IV-14 The page contains a map of European Russia at a scale of 1/2,000,000.

IV-15 The page provides a list of important considerations for writing about Southern literature.

IV-16 The page describes the geography and features of a river and coastline, including shifting sands, meadows, woods, marshes, sand hills, and shallow waters. There are also mentions of transportation routes, seaplane bases, and specific locations along the coast.

IV-18 The page describes a geographical area with improved roads, sandy terrain, canals, and various landmarks.

IV-19 The page discusses the approximate position and navigation routes near Onega, including channels extending to the Onega. It also mentions the importance of continental communication and provides coordinates for reference.

IV-20 The page describes the coastal area of the White Sea and Kandalaksha Bay, including the presence of hills, a railroad, and mineral deposits.

IV-22 This page appears to be a chart or map related to the location of a beach called Rose Ts. It mentions specific details such as the smooth shoreline, sandy beaches, and its offshore extent. The page also includes technical information, such as chart numbers and approvals.

IV-24 The page describes the coastline of Pope 120, located in the Northeast, with steep and rocky cliffs, offshore rocks, and tundra vegetation. It also mentions a landing field for airplanes and sandy beaches along the White Sea.

IV-27 The page describes the geography and features of the Kola Peninsula in Russia, including its coastline, rivers, bays, and towns. It also mentions the potential for cultivation and the presence of forests.

IV-30 The page describes the location and geography of a town called Amman, including its surrounding terrain, nearby bodies of water, and neighboring towns.

IV-31 The page discusses various topics, including beaches, conditions, and errors.

IV-34 The page contains a test that is being continued from Figure 1-50.

IV-35 This page provides information on the West Coastal Sector, specifically the area from Kryuserort to Stutthor. It mentions the formation of solid ice in the northern part of the sector during the early spring and describes the dangerous conditions for navigation in certain areas. The page also discusses the varying depths and bottom compositions of the sea in different parts of the sector.

IV-36 This page provides information on Petrograd Bay, including its width, depth, and surrounding landmarks. It also mentions the villages and transportation connections along the shore. The page highlights the importance of Leningrad as a commercial port and describes the canal system in the city. Additionally, it mentions the marshy nature of the Neva River and the presence of other rivers along the coast.

IV-37 This page provides a description of the coastal geography and features of various locations, including bays, rivers, and islands. It mentions specific landmarks, depths, and characteristics of the coastline.

IV-38 The page describes the coastal features of a specific area, including sand strips, rocky points, and occasional sandy and gravel beaches. The bottom near the shore consists of sand and sediment.

IV-40 The page contains various technical terms and symbols related to a subject that is not explicitly stated. It appears to be an approval or authorization for something.

IV-43 The page describes the geographical features of a coastal area, including rocky shores, sandy beaches, meadows, and woodlands. It also mentions the presence of lakes and various types of vegetation.

IV-45 The page provides information about the geographical location and shoreline trends of a specific area, including points of reference and charts.

IV-46 The page describes the geographical features of a coastal area, including cliffs, sandy beaches, bays, and depth measurements. It also mentions specific locations and their relevance for trade and harbors.

IV-47 The page provides information about various islands and shores, including Osmussaar, Suur Pakri, Viike Pakri, and Kelbu Lant. It mentions their sizes, geographical features, and anchorage options.

IV-52 The page provides a brief description of the geography and coastal features of various areas, including Ooty, Vormsi, and Saaremaa. It mentions the presence of reefs, shoals, and wooded hills, as well as specific points of interest such as Muha Vin and Taba. The page also highlights the depth and width of certain channels and bays, and notes the obstacles and hazards that may be encountered in the different coastal regions.

IV-53 The page provides information about the geography and navigation of the Daugava River, its entrance, and the Gulf of Riga. It mentions the depth, sandbars, harbors, and surrounding areas. The coastline is described as sandy with some wooded areas.

IV-54 The page contains a document titled "PTROVA EZR1084S" with various symbols and numbers.

IV-58 This page describes the geographical features and navigability of a specific area along the coast. It mentions sand deposits, orientation of files, and lack of protection. The page also provides information on the depth and navigability of the water in the area.

IV-59 The page discusses the topic of "goons" and includes various symbols and abbreviations. It appears to be related to intelligence or security matters.

IV-60 The page discusses the geography of a coastal area, specifically the presence of dunes, woods, and cultivated land. It mentions the proximity of roads and the types of vegetation found in different areas.

IV-64 The page describes the high and wooded shores of a coastal village called Ronen, located 9 miles north of Bl. It also mentions other nearby points and describes the appearance of the rocky and sandy shores in the area.

IV-65 The page provides information about the depths and positions of various locations near GroseSkaen, including the beach and coastline. It also mentions specific depths and directions for navigation.

IV-69 The page discusses the approval of something related to European Russia, with specific details and codes provided.

IV-70 The page discusses the South Coastal Sector, specifically the Danube river mouth to Port-Katon. It mentions charts and provides information about the geography, currents, and coastline of the area.

IV-72 This page appears to contain information about various locations and their geographical features, including entrances, sandy spits, and beach areas.

IV-73 The page contains a description of the town of Odessa and its surroundings, including nearby bodies of water and landmarks.

IV-74   The page provides information about the geographical location and features of a specific area, including rivers, ports, beaches, and lagoons.
IV-77   The page describes the geographical features and location of a beach in eastern Crimea, including its length, orientation, and proximity to a bay.
IV-80   The page describes the geography and navigation of Sevastopol harbor, including the direction in which the coast trends, the rivers that flow into the sea, and the presence of sunken rocks. It also mentions the entrance to the harbor and provides some depth measurements.
IV-81   The page provides a brief description of beaches in the subsector 45B, including locations such as Mys Khersonesskiy and Simferopol.
IV-83   The page describes the southern coast of Crimea, highlighting its gently descending mountain slopes and numerous bays. It also mentions the dry brook basins in summer and the westward current of the Black Sea.
IV-85   The page discusses the importance of railroad connections, specifically the need to connect a road with the coastal terrain at Khrebet Yaya.
IV-86   The page describes partially sheltered anchorage in a small bay between Mys 1's and Mys Chauda. It provides details about the location, nearby rocks, and coastal features.
IV-87   The page provides information about various beaches and their geographical locations, including details about specific features and characteristics.
IV-94   The page provides information about the geography and features of the Kerch Strait and the surrounding areas, including the salt marshes, narrow channels, and sandy beaches. It also mentions the towns of Kerch and Feodosiya, as well as the industrial and transportation activities in the region.
IV-95   The page contains a mixture of symbols, letters, and numbers with no discernible meaning or purpose.
IV-96   The page describes the geographical features and locations along the coast of the River Kosa, including villages, beaches, cliffs, and spits. It also mentions the town of Osipenko and the harbor connected to it.
IV-97   The page provides information about the town of Taganrog, its location, geography, and transportation connections. It mentions the river Don, the gulf, and the various roads and railways that connect the town to other cities. The page also briefly discusses the beaches in the area and their suitability for navigation.
IV-99   The page discusses various topics including correks, NL, BE, and HH. It mentions different numbers and percentages, as well as the concepts of wit, mobo, and Boma. There are also references to Pood, Vom, and a contact email address.
IV-100 The page discusses principal sources related to a study, including German and French materials. It mentions the value of coastal pilots and hydrographic data, as well as the abundance of information in Sector 42.
IV-101 The page contains a list of references related to various topics, including geography, cartography, weather, and naval command.
IV-110 The page discusses European terrain.
IV-111 The page discusses the European USSF South Coastal Sector Terrain.
IV-112 The page discusses the Conran ST chair by DNeE3, highlighting its design and features.

IV-113 The page discusses European coastal divisions and beach areas.
IV-116 The page contains a document with the title "CIARDPTS.01144A0002000100045" and the reference number "2003105114".

Notable Passages

"COASTS AND LANDING BEACHES"
"INTRODUCTION This chapter is based upon material available in Washington, D.C. on 1 May 1944.

IV-1 "The positions of coastal sectors and subsectors and the essential location of beaches are shown in Figure 1. General summary (page 1v-1) provides a summary of coasts and landing beaches (pages 19-11 to 1-11)."

IV-2 "Coastal descriptions follow the same order as the beach. Such commonly known terms as Kola Peninsula, Barents Sea, and Gulf of Bothnia often denote only an enlarged bay, inlet."

IV-5 "The many large rivers provide excellent drainage and are a primary source of the lumber which is by far the most important. The distance, however, between sector soil add somewhat to trafficability. Reindeer and sleds extend to about 300 miles. The large and Norn Zemin extends to 500 miles northward of the Barents and Kars Seas. With the exception of the White Sea coast, the entire sector lies north of the Arctic Circle and is subjected to Arctic conditions. The annual temperature average is below freezing for most of this sector. Winter lasts from November to March, spring until May, summer from June to August, and autumn from September to October. The sun does not rise between December and January, and there is a period of continuous darkness. Navigation is therefore limited to periods of daylight between May and August. The polar day lasts for about 15 days in June, with the midnight sun occurring between April and September."

IV-7 "The port is a narrow strait on the eastern coast of Nova Zemlya. It is 11 miles wide with an excellent channel. However, fog often prevails during the summer months, which poses a risk for navigation. Shoals and rocks extend far off the shores. The mountainous terrain along the northern half of the southern sandbar is covered with thick forests. Elevations of 3000 feet can be found in the mountainous portion, which meets the mountains about 30 miles inland. The coastal terrain along the southern half of the southern sandbar is low and sandy, with wide sandy beaches. The shores are lined with many bays, islands, rocks, and shoals. The entrance ranges with many beacons and is reached by cliffs. The port is reported to have a depth of 60 yards and is navigable without hazards. The highest point in the area rises 10,300 feet along the shores."

IV-8 An isolated mountain reaching 90 feet in elevation is the Traps, which extends outward to the Khrebet Pay-Khoy. Pechorskaya Guba (Pechora Bay) extends 10 miles inland and 15 miles west. It shallows and has a sandbar covered by 10 feet of water at high tide. The access to the bay is through the Pechora River, as well as an entrance point to Pechorskaya

Guba (Pechora Bay). The bay is surrounded by sandy beaches extending 20 miles eastward. The Southeastern Barents Sea experiences severe storms from October to August, with navigation being possible in the southern part throughout the year. The main landing beaches are located in subsector 41A, including the mainland beaches and islands such as Vaygach and Novaya Zemlya. The terrain of these areas consists of ridges with ponds and bogs in between, particularly when the ground is icy and snowy.

IV-13 "The western coast, from the mouth of the Pechora River to Mys Kanin Nos, is a series of sandy beaches, shallow inlets, and river mouths. The western coast is generally of rolling hills, in few places exceeding 650 feet in elevation. The eastern coast, from Mys Kanin Nos to Svyatoy Nos, is steep and rocky, with drying sandbanks and a ridge that reaches almost to the point. The highest point on the island is a coneshaped hill, about 300 feet high. The winters in this region are severe, with pack ice forming in October and lasting until June. The warm river waters in the spring usually melt the ice and clear the coast. The coastline extends along the valley of the Mezen River, gradually extending westward toward its limit north of Mys Kanin Nos. The only road in the area is located on Mezenskays Guba."

IV-18 "The river is important as a transportation route for Hime from the x. of the cape."

IV-25 "Original Approved For Release 20030814 GIA ROPTB0114AOHGZ00100085"

IV-26 "Offshore rocks exist for a short distance seaward and tundra type vegetation grows on the rock slopes. There are many hills, with areas of grassy and shrubby vegetation showing on the slopes. The beaches along the shores of the White Sea vary considerably. Along the east shore, the beaches are most extensive; they are backed rather generally with sand and clay cliffs. Beaches of beach areas (33) to (37) along the west shore are more narrow, short, and sandy. Some are indented and rocky. The coastline extends through the coastal zone."

IV-38 "The city of Leningrad is one of the principal commercial ports of the USSR, has telegraph and railroad communications with all parts of Europe. Several operational airfields are located at and near Leningrad. The period of heavy winds, which occur in the spring and fall, as well as the effect of backwash during the period of high water, makes navigation on the Neva River uncertain whether at normal water level or at high water."

IV-47 "About mid-way between these two points the shore trends more to the northwestward for nearly 8 miles to Rohneem, the northernmost area of the Vimsi peninsula."

IV-48 "Near the middle there is a depth 'of 11 fathoms over sand."

IV-54 "The principal northern approach to the ... island is surrounded by scattered reefs and shoal water. The mainland coast from Rooslepa for 53 miles southward to Noarooss peninsula is low and rocky with scattered stretches of sand. The interior is flat and marshy, rising gradually to a height of 8 feet on the northeastern coast. The northwestern coast is lower and less wooded. The shoreline between the point of Matsa Lan and Pika

Nina, on the thickly wooded Kopu Polsar peninsula, is 23 feet high while the southwestern coast is low and slightly above sea level. The land is entirely surrounded by reefs and shoal waters extending between it and Muna, with a depth of 1 to 7 miles seaward. There is a landing strip at Dina on the southeastern coast."

IV 60 "The files along this coast are oriented diagonally to the sea. Rail lines run parallel to the coast for about 120 miles to the north and south. The coastline is irregular, with numerous small bays and coves which greatly hinder movement. The shoreline consists mostly of sand, which varies in composition from fine to coarse. Over to the east, 31 miles offshore, there is a chain of small islands which provide some protection from the open sea. The water depth along this coast tends to be shallow, with depths ranging from 3 to 15 feet. The area is entirely unprotected and is not favorable for navigation. There are many rocks and shoals which pose a

IV-66 "From this point the coast extends southward for 10 miles to Baklokhaloeiy Les, and around the peninsula from there to Mya Brywsterot and Vantamyy Dac Sen. Northward of the tors, the shores of the bay are scenic and high with a yellowish appearance. Rocky shoals near Bay are sandy highs lined by trees on the shore. The coastal village about 9 miles northward of Bl (105) and (100), Foon, 10:18 to 19:50, is Ronen. Between Mya Brywsterot and Vantamyy Dac Sen, the bay, Zan isnkhausen (formerly Palmiken) (BA. Chars 23), the shore consists of rocky cliffs. Near Bay, sandy beaches extend several miles offshore from the shore."

IV-72 "In addition, the waters off the coast are almost constantly affected by strong currents flowing out of the Sea of Azov and the mouths of the Danube River, making them unsuitable for anything other than small local craft. The coastline is characterized by continuous cliffs, with barely visible land in many places along the outer edge of the flat. A pine forest can be found about 5.5 miles northwestward from the shore. The coastline is a continuous cliff, reaching heights of about 130 feet. The waters off the coast experience general counterclockwise current flows, with variations due to wind. The island of Ostrov Zmeinyy (Fidonisi, or Zmeini) is situated about 31 miles southeast of Gor VeSmt, and it stands at a height of approximately 106 feet. The area encounters strong winds and rough seas, making navigation challenging."

IV-74 "Looking inwards, chasers could extend to other important inland cities. Steamship companies offer easy transportation to these areas."

IV-82 "From Mys Lukull the coast trends south-southwestward, and is pierced by the valleys of the Kacha (Kagas) and Belbek rivers which flow into the sea southward of Lukull Bluff. Sevastopol harbor is entered between Konstantinovka Point on the north and Alupka Point on the south, about 6 miles apart. The depth at the entrance is about 30 meters, decreasing to 18 meters inside the harbor. The harbor is sheltered from all winds except those from the south and southeast. The bottom is sandy and rocky, with depths of 2 to 28 meters. Lacking cast-up shoals, it affords good anchorage for vessels of any size."

IV-83 "The beaches of subsector 45 B are described briefly in this paragraph. Some of the notable features include the northern side of Mys

Khersonesskly (Cape Khersonyes) and its southern side along the southwestern coast. The description provides insight into the geographical location and characteristics of these beaches."

IV-98 "Between the mouths of these rivers the coast is fronted by a beach of fine sand fringed by a bank with small patches with depths from 10 to 17 feet extending 0.5 mile offshore."

IV-102 "Sector 42 were most plentiful. They were of considerable value in the descriptions where available, with spring tides and neap tides being mentioned. Coastal pilots and hydrographic charts were of relatively little value. Aerial photographs and captured material were more informative. The study was adequate."

JANIS 40
CHAPTER IV

JOINT ARMY-NAVY INTELLIGENCE STUDY

EUROPEAN U.S.S.R.

COASTS AND LANDING BEACHES

This document contains information affecting the national defense of the United States within the meaning of the Espionage Act, 50 U.S.C., 31 and 32, as amended. Its transmission or the revelation of its contents in any manner to an unauthorized person is prohibited by law.

LIST OF EFFECTIVE PAGES, CHAPTER IV

Subject Matter	Change in Effect	Page Numbers
Cover Page	Original	unnumbered
List of Effective Pages and Table of Contents, Chapter IV (inside front cover)	Original	unnumbered
Text	Original	pp. IV-1 and IV-2
Figure (insert, reverse blank)	Original	Figure IV-1
Text and Figures	Original	pp. IV-3 to IV-8
Figure (insert, reverse blank)	Original	Figure IV-8
Text	Original	pp. IV-9 and IV-10
Figure (insert, reverse blank)	Original	Figure IV-9
Text and Figures	Original	pp. IV-11 to IV-30
Figure (insert, reverse blank)	Original	Figure IV-30
Text and Figures	Original	pp. IV-31 to IV-44
Figure (insert, reverse blank)	Original	Figure IV-56
Text and Figures	Original	pp. IV-45 to IV-60
Figure (insert, reverse blank)	Original	Figure IV-81
Text and Figures	Original	pp. IV-61 to IV-68
Figure (insert, reverse blank)	Original	Figure IV-89
Text and Figures	Original	pp. IV-69 to IV-80
Figure (insert, reverse blank)	Original	Figure IV-112
Text and Figures	Original	pp. IV-81 to IV-88
Figures (inserts, reverse sides blank)	Original	Legend for Figures IV-116 to IV-118; Figures IV-116 to IV-119
Imprint (inside back cover, reverse blank)	Original	unnumbered

TABLE OF CONTENTS

Note: This chapter is based upon material available in Washington, D. C., on 1 May 1947.

40. INTRODUCTION . . . . IV- 1	A. Mys Kryuserort (Ristniemi) to Rooslepa . IV - 31
A. General Summary . . . . IV- 1	(1) Coast . . . . IV - 31
B. Figures . . . . IV- 1	(2) Landing beaches . . . . IV - 41
C. Organization of text . . . . IV- 2	B. Rooslepa to Oviši . . . . IV - 45
D. Beach selection and description . . . . IV- 2	(1) Coast . . . . IV - 45
(1) Basis for beach selection . . . . IV- 2	(2) Landing beaches . . . . IV - 46
(2) Reliability of beach descriptions . . IV- 2	C. Oviši to Klaipėda (Memel) . . . . . IV - 51
(3) Bottom gradient . . . . IV- 2	(1) Coast . . . . IV - 51
E. Navigational instructions . . . . . . IV- 2	(2) Landing beaches . . . . IV - 53
F. Nautical and statute miles . . . . . . IV- 2	D. Klaipėda (Memel) to Sztutowo (Stutthof) IV - 55
G. Glossary . . . . IV- 2	(1) Coast . . . . IV - 55
41. NORTH COASTAL SECTOR—KARSKAYA GUBA TO NORWEGIAN BOUNDARY . IV- 3	(2) Landing beaches . . . . IV - 58
	43. SOUTH COASTAL SECTOR—DANUBE RIVER MOUTH TO PORT-KATON . . . IV - 61
A. Karskaya Guba to Mys Russkiy Zavorot . IV- 4	A. Danube river mouth to Mys Kartkazak . IV - 61
(1) Coast . . . . IV- 4	(1) Coast . . . . IV - 61
(2) Landing beaches . . . . IV- 6	(2) Landing beaches . . . . IV - 65
B. Mys Russkiy Zavorot to Mys Kanin Nos . IV- 9	B. Mys Kartkazak (Kartkazak Point) to Sevastopol' . . . . IV - 68
(1) Coast . . . . IV- 9	(1) Coast . . . . IV - 68
(2) Landing beaches . . . . IV- 9	(2) Landing beaches . . . . IV - 70
C. Mys Kanin Nos to Mys Svyatoy Nos . . IV - 11	C. Sevastopol' to Mys Takil' . . . . . . IV - 72
(1) Coast . . . . IV - 11	(1) Coast . . . . IV - 72
(2) Landing beaches . . . . IV - 20	(2) Landing beaches . . . . IV - 76
D. Mys Svyatoy Nos to the Norwegian Boundary . . . . IV - 23	D. Mys Takil' to Port-Katon . . . . . . IV - 81
(1) Coast . . . . IV - 23	(1) Coast . . . . IV - 81
(2) Landing beaches . . . . IV - 27	(2) Landing beaches . . . . IV - 84
42. WEST COASTAL SECTOR—MYS KRYUSERORT (RISTNIEMI) TO SZTUTOWO (STUTTHOF) . . . . IV - 31	44. PRINCIPAL SOURCES . . . . IV - 87
	A. Evaluation . . . . IV - 87
	B. List of References—Coasts . . . . . IV - 87
	C. List of References—Landing beaches . . IV - 88

Chapter IV

COASTS AND LANDING BEACHES

*Prepared under supervision of Office of Naval Intelligence by
Strategic Studies Section, Office of Naval Intelligence;
and by Beach Erosion Board, Corps of Engineers*

40. INTRODUCTION

A. General summary (TABLE IV-1)

B. Figures

The positions of coastal sectors and subsectors and the general location of beaches are shown on FIGURE IV-119.

TABLE IV-1

SUMMARY OF COASTS AND LANDING BEACHES (FIGURES IV-116 to IV-119)

Sector	Sea approach	Coastal terrain	Beaches
41. North Coast: Arctic and White Sea Coasts (Karskaya Guba to the Norwegian Boundary)	E of White Sea (Beloye More), projecting shoals, rocky areas, and obstructed by ice except during August and September. Sandbanks in Gorlo. Many offshore islands in W part of White Sea. Murmanskiy Bereg ice free year around; clear approaches with great depths and nearshore rocks.	Low, mildly undulating marshy tundra W to White Sea. SE and S coast of White Sea moderately high, undulating and forested. W coast of White Sea low, with many lakes and marshes; forested. Kola Peninsula (Kol'skiy Poluostrov) and westward along Murman Coast (Murmanskiy Bereg), high bare granite hills. Frozen subsoil except in White Sea area.	Arctic coast: rock, pebbles, sand and mud, fronted by shoals and flat bottom slopes, and backed by tundra to E; short beaches in shallow bays along steep indented coast to W; exits either unknown or limited to trails or local roads. White Sea beach areas, sand and pebbles fronted by shoals, rocks, and islets. Shore approaches open. Roads inland.
42. West Coast: Coasts of Gulf of Finland, Gulf of Riga and the Baltic Mys Kryuserort (Ristniemi) to Sztutowo (Stutthoff)	S shore Gulf of Finland obstructed by islets, rocky shoals, and reef patches. Gulf of Riga obstructed by islands with shallow sounds between, coast fringed by shallow flats extending 1.5 to 3.5 miles offshore. Coast of open Baltic Sea clear.	N shore Gulf of Finland high and wooded. Broad coastal plain from Leningrad W to Ledipaa Nina. N coast of Estonian SSR, rocky platform with precipitous cliffs and numerous indentations. W coast low and rocky to Gulf of Riga. Low and flat coast around Gulf of Riga. Kolkasrags to Klaipėda low and sandy backed by dune barrier. Klaipėda to Sztutowo low sandspits separated by Zamland Peninsula.	Gulf of Riga and Baltic, almost continuous sandy beaches, backed by dunes or low bluff, with roads inland. Elsewhere, short beaches of sand, pebbles, rock, or mud; approach obstructed by rocks. Exits into towns or roads.
43. South Coast: North coasts of Black Sea and Sea of Azov (Danube river mouth to Port-Katon)	Danube, Dniester, Dnepr, and Donets deltas and E half of Karkinitskiy Zaliv fronted by extensive shallow flats. S coast of Crimea clear, with 5-fathom line close inshore. Kerch Strait (Kerchenskiy Proliv) obstructed by shoals and banks. N coast of Sea of Azov obstructed by many spits projecting SW and bordered by shallows.	Low coastal plain from marshy Danube Delta to Dniestrovskiy Liman. N coast of Black Sea moderately high and steep. From Dnepr delta S to Kalamitskiy Zaliv, coast low and flat except for cliffs at Mys Tarkhankut. Steep clay and rock cliffs S to Mys Khersonesskiy. Precipitous cliffs backed by mountains along S shore of Crimea. E and N shores of Kerchenskiy Poluostrov, high, backed by hills. W shore Sea of Azov, low, sandy spit. N coast Sea of Azov, high and cliffy and backed by steppes. Don delta low and marshy. SW to Port-Katon terraced clay cliffs intersected by ravines.	Generally extensive sand beaches, many along narrow spits, except S coast Crimea, where short sand or cobble pocket beaches in coves or breaks in steep rocky coast.

Note: The Caspian coast of European USSR is covered in JANIS 41.

Original

Beaches are shown by heavy purple bands along the appropriate section of the coast; purple dots represent small beach areas. FIGURES IV-116 to IV-118 show by means of patterns the coastal terrain types, vegetation, and trafficability.

PLANS 12 to 19 present in greater detail the distribution of landing beaches or landing areas. All landing beaches designated by encircled numbers on these PLANS are described briefly in tables in the text. Beach areas are numbered clockwise around the shores of each body of water involved, from Karskaya Guba to Port-Katon.

The text description of each subsector of the coast is accompanied by annotated strip maps reproduced from B.A. Chart 2962 and from A.M.S. maps, varying in scale from 1:300,000 to 1:1,000,000. Each map bears a number and letter corresponding to the subsector shown. Each sector is subdivided into four subsectors, lettered from A to D. Beach areas are numbered in circles on illustrations and strip maps, but in the text and tables are printed in italic type enclosed in parentheses.

C. Organization of text

Coastal descriptions follow the same order as the beach numbering, beginning at Karskaya Guba and ending at Port-Katon. For each coastal sector the chapter presents a general characterization of the coasts, winds, ocean currents, ice conditions, and landing beaches; and for each subsector a more localized and detailed description, in the following order:

1) Coast
   Brief description of offshore approaches, the coast proper, and the terrain immediately inland.
2) Landing beaches
   Tabulated descriptions of beaches within the subsector, usually preceded by a brief introduction characterizing prevailing types of beaches in the subsector. In the tables, figures giving the width of beach and gradient of beach often denote only an order of magnitude; such approximations are necessary for areas where good source materials are lacking.

D. Beach selection and description

(1) Basis for beach selection

Beaches were chosen on the basis of their physical characteristics alone, and not because of proximity to important objectives or relative quality of the beaches in a given area.

(2) Reliability of beach descriptions

The reliability of each beach description is stated in the heading relative to the following scale:

EXCELLENT—Aerial coverage available; excellent literature; good source maps, few or no factual conflicts.
FAIR—No aerial coverage; fair to good literature; fair to good source maps.
POOR—No aerial coverage; literature poor; source maps indifferent.

In all beach descriptions some interpretation is necessary. With higher reliability ratings this generally involves only minor beach features, but in the lower ratings the facts are often so meager that interpretation involves some of the major beach features as well. This interpretation is in all instances made in accordance with established principles of beach mechanics.

(3) Bottom gradient

In describing beach gradients and bottom slopes within the 30-foot depth off landing beaches the following standard descriptive terms are used:

STANDARD TERM FOR SLOPE	GRADIENT	DISTANCE FROM SHORE TO 30-FOOT DEPTH
Steep	Greater than 1 on 15	Less than 450 feet
Moderate	1 on 16 to 1 on 30	450 feet to 900 feet
Gentle	1 on 31 to 1 on 60	900 feet to 1,800 feet
Mild	1 on 61 to 1 on 120	1,800 feet to 3,600 feet
Flat	Smaller than 1 on 120	Greater than 3,600 feet

E. Navigational instructions

For sailing directions and information on approaches, anchorages, and dangers to navigation the reader should consult the Arctic Pilot, Vol. I; Baltic Pilot, Vols. I and III; Black Sea Pilot, with latest supplements; and U.S.H.O. and British Admiralty Charts of the coastal regions.

Ports, naval facilities, and anchorages are described in detail in Chapter VI; air facilities in Chapter XII.

F. Nautical and statute miles

Under the heading "Coast," distances across water and distances measured in a direct line between points on the coast are in *nautical* miles.

In descriptions of landing beaches, all mileage is given in *statute* miles.

G. Glossary

Terms describing natural features have been left in the transliterated Russian form, with the exception of such commonly known terms as Kola Peninsula, Barents Sea, White Sea, and Gulf of Riga. Alternate names are provided in parentheses where believed useful for map identification. English equivalents of the more common terms are:

RUSSIAN	ENGLISH
Bereg	coast
Bol'shoy	great, large
Gora	mountain
Guba	bay, inlet
Krasnyy	red
Liman	estuary
Malyy	little, small
Mys	cape, point
More	sea
Navolok	headland
Nos	cape, headland
Novyy	new
Obryv	bluff
Ostrov	island
Ozerko	salt water lake with a narrow channel leading to the sea; also, little lake
Peschanyy	sandy
Poluostrov	peninsula
Proliv	strait
Shar	strait
Staryy	old
Strelka	sandspit
Vorota	gate, passage
Zaliv	bay, gulf
Zemlya	land

FINNISH	ENGLISH
Niemimaa	peninsula
Saari	island

RUMANIAN	ENGLISH
Bratu	(the) branch, arm
Golful	(the) gulf
Gura	(the) mouth
Insula	(the) island
Liman	harbor
Ostrovu	(the) island
Sfantul	(the) saint
Vechiu	old

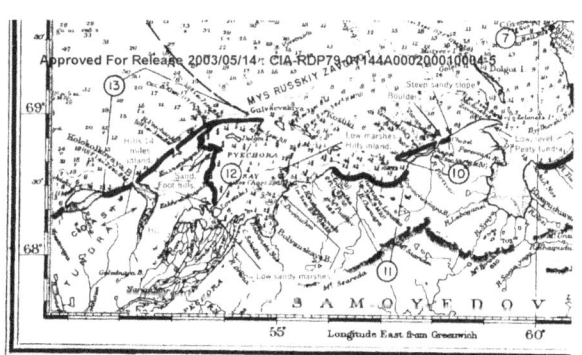
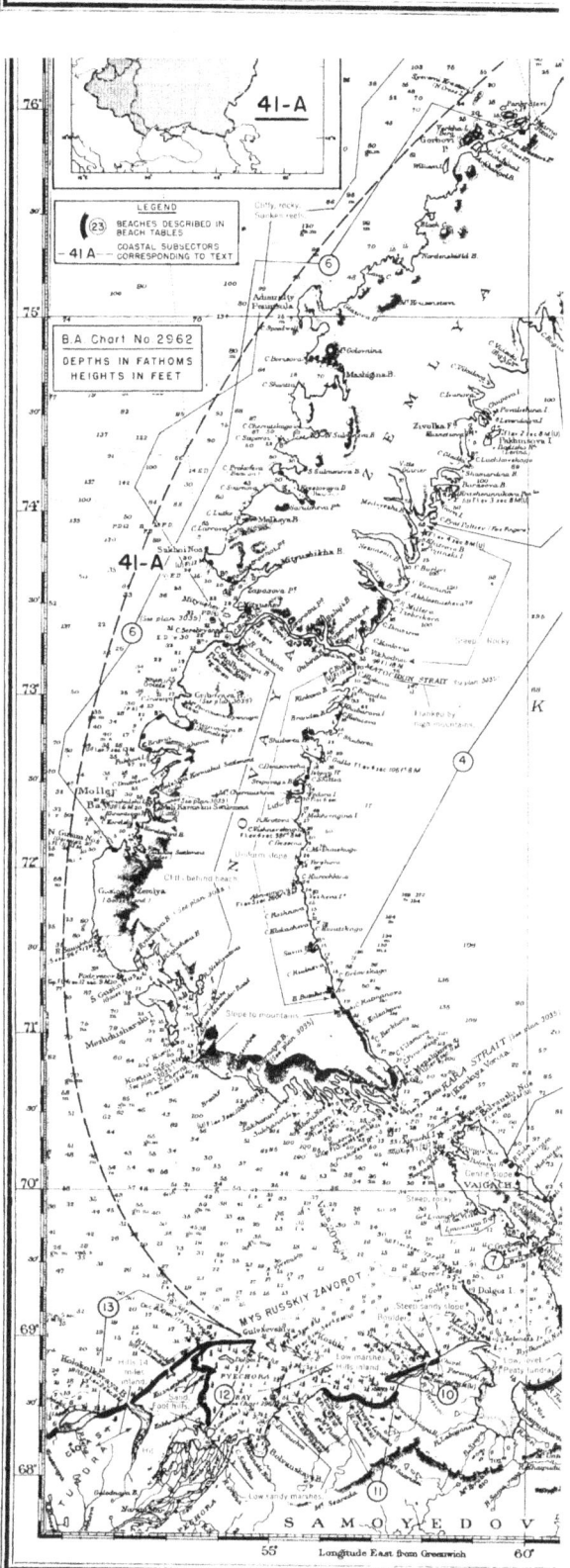

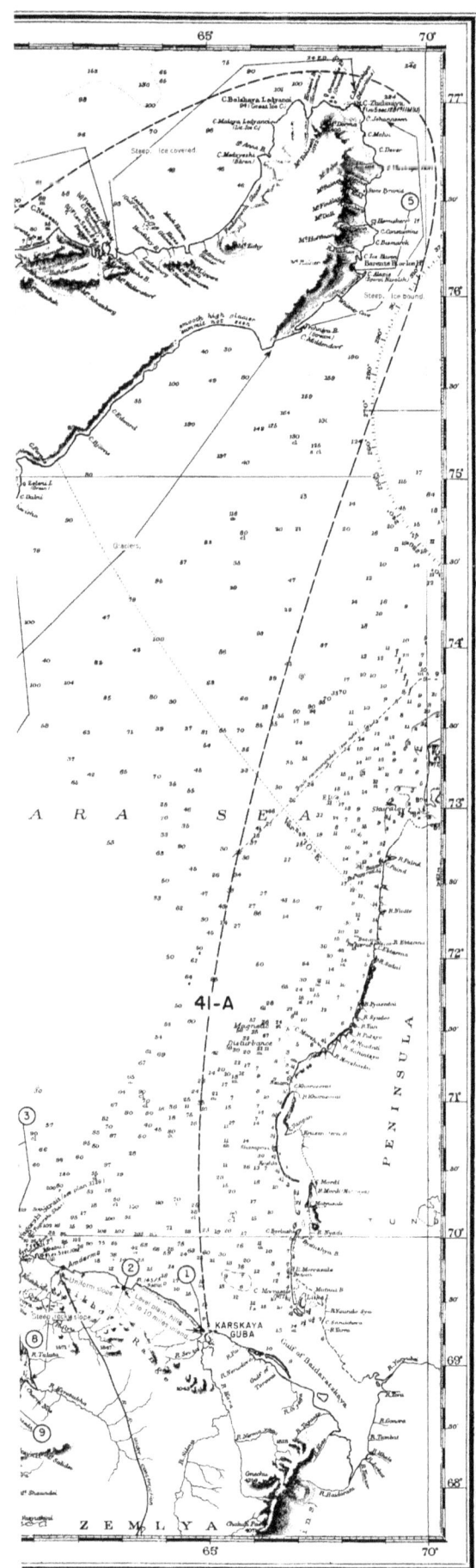

LATVIAN	ENGLISH
Krasts	shore
Osta	harbor
Rietumi	west
Sala	island
Upe	river
Veca	old

ESTONIAN	ENGLISH
Kari	reef
Laht	gulf, bay
Madalik	shoal
Neem	point
Poolsaar	peninsula
Saar	island
Sadam	harbor

41. NORTH COASTAL SECTOR— KARSKAYA GUBA TO NORWEGIAN BOUNDARY

(69°20′N, 65°E; 69°47′N, 30°50′E) (PLANS 12 and 13; FIGURES IV-116 and IV-119; U.S.H.O. Chart 6602; B.A. Charts 2282 and 2962; A.M.S. Map Northern Europe, scale 1:4,-000,000, G.S.G.S. No. 2957, Key No. 100234)

The north coastal sector of European USSR exceeds 2,200 statute miles in length, about 100 miles of which lies on the Kara Sea (Karskoye More), over 1,000 miles on the White Sea (Beloye More), and the remainder on the Barents Sea. The distance, however, between sector limits is only 800 miles. The large island Novaya Zemlya extends about 500 miles northward of the mainland and has over 1,000 statute miles of coast bordering on the Barents and Kara Seas.

With the exception of the White Sea coast, the entire sector lies north of the Arctic Circle and is subjected to conditions peculiar to Arctic regions: the polar day, ice, frozen soil, and Arctic vegetation. Above the Arctic Circle winter lasts from 1 November to 1 March, spring until 15 July, summer to 15 September, and autumn to 1 November. The sun does not rise between 27 December and 17 January, and there is sufficient light for reading only within one hour of noon. From 28 March to 1 May, as the daylight period lengthens, there are only four hours of darkness, between 2200 and 0200. This is followed by a period of all-night twilight until 26 May, after which the sun remains above the horizon until 18 July. All-night twilight again exists until 15 September, but observations of the stars cannot be made until after August. The nights lengthen after 15 September, until the above-mentioned conditions of 27 December prevail. Celestial navigation is therefore limited to observations of the sun, between 1 May and 30 August. The polar day at Arkhangel'sk typifies conditions in the White Sea. There the midsummer day is 22 hours in length. A ruddy glow remains in the sky at midnight between 1 April and 30 August. At the end of December there are only three hours of daylight each day.

Barren tundra, peculiar to the Arctic, characterizes the terrain. Vegetation is limited to moss, grass, bushes, and stunted trees covered with lichens. The soil is extremely humic in nature and there are considerable peat deposits. Two feet below the surface the subsoil is permanently frozen, enhancing trafficability and limiting the depths of the extensive marshes of the region. Coniferous forests extend inland, beginning at distances of 50 to 100 miles from the coast. They are separated from the tundra by a belt of dwarfed trees and forest islands which represent the gradual change from tundra to forest. The forests approach the coasts of the White Sea and are the source of the lumber which is by far the most important resource of the area. Geologically the area consists of quarternary deposits of glacial and marine origin. Only in the Ural and Timanskiy ridges do folded, older basement rocks appear; while igneous rocks appear in the granite hills of Kol'skiy Poluostrov.

The many large rivers provide excellent drainage. Navigable for many miles inland, they also serve as primary communication routes. Shifting sandbanks in river mouths bar navigation by other than small boats. Channels have been dredged through the mouths of several rivers flowing into the White Sea. Elsewhere high water must be awaited to assist passage. Kol'skiy Zaliv, the largest and most important gulf on the Murman Coast (Murmanskiy Bereg), is an exception to this rule as far up as the mouth of the Kola, 28 miles inland.

Roads in this sector are limited to winter roads and unimproved roads, except along the southern and western shores of the White Sea, where there are also railroads. Murmansk, 26 miles inside Kol'skiy Zaliv, is served by rail, but good roads in the vicinity are local. A spur of the Pechora railroad, which lies far southward of the coast, is reported as under construction to Amderma, on the Kara Sea. Soil trafficability is generally considered poor throughout the coastal area. Warm weather reduces the sandy humus tundra areas to shallow marshes in the summer, but good drainage and the frozen subsoil add somewhat to trafficability. Reindeer and sleds are the native mode of transportation, with or without snow cover on the ground. The terrain around the White Sea is fair for trafficability and bears the normal obstacles of forests, marshy localities, hills, and some rocky areas.

Ice forms a hazard to navigation or landing throughout most of this sector. The annual temperature average is below freezing, the coldest months being January and February, while July is the warmest. From March to April air temperatures rise rapidly. Variations in ice conditions, generally consistent with seasonal variations, are also influenced by the North Atlantic current, which flows southeastward from the coasts of Norway along the Murman coast and keeps the southwestern part of Barents Sea open to navigation the entire year. This current continues eastward and reduces the period of ice coverage along the entire western coast of Novaya Zemlya. Effects of the current on ice conditions in the White and Kara Seas, however, are negligible. Ice is present in the White Sea from about November until May, moving toward the mouth about that time and remaining longest along the shore at the mouth. The White Sea is closed to navigation between 15 December and 15 May. Parts of the sea do not always freeze solidly, but shore ice extends seaward for 3 to 5 miles and lies in narrow channels between islands or shoals. Spring thaws make the White Sea particularly hazardous with drifting ice, which moves into the Barents Sea. Pack ice seldom enters the coastal waters west of Mys Kanin Nos, but in the waters to the east ice is present from late fall until late June or July, and the area is unnavigable from January until May. There is open sea to Ostrov Kolguyev by 15 June and Novaya Zemlya may be reached early in July. Although Proliv Karskiye Vorota (Kara Strait) does not freeze solidly except during especially severe winters, the greater part of the Kara Sea is covered with ice throughout the year. The location of open water in the Kara Sea, even during the navigation seasons, varies widely, depending upon the force and direction of the wind and current. August and September are the best months for navigation. During this period icebergs may be present off the northeast coast of Novaya Zemlya. In October the ice commences its growth westward to attain again its January limit. Land ice forms in the bays and inlets along the entire coastal sector. Even Kol'skiy Zaliv, on the Murman Coast, may freeze for several days during the winter, but is easily opened by ice breakers. Spring thaws bring warmer water from rivers and streams, pushing land ice seaward, where it becomes an added hazard to navigation.

Prevailing winds are generally onshore during the summer months from about May to September and offshore during the winter months, but vary considerably from place to place as the configuration of the coast changes. Through the narrow throat of the White Sea and in narrow channels between islands and the mainland, the winds generally blow with the direction of the channel. Land and sea breezes are predominant along some sections in the inner parts of the White Sea during summer months.

The flood tidal current flows eastward along the shore of the Barents Sea as far as Proliv Yugorskiy Shar (Yugorski Strait), and south and southwest into the White Sea. The flood current from the Kara Sea usually sets westward through Proliv Yugorskiy Shar and southwest and southeast along the eastern shores of Novaya Zemlya and Ostrov Vaygach (Vaigach Island). The spring range of the tide is greatest near the mouth of the White Sea and along the Barents Sea coast to the west, varying from about 11 to 20 feet; in other parts of the sector the range varies from about 3 to 7 feet.

The relatively few known beaches in the western half of this sector are widely scattered. Along the coast of the White Sea and eastward along the Barents and Kara Seas to the sector limit at Karskaya Guba (Kara Bay), the beaches are more abundant and extensive, with terrain and transportation conditions varying considerably.

A. Karskaya Guba to Mys Russkiy Zavorot

(69°20′N, 65°E; 68°58′N, 54°34′E) (FIGURE IV-1; B.A. Charts 2282, 2294, 2961, 2962, and 3129)

(1) Coast

Karskaya Guba (Kara Bay) lies on the south coast of the Kara Sea (Karskoye More) at the mouth of the river Kara, which forms the boundary between European and Asiatic USSR, and has its source in the Ural Mountains to the southeast (B.A. Charts 2282 and 2962). Karskaya Guba extends about 12 miles inland and is 9 miles wide. The mouth of the bay (beach area (1))* is narrow and is obstructed by a drying sandbank.

The coastal terrain northwestward to Proliv Yugorskiy Shar is a narrow belt of marshy tundra, low and level for the first 13 miles from Karskaya Guba to Cape Yagoz. The next 65 miles to Amderma is uniform, gently sloping terrain broken by Zaliv Shpindlera (beach area (2)). The Khrebet Pay-Khoy (Paikhoi range), a spur of the Urals reaching 1,800 feet in elevation, extends northwestward parallel to the coast at a distance of 10 to 20 miles inland. Amderma has air facilities, a pier, and projected railway connections to Pechora. Approaches appear to be clear along the coast between Karskaya Guba and Amderma with the 10-fathom curve about 1 mile offshore. There are sandbanks off Amderma and the coast northwestward to Proliv Yugorskiy Shar.

Ostrov Vaygach and Novaya Zemlya extend northward

---
* Italic numbers in parentheses refer to beach areas described in beach tables and shown on strip maps and PLANS.

---

for 500 miles, separating the Kara and Barents Seas. Both islands evidence gray limestone deposits of the Khrebet Pay-Khoy. Ostrov Vaygach, 60 miles long and 20 miles wide, has an even plateau along its northwest axis, varying in elevation from 150 feet in the southeast to 300 feet in the northwest. Along the east coast (beach area (3)) the terrain rises gently inland; the northwest, west, and south coasts are rugged, with bluffs, inlets, and offshore rocks and shoals.

Novaya Zemlya (beach areas (4) and (6); FIGURES IV-2 to IV-4) is 300 miles long and 46 miles wide and consists

FIGURE IV-2. *Novaya Zemlya, West Coast. Beach area (6).*
Typical beach along north half of beach area. Date unknown.

FIGURE IV-3. *Novaya Zemlya, West Coast. Beach area (6).*
Looking southwestward along beach bordering narrow isthmus at north end of beach area. Approximate position 75°53′N, 59°50′E; B. A. Chart 2962. 1921.

FIGURE IV-4. *Novaya Zemlya, Cape Larrova.*
Typical cliffed coast between beaches in area. Approximate position 74°N, 54°E; B. A. Chart 2962.

of two islands separated by a narrow strait, Proliv Matochkin Shar (FIGURES IV-5 and IV-6). The southern half of the southern island is low, with wide sloping terraces which meet the mountains about 50 miles northward (B.A. Chart 2294). Mountainous terrain covers the northern half and extends to the glaciers of the northern island. Elevations of 3,000 feet exist in the mountains bordering Matochkin Shar. The northern island is almost entirely covered with glaciers. The coastal terrain along the rocky northern tip of Novaya Zemlya is generally low tundra, sloping gently inland. There is no soil on the island, only a sandy humus tundra surface interspersed with granite. The coast of the remainder of the island is generally rugged with many bays, islands, rocks, and shoals in the approaches. Isolated landing places, in the form of narrow pebble beaches at bay heads, are backed by cliffs.

Navigation of the three straits through these islands is precarious. Proliv Yugorskiy Shar (B.A. Chart 3129) is shallow, with shifting sandbanks and a narrow irregular 60-mile fairway. Its shores are low and sloping, with rocks and shoals extending far offshore. The port village of Khabarovo (FIGURE IV-7) lies in the strait on the mainland coast. Proliv Karskiye Vorota is 17 miles wide with an excellent channel. However, fog prevails during 60% of the navigational period. Shoal water is far offshore in the strait. Proliv Matochkin Shar is reported to be the chief passageway for trade, despite its narrow winding channel, which is 660 yards wide at its narrowest point. It is deep and without hazardous shoals. The mountains rise to 3,000 feet along its shores. Ice conditions in the Kara Sea control conditions in the straits. Pack ice is driven against the western shores of the Kara Sea, blocking the straits. Passage is normally possible from 15 August to 15 September, unless the pack ice of the Kara is driven northward, which extends the period from August to October. Polar stations are located in each strait for observation of ice and meteorologic conditions.

The mainland coast southwestward from Proliv Yugorskiy Shar (beach areas (7) and (8)) is steep and rocky for 34 miles; the approaches are filled with rocks and sand-

FIGURE IV-5. *Novaya Zemlya, Matochkin Shar.* Middle reach of strait.

FIGURE IV-6. *Novaya Zemlya, Matochkin Shar.* Eastern entrance of strait. Prior to 1943.

FIGURE IV-7. *Proliv Yugorskiy Shar, Khabarov Point.*
View southeastward across Khabarovo. River Bol'shaya O-yu at (a). Approximate position 69°39′N, 60°26′E; B. A. Chart 3129.

Original

banks. Scattered hills of the Khrebet Pay-Khoy lie close to the coast. The coastal area southward to Khaypudyrskaya Guba (beach area (9)) and thence northward to Mys Medynskiy Zavorot is low, barren tundra, with marshes at the shallow river mouths and sandbanks off the entire coast. Inland the Bol'shezemel'skaya Tundra extends southward and westward to the river Pechora. Scattered hills lie about 30 miles south-southwestward, reaching elevations of about 650 feet. A chain of islands extends about 40 miles northwestward from Mys Medynskiy Zavorot. These are low, rocky, and covered with peat. Ostrov Dolgiy is the largest of the group. Since this coast is off the usual sea routes of the area, investigation and survey have been limited.

Southwestward to Pechorskaya Guba (Pyechora Bay) the coast is generally low and sandy with some steep sand slopes near Mys Medynskiy Zavorot. Ostrov Pesyakov is low and sandy (beach area (10)). Sand hills and marshes lie along the mainland coast southeastward (beach area (11)). An isolated mountain reaching 900 feet in elevation lies 20 miles south of Mys Gorelka (Cape Goryelka), the eastern entrance point to Pechorskaya Guba. This hill is part of a series of scattered hills, which extends eastward to the Khrebet Pay-Khoy.

Pechorskaya Guba (B.A. Chart 2961) extends 50 miles inland and is about 40 miles wide. It is shallow and has a channel 20 feet deep along its southeastern side leading into the Pechora. A sand bar covered by 10 feet of water at high water (1932) limits access to the river. The Pechora is the key inland communication route of this area. The shores of the bay are low and marshy on the east, swampy delta on the south, and marshland fronted by sand on the west (beach area (12)). The bay is protected from the sea by Mys Russkiy Zavorot, a low narrow sandspit extending 26 miles eastward. A number of small, rocky islands surrounded by many shoals extend farther eastward across the entrance to the bay.

The southeastern Barents Sea, sometimes referred to as the Pechorskoye More (Pechora Sea), is generally icebound from October to August. However, even in September ice from Proliv Yugorskiy Shar and Proliv Karskiye Vorota may exist here, moving slowly northward in large detached masses along the eastern coast of Novaya Zemlya. The greater part of the Kara Sea is covered with ice throughout the year, navigation being possible in the southern portions during August and September.

(2) Landing beaches

The mainland beaches included in subsector 41 A are generally long sand or sand-and-mud areas fronted by wide drying flats. The smaller beaches located on the islands, Vaygach and Novaya Zemlya, and along the mainland shore near the east limit are narrower, pebbly, and fronted by deeper water. Behind the mainland beaches and on Ostrov Vaygach is typical marshy tundra country. It consists of grass-covered low ridges with ponds or bogs between. Exit through the inland area is generally possible only when the ground is frozen and snow-covered. Novaya Zemlya valley glaciers lie close inland of some of the beaches on the northern island. Beach areas are described briefly in TABLE IV-2.

TABLE IV - 2

LANDING BEACHES OF COASTAL SUBSECTOR 41 A

Reliability POOR. (FIGURE IV - 1)

Number and location of beach area	Nearshore	Length	Width at H.W. and L.W.	Gradient in H.W. zone	Surf and shore drift	Material and firmness	Terrain immediately behind beach	Connections inland
(1) NW entrance to Karskaya Guba.	Bottom slopes flat; other details unknown.	About 2 mi.	500 ft. at H.W., probably 1,000 ft. or more at L.W.	1 on 100.	Moderate-to-heavy surf; drift to SE.	Sand; firm below H.W.	Backed by soft sand of spit; bordered to NW by gentle slopes of tundra area.	Unknown.
(2) Zaliv Shpindlera.	Details unknown.	About 1 mi. along river mouth at bayhead.	Probably 50 to 100 ft. at H.W., width at L.W. unknown.	Probably 1 on 50.	Generally moderate-to-heavy surf; drift to SE.	Muddy sand and pebbles; relatively firm above H.W.	Gentle slopes of tundra area; details unknown.	Unknown.
(3) Ostrov Vaygach, E shore.	Bottom slopes gentle to flat; other details unknown.	River mouth beaches; average length probably 500 ft.	About 50 ft. at H.W., width at L.W. unknown.	1 on 30.	Moderate-to-heavy surf; drift probably to SE.	Pebbles with some sand and mud; firm but slippery.	Swampy tundra.	Unknown.
(4) Novaya Zemlya, E shore.	Approach generally through narrow deep bay entrances; bottom slopes probably moderate.	Probable beach areas along deltas of small streams, range from 500 ft. to 0.5 mi.	10 to 15 ft. at H.W., probably 1,000 ft. or more at L.W.	Probably about 1 on 15.	Moderate surf along more exposed areas.	Probably sand and pebbles with some mud; relatively soft.	Moderate terraced rocky slopes at valley heads, glaciers may back northern areas; steep rocky cliffs border area.	None are known.

COASTS AND LANDING BEACHES

TABLE IV - 2 (Continued)

Number and location of beach area	Nearshore	Length	Width at H.W. and L.W.	Gradient in H.W. zone	Surf and shore drift	Material and firmness	Terrain immediately behind beach	Connections inland
(5) Novaya Zemlya, NE shore.	Steep bottom slopes; approach clear.	About 1 mi.	10 to 15 ft. at H.W., width at L.W. not known.	1 on 10.	Surf heavy with NE winds.	Pebbles and cobbles; firm.	Steep cliff.	None are known.
(6) Novaya Zemlya, W shore. (Figs. IV - 2 and IV - 3.)	Approaches generally obstructed by islets or rocks; bottom slopes probably moderate.	Numerous short beaches along bayheads, river mouths, or bay shores between rocky points.	Probably range to 50 ft. at H.W., widths at L.W. not known.	1 on 30.	Surf generally heaviest along areas exposed to N or NW; drift variable.	Pebbles and sand, driftwood common; generally firm except at river mouths.	Low stony terraced plateau or flat delta land.	None are known.
(7) Khabarovo.	Flat bottom slopes; otherwise clear.	Probably about 0.3 mi. between streams.	25 ft. at H.W., probably 150 ft. at L.W.	1 on 30.	Light-to-moderate surf general; drift variable.	Sand and pebbles; firm.	Town lies immediately inland; inland is typical tundra region.	Unknown.
(8) N of Belkovskiy Nos.	Covered rocks at S end; bottom gentle to flat.	About 6 mi., center may cover at H.W.	50 to 100 ft. at H.W., width at L.W. unknown.	1 on 50 average.	Light-to-moderate surf; drift mainly to S.	Sand and rock; generally firm.	Narrow low peninsula; inner shore is marshy and borders drying bay.	Unknown.
(9) E of Sin'kin Nos.	Obstructed by many rocky islets; bottom slopes flat.	About 17 mi. interrupted by shallow river mouth.	Probably 50 to 75 ft. at H.W., width at L.W. unknown.	1 on 30.	Surf light-to-moderate; drift probably variable.	Sand and pebbles; firm near H.W.; may be muddy and soft near L.W.	Low tundra area.	Unknown.
(10) Ostrov Pesyakov, Ostrov Varandey, and E.	Shoals off island; approach probably better along E end; details unknown.	Total about 20 mi., interrupted by channel between islands and between islands and mainland.	Probably 100 to 150 ft. at H.W., width at L.W. unknown.	Average 1 on 30.	Surf moderate-to-heavy in summer; drift variable.	Mainly sand along islands; sand and boulders to E. Driftwood common along entire area.	Steep sand hills alternate with low swampy areas on islands; to E inland is low grassy tundra.	Probably trails from E end to chapel and settlement on river bank.
(11) Guba Pogancheskaya and W.	Bottom slopes flat; other details unknown.	About 30 mi., interrupted by small rivers and streams.	About 100 to 150 ft. at H.W., probably 500 ft. or more at L.W.	Average 1 on 50.	Surf moderate-to-heavy; drift probably mainly to W.	Mud with some sand grading to all sand at W end; soft.	Low marshy tundra with higher land beginning W of W end.	Unknown.
(12) W shore of Pechorskaya Guba.	Flat bottom slopes; N end obstructed by island.	About 50 mi., interrupted by numerous small rivers.	About 150 ft. at H.W., width at L.W. unknown.	1 on 50 to 1 on 100.	Surf usually light or absent along N half; drift variable.	Mainly sand, covered in places with driftwood; firm near H.W.	Low land, generally swampy.	Unknown.

(Text continued following Figure IV-8)

FIGURE 5
COASTAL SUBSECTOR 41-B
JANIS 40

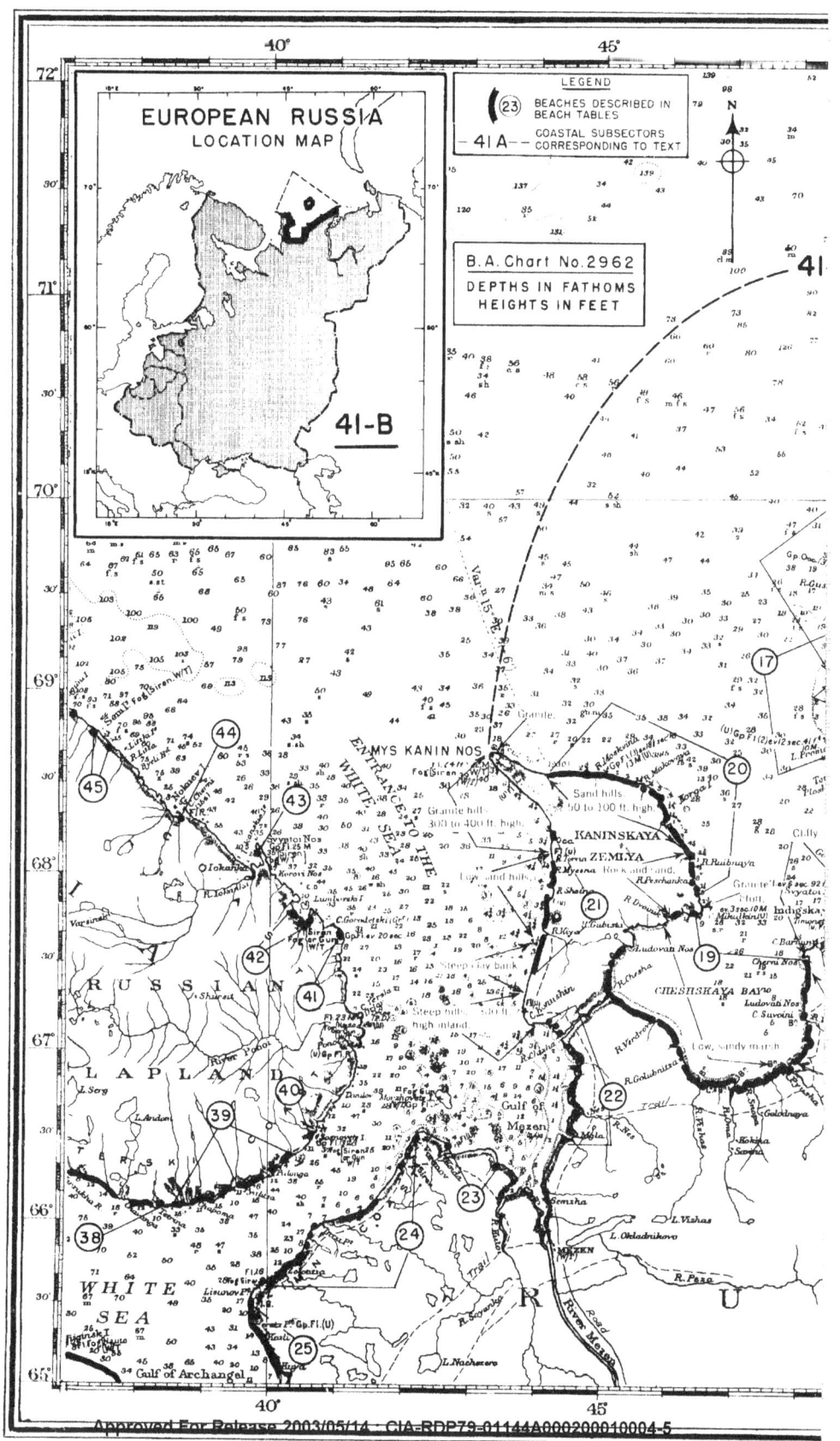

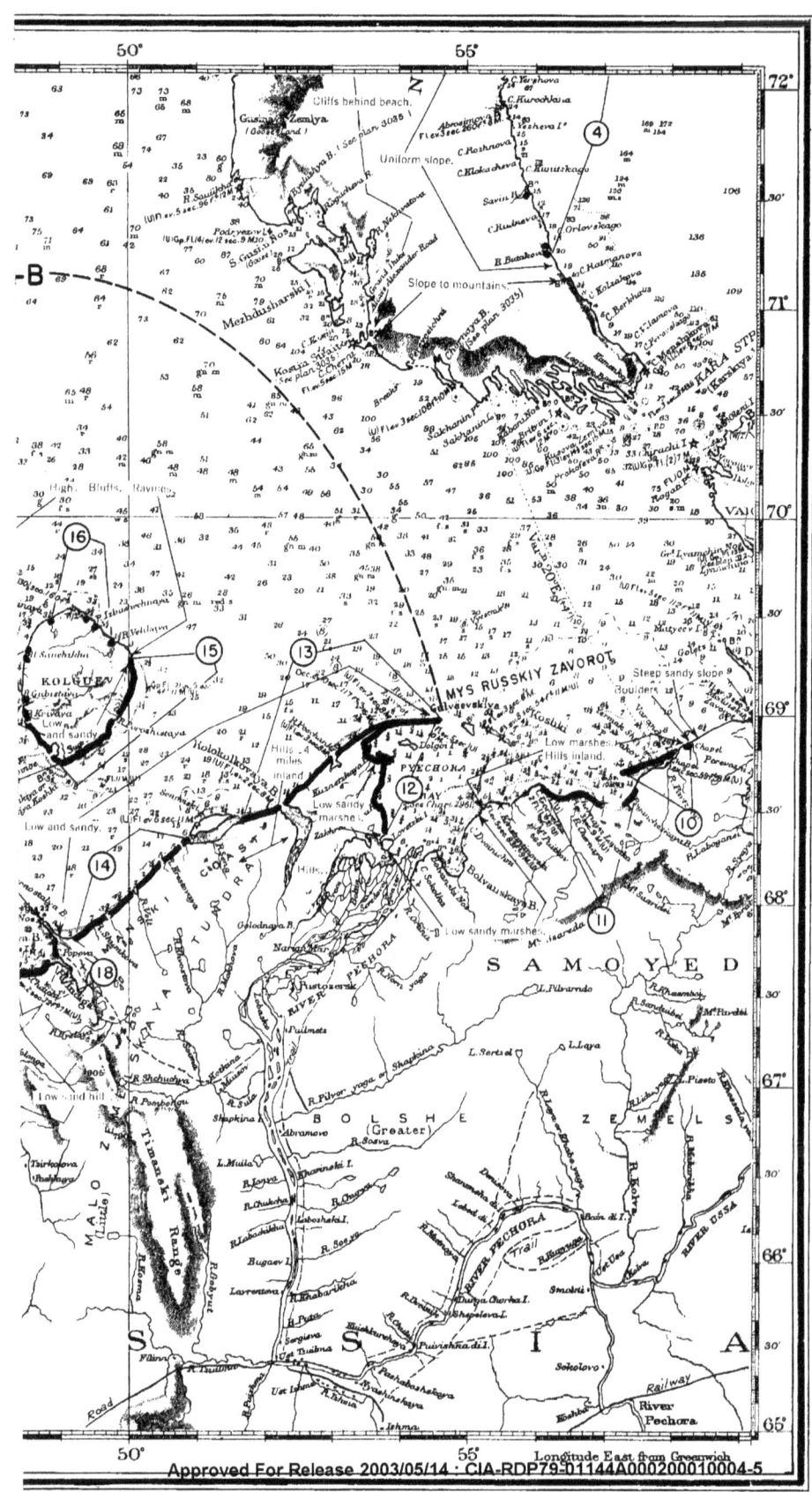

B. Mys Russkiy Zavorot to Mys Kanin Nos

(68°58′N, 54°34′E; 68°40′N, 43°17′E) (PLAN 12; FIGURE IV-8; B. A. Charts 2284 and 2962)

(1) Coast

The Malozemel'skaya Tundra lies between the Pechora and the Mezen' rivers southwestward of Mys Russkiy Zavorot (B.A. Chart 2962). It is flat tundra broken only by the Timanskiy Kryazh (Timan Range). The Timanskiy Bereg (Timanski Coast) lies between Mys Russkiy Zavorot and Mys Svyatoy Nos north of Indigskaya Guba. This coast is low and sandy, not exceeding 30 feet in height (beach areas (13) and (14)). Between Pechorskaya Guba and Kolokolkova Guba, a large shallow bay, the terrain is impassable because of lakes and marshes. A low hill group lies southward of the marshes along the western banks of the Pechora delta. The coast southwestward to Mys Svyatoy Nos is low and sandy, backed by undulating tundra. Ostrov Sengeyskiy, 22 miles southwestward of Kolokolkova Guba, is steep and sandy, conspicuous for its height, and surrounded by sandbanks. It is separated from the mainland by the shallow Proliv Sengeyskiy Shar.

Ostrov Kolguyev lies about 50 miles northward of Mys Svyatoy Nos. It is 59 miles long and 44 miles wide (beach areas (15) to (17)). Its terrain is very low, level, and marshy for about 10 miles inland along the shores of the southeastern half of the island. However, this coast is fronted by a sandspit, and drying sandbanks extending 4 miles offshore. The remainder of the island consists of rolling terrain and plateau about 300 feet high. The highest point on the island, a cone-shaped hill, is 444 feet high. The coast of the northwestern half of the island is steep and cliffy, between 80 and 130 feet high.

Mys Svyatoy Nos, the northern entrance point to Indigskaya Guba, is a long spit 25 feet high. A valley lies between this point and the Indiga and is about 10 miles wide, extending 140 miles southeastward to the Pechora river valley. A winter road extends along this valley. This same road passes southward and westward from Indiga to Nes' on Mezenskaya Guba and is the only road in this subsector. Vessels of 15- to 17-foot draft may enter the Indiga at high water; the river is from 12 to 26 feet deep 8 miles from the mouth. Steep cliffy shores border Indigskaya Guba (beach area (18)) for 6 miles northward of Mys Popova and at the center of the southern coast.

The Timanskiy Kryazh extends from the southern shores of Indigskaya Guba south-southeastward to its junction with the Urals, is about 50 miles wide, and consists generally of rolling hills, in few places exceeding 650 feet in elevation. To the southwest, bounded on the west by Poluostrov Kanin, lies Chëshskaya Guba (PLAN 12). This bay, which extends 60 miles inland, is about 75 miles wide, and is navigable, affording a good anchorage (beach area (19)). Gently sloping spurs of the Timanskiy Kryazh approach the eastern shores, which are low and sandy. Flat marshes back the head of the bay, which has many shallow inlets and river mouths. The western coast is low and sandy. Broad marshes extend across the Poluostrov Kanin along the river Chësha. Along the northern shores of the bay, which extend in an easterly direction, the coast consists of sandy banks from 50 to 100 feet high backed by gently sloping tundra. At the western entrance point to Chëshskaya Guba, Mys Mikulkin, the coast becomes cliffy. Here the Kryazh Kanin Kamen' approaches within 2 miles of the coast. This ridge, which reaches 690 feet in elevation, extends northwestward across the peninsula to Mys Kanin Nos. The northeast and north coast of Poluostrov Kanin (beach area (20)) consists of steep sand banks 40 to 100 feet high, and slopes moderately to the hills 10 miles inland. Rock and shoals along this coast (B.A. Chart 2284) are particularly hazardous in the vicinity of Ostrov Korga, a low island covered with sandy hillocks. The 21-mile coast to Mys Kanin Nos is steep and rocky. The ridge reaches almost to the point, which is rocky and only 25 feet in height.

Ice conditions in this subsector vary annually according to severity of the winters. Pack ice limits normally extend north-northwestward from Mys Kanin Nos from January to April. The limit recedes to the 50th meridian, east of Ostrov Kolguyev, by 15 June; and the entire western coast of Novaya Zemlya is clear of ice in July. September is the best month for navigation in this area. Ice again forms in the east in October, gradually extending westward toward its limit north of Mys Kanin Nos until conditions of March and April are reestablished. Warm river waters in the spring usually melt and clear the coastal ice relatively early.

(2) Landing beaches

The beaches of subsector 41 B are described briefly in TABLE IV-3.

TABLE IV - 3

LANDING BEACHES OF COASTAL SUBSECTOR 41 B

Reliability POOR. (PLAN 12; FIGURE IV - 8)

Number and location of beach area	Nearshore	Length	Width at H.W. and L.W.	Gradient in H.W. zone	Surf and shore drift	Material and firmness	Terrain immediately behind beach	Connections inland
(13) NE and SW of Kolokolkova Guba.	Mild to *flat* bottom slopes; no other details known.	About 60 mi. interrupted by several large river mouths; E end along spit may cover during storms.	50 to 150 ft. at H.W., widest near E end; width at L.W. unknown.	Average 1 on 50.	Surf light to moderate, most heavy along E end; drift mainly to E.	Sand; firm near H.W.	Low narrow soft sandspit along 20 mi. at E end; sand hills generally back remainder.	Unknown.
(14) Gornostal'ya Guba and E.	*Mild* bottom slopes flattening to E; other details unknown.	About 40 mi. interrupted by river mouths.	50 to 75 ft. at H.W., width at L.W. unknown.	Average 1 on 30.	Surf moderate to heavy, lightest at W end; drift mainly to E.	Sand; firm near H.W.	Moderately high sand hills.	Unknown.
(15) Ostrov Kolguyev, E shore.	Drying sand banks extend as much as 4 mi. offshore enclose mud, sand and pebble flat partially dry at L.W.	About 40 mi. interrupted by river mouths usually blocked with sand and pebbles.	Average 25 ft. at H.W.	1 on 30.	Surf generally light, extends over wide belt; drift weak.	Sand; firm near H.W.	A fairly level peat-and-grass tundra.	Trails from scattered settlements.
(16) Ostrov Kolguyev, N shore.	*Gentle* to *mild* bottom slopes; details unknown.	River mouth beaches; probably range from 100 to 500 ft.	10 to 25 ft. at H.W.	1 on 15.	Generally heavy surf; drift mainly to E and SE.	Pebbles; firm.	Steep cliffs 80 to 130 ft. high.	Unknown.
(17) Ostrov Kolguyev, W shore.	Drying sand spits lie from 5 to 9 mi. offshore along S half.	Total about 25 mi., interrupted by rivers; N half may be more continuous than shown.	25 ft. at N, widens to 150 ft. at S at H.W.	1 on 30 average.	Surf moderate to heavy; drift probably varies over area.	Sand; firm.	Low bluffs along N half; low moss and grass plain to S.	Unknown.
(18) Indigskaya Guba.	Bottom slopes probably *gentle*; details unknown.	About 15 mi. interrupted by river mouths and adjacent steep cliffs.	Average 50 ft. at H.W., about 15 ft. on E; L.W. widths not known.	Average 1 on 30, steepest on E.	Surf moderate to heavy, heaviest to W; drift varies.	Sand and pebbles; firm at H.W.	Low sand terrain on W; steep sand and clay cliffs locally along E.	Unknown.
(19) Chëshskaya Guba.	Shallow bay with drying shoals and flats near head; details are not known.	About 160 mi. interrupted by numerous rivers and by rocky ledge along NW shore.	Probably 100 to 150 ft. at H.W. along E and S shores, 25 ft. along NW shore; L.W. width not known.	Average 1 on 100, flattest near head of bay.	Surf light, most heavy along W shore; drift varies.	Mainly sand along E and S, sand and rock along NW; generally firm near H.W.	Peat-covered tundra generally, steep sandy cliffs along NW shore.	Unknown.
(20) NW of Mys Mikulkin.	Obstructed by shoals and sand islands which partly cover; rocks along parts of shore near SE end.	About 85 mi. interrupted by rivers and some cliffed shore.	Probably 15 to 50 ft. at H.W., widest parts along SE half; L.W. widths not known.	Average 1 on 30.	Surf generally heavy, breaks in wide belt; drift mainly to E and SE.	Sand with scattered rock; firm near H.W.	Generally a sand-and-clay cliff ranging from 40 to 100 ft.; inland is hilly tundra with some bog or marsh.	Unknown.

FIGURE IV
COASTAL SUBSECTOR 41-C
JANIS 40

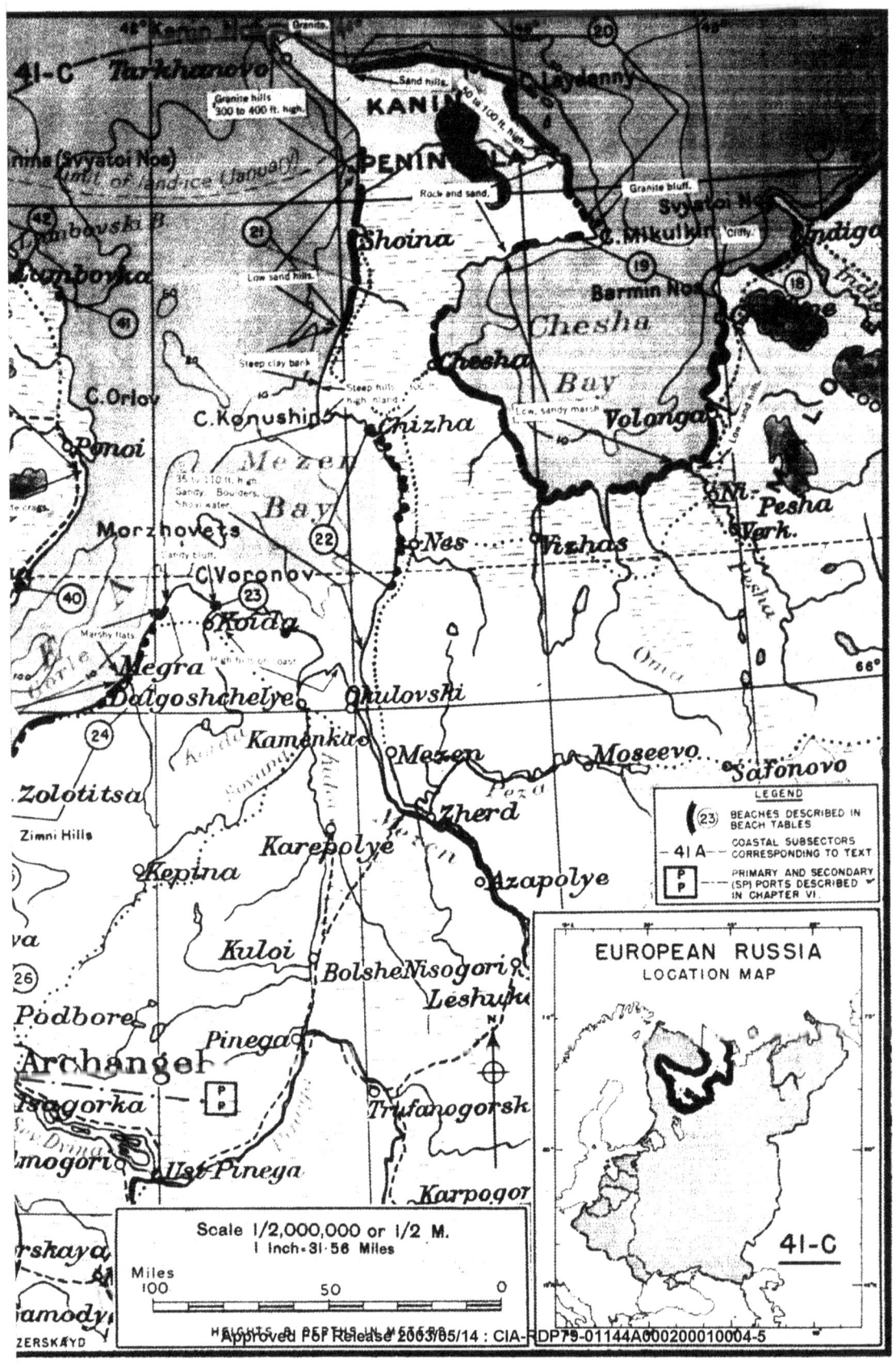

C. Mys Kanin Nos to Mys Svyatoy Nos

(68°40′N, 43°17′E; 68°09′N, 39°49′E) (PLAN 12; FIGURE IV-9; U.S.H.O. Chart 5784; B.A. Charts 2269 to 2278, 2280, and 2284; A.M.S. Map, North West Russia, scale 1:2,000,-000, G.S.G.S. No. 4464, Key No. 312625)

(1) Coast

The White Sea (Beloye More), most of which is south of the Arctic Circle, has a wide variety of coastal terrain (U.S.H.O. Chart 5784; B.A. Chart 2278). The northern and eastern shores are strategically important only as control points of sea routes, while the southern and western shores contain important communication centers and transportation routes.

The entrance to this sea (B.A. Charts 2284 and 2270) contains sandy shoals, and the preferred route is close to the western shores. The throat of the sea, the Gorlo (B.A. Chart 2272), is 30 miles wide for a distance of 115 miles. Approaches to the southern shores are generally good, while those to the western shores are extremely hazardous, as a natural barrier of rocks, shoals, and islets lie along the entire coast. The cities on this sea are of importance largely as key communication points through which flow the natural resources of the Soviet Arctic and foreign trade. The Murmansk railroad passes southward along the west coast of the White Sea, serving the port cities of Kandalaksha, Kem' and Belomorsk. The Arkhangel'sk railroad serves Molotovsk and passes southward also. These north–south railroads have an east–west lateral connection between Obozerskaya and Belomorsk which serves Onega. Air facilities are scattered throughout the coastal area.

Ice conditions in the White Sea are important considerations. The rivers begin to freeze in October and the basin in November. The Gorlo is never frozen solidly across, but becomes unnavigable between mid-December and mid-January, even with ice breaker assistance, and remains so until the second week of May. In a particularly mild winter, however, with several large ice breakers available, the White Sea can be kept open. Arkhangel'sk may be

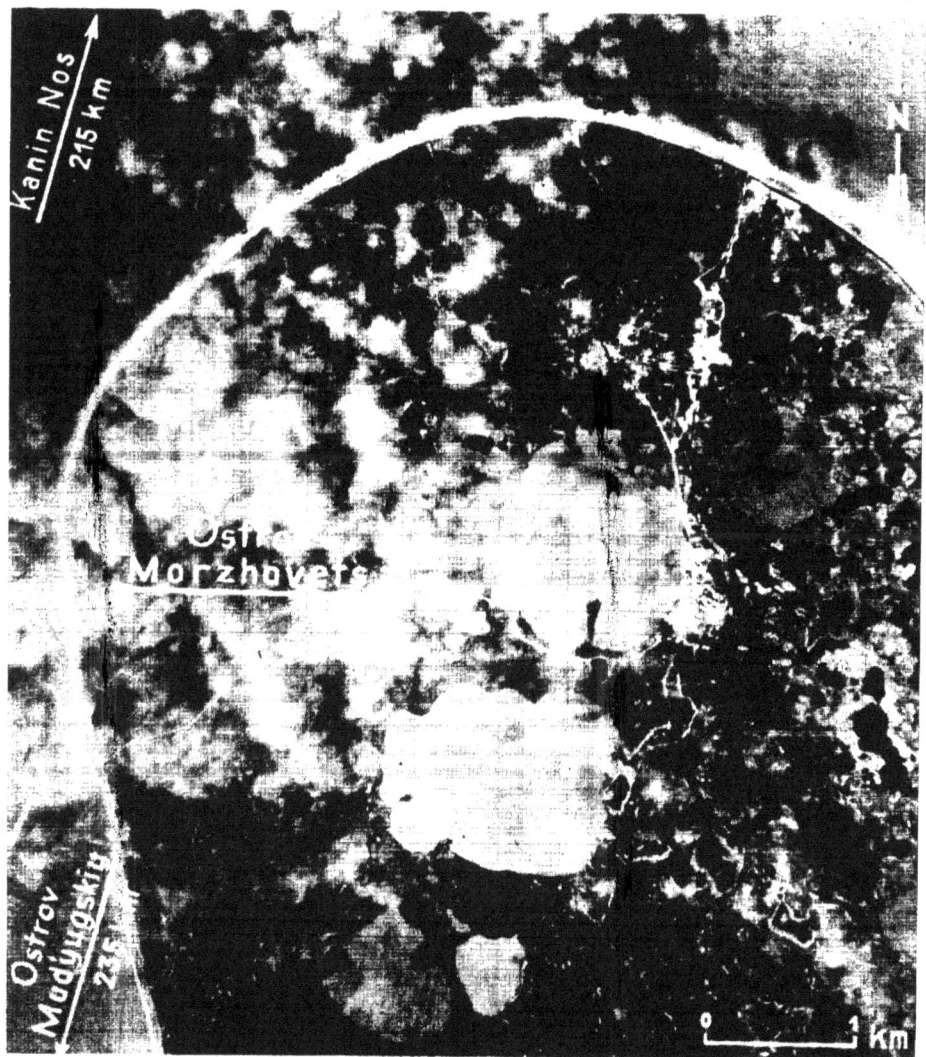

FIGURE IV-10. *Mezenskaya Guba, Ostrov Morzhovets.*
Aerial view of northwest end of island. Seaplane base at (a). Prior to 1943. Approximate position 66°45′N, 42°27′E; B. A. Chart 2271.

reached, on the average, from 15 May to 15 December. Thaws begin in late April; ensuing floods move the ice to the Barents Sea, creating added hazards to navigation.

Mys Kanin Nos (B.A. Chart 2284) is the eastern entrance point of the White Sea. The foothills of the Kryazh Kanin Kamen' lie along the first 35 miles of coast southeastward of the cape. Close inland granite hills reach elevations of 420 feet. The next 35 miles of coast is low and sandy, backed by separated hills and marshes (beach area (2)). At Shoyna there is a landing ground and from here a winter road runs southward to join a secondary road at Mezen'. The 22 miles of coast southward to Mys Konushin consists of a series of high sand hills which reach an elevation of 300 feet and extend inland about 10 miles to marshes. Moss, peat, and tundra appear along this entire coast. The rivers are shallow and approaches to the shores are poor. A rocky, sandy bank lies along the coast. The 5-fathom curve lies 2 to 8 miles offshore. Sandbanks lie even farther from shore and the depths are very irregular.

Mezenskaya Guba (B.A. Chart 2271) lies between Mys Konushin and Mys Voronov with the rivers Mezen' and Kuloy at its head. The eastern part of the Gulf is unnavigable because of shallow water and drying sands which extend 2 to 6 miles offshore (beach area (22)). The 3-fathom curve lies from 5 to 9 miles offshore. The coast is steep, from 35 to 110 feet high, and composed of sand and clay, with some boulders. The rivers are also shallow and those from the Nes' southward have trees along their banks. It is here that the tundra gives way to forest. The river Mezen' is shallow. At high tide vessels drawing not more than 7 feet can reach the port of Mezen', about 20 miles upstream. The channel changes annually because of shifting sands. The banks are bluff, generally sand and clay, and are covered with meadows and woods. Along the eastern bank a secondary road follows the river southward to join better roads inland. The river is important as a transportation route for lumber from the extensive forests for several hundred miles southeastward. The Kuloy, west of the Mezen', extends southward where a canal joins it with the Pinega, an important tributary of the Severnaya (northern) Dvina. The coast from the Kuloy westward to Mys Voronov is from 80 to 100 feet high, backed by hills reaching 300 feet in elevation. Drying sands lie along the coast (beach area (23)) and approaches are poor because of shallow water. The terrain is of a tundra nature, and a winter road roughly parallels the coast 10 to 20 miles inland. Ostrov Morzhovets (FIGURE IV-10), 8 miles long and 5 miles wide, lies about 12 miles northeastward of Mys Voronov. The coasts are steep sandy clay; there are no trees, and peat and bushes cover the island. Two large lakes are used by seaplanes and an auxiliary seaplane base is reported on the island. The northwestern end is 70 to 100 feet high and the southeastern end is 200 feet high. Sandbanks surround the entire island, extending offshore as much as 4 miles in places. Much land ice forms in the shallow waters of Mezenskaya Guba. Strong currents from the Mezen' and Kuloy cause the three gulf channels to shift frequently.

The coast between Mys Voronov and Arkangel'sk, a distance of 175 miles, is known as the Zimniy Bereg (Winter coast) (B.A. Charts 2272, 2273), and is backed by the Zimniye Gory, which reach an elevation of 650 feet. A trail

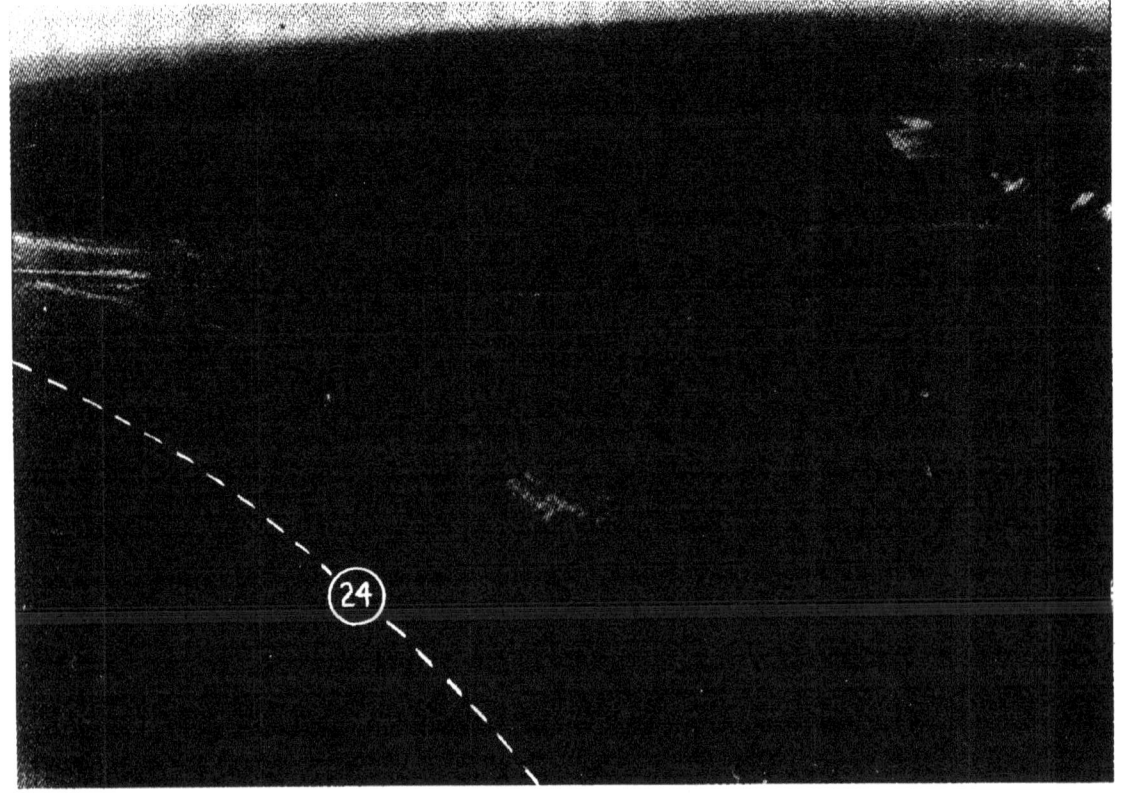

FIGURE IV-11. *Zimniy Coast, Nizhnyaya Zolotitsa. Beach area (24).*
Aerial view northeastward across Zolotitsa river mouth and village, at southwest end of beach area. Note steep coasts and narrow beach. Date unknown. Approximate position 65°41'N, 40°13'E; B. A. Chart 2273.

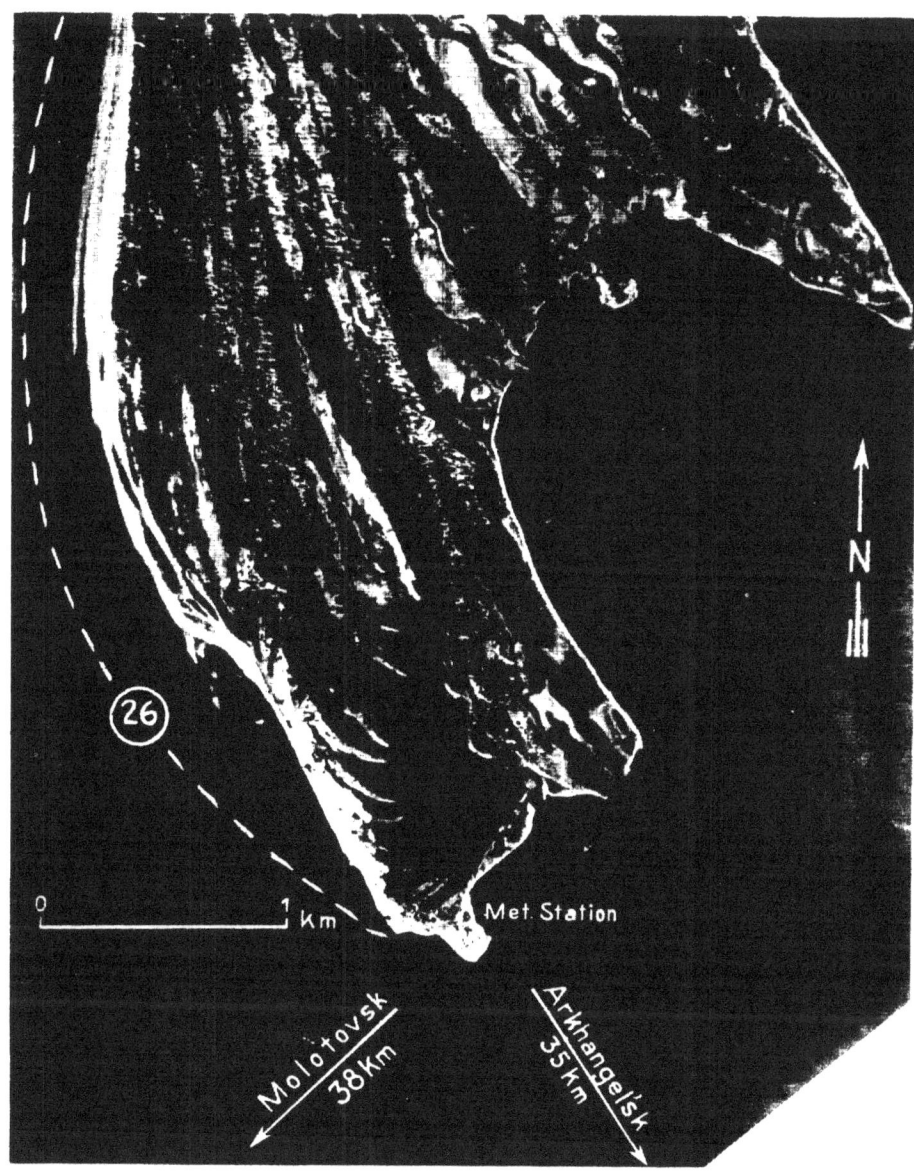

FIGURE IV-12. *Dvinskaya Guba (Gulf of Archangel), Ostrov Mud'yugskiy. Beach area (26).*
Sparse woods, dunes and shoals at southern tip of the island, which borders the channel to Arkhangel'sk. Prior to 1943. Approximate location 64°51'N, 40°17'E; B. A. Chart 2273.

runs along this coast. Southwestward of Mys Voronov the shores are sandy hills 50 to 130 feet high for about 50 miles southwestward to Mys Intsy (beach area (24)). The hills inland have marshes between them. The 10-fathom line lies 4 to 8 miles offshore and except for a few sandbanks the approaches are fair. Southwestward of Mys Intsy for 49 miles to Mys Kerets (Cape Keretski), the westernmost projection of the Zimniy Bereg, the coastline is extremely rugged with steep shores, bluffs, and cliffs (FIGURE IV-11). The hills here reach 650 feet in elevation 4 miles inland. Forest extends to the coast from Mys Intsy southward. Thirteen miles of cliff lie behind the steep sandy coast southward to Mys Kerets (beach area (25)), and surf on this shore is hazardous. The coast from Mys Kerets 18 miles southeastward to the river Kuya lies on Dvinskaya Guba (the Gulf of Archangel). It is generally steep sand and clay slopes, in places 40 feet high. The 10-fathom curve lies 2 miles off Mys Kerets and 7 miles off the mouth of the Kuya.

The coast southward of the Kuya (beach area (26)) becomes lower, and at a distance of 3.5 miles Nikolskaya Kosa commences. The spit trends southward 3.5 miles, and is covered with sand dunes from 15 to 20 feet high and wooded growth. The mainland coast is high, but the hills inland decrease in elevation as they approach the high plateau of the northern bank of the Severnaya Dvina. Ostrov Mud'yugskiy (Mudyugski Island) extends 8.5 miles southward of Nikolskaya Kosa and is separated from it by a shallow strait 300 yards wide and between 6 and 8 feet deep. The island (FIGURE IV-12) is about 2 miles wide at the center and tapers northward and southward. The west coast is steep sand 10 to 15 feet high, and the terrain inland consists of sandy hillocks 40 feet high, covered with moss, bushes, and pine trees. The southern and eastern shores are low, with occasional sand dunes. Between the island and the mainland lies a shallow bay; its northern part nearly dries and the southern part is very shallow. West of the island the approaches to Arkhangel'sk commence (B. A. Chart 2280); the northern channel, which is the best of three, passes southeastward close to the southwestern extremity of the island. Vessels up to 24 feet in draft use this channel to Arkhangel'sk which lies 26 miles up the Severnaya Dvina (Chapter VI). The Severnaya Dvina estuary, which extends 21 miles between Ostrov Mud'yugskiy and Molotovsk, consists of many low sandy islands. Those on the gulf are covered at high tide. They are generally marshy, with some trees. The loss of time and supply via Arkhangel'sk during World War II, because of ice, resulted in the construction of a channel to Molotovsk and the installation of naval, railway, and air facilities (FIGURE IV-13). The port of Molotovsk (Chapter VI) is situated at the western extremity of the delta of the Severnaya Dvina. Ostrov Yagry lies northward of Molotovsk, protecting it from the sea. The island is low and sandy and has many installations built upon it. A bridge connects it with Molotovsk across Nikol'skoye Ust'ye (Nikolski Inlet). Off the southwestern extremity of Ostrov Yagry the mainland coast is low and sandy for a distance of 10 miles. Marshes exist inland but have not prevented road and rail construction, as both extend across them. The railroad is close to the coast and terminates 8 miles west of the town. The railroad runs southeastward from Molotovsk for 25 miles to a junction with the main line about 5 miles south of Arkhangel'sk. A road is reported to parallel the railway. An improved road passes from the coast northwestward of Molotovsk close to the railroad termination from which it trends southeastward for 6 miles then east-northeastward 12 miles to the Severnaya Dvina. It crosses the railroad about 6 miles southeast of Molotovsk. The inland terrain here is undulating, and on the west hills rise along a generally southeast line, commencing about 15 miles west of Molotovsk. Approaches to the Northern Dvina estuary are fair. The 5-fathom line lies within 2 miles of the coast and islands, while the 10-fathom curve lies between 10 and 12 miles from the shores. Sandbanks extend to 1 mile off Ostrov Yagry and 3 miles off the adjoining mainland coast at the mouth of Nikol'skoye Ust'ye. A channel has been dredged here admitting vessels of 21-foot draft to reach Molotovsk. There are 4 miles of clear beach approach (beach area (27)) at the western extremity of the sandbanks 6 miles southwest of Molotovsk with the railway termination at the center of the beach. Airfields and seaplane facilities of this area are good.

For 35 miles northwestward to Unskaya Guba the coast (beach area (27)) is sand and clay covered with grass and woods (FIGURE IV-14). The hills inland reach 300 feet in elevation. The road from Molotovsk passes along the coast to within 4 miles of Unskaya Guba, where it turns southwestward across the peninsula toward Onega; inland sections of this road are unimproved. Vessels with maximum draft of 14 feet can enter Unskaya Guba (B. A. Chart 2274) at any time through the 5-mile-long channel leading into a shallow basin 2.5 miles southeastward of the inlet. This inlet is frozen from November to May. The eastern entrance is bluff and 45 feet high; low sandy shores lie at the western entrance point. Northwestward of the inlet the coast is low and sandy for a distance of

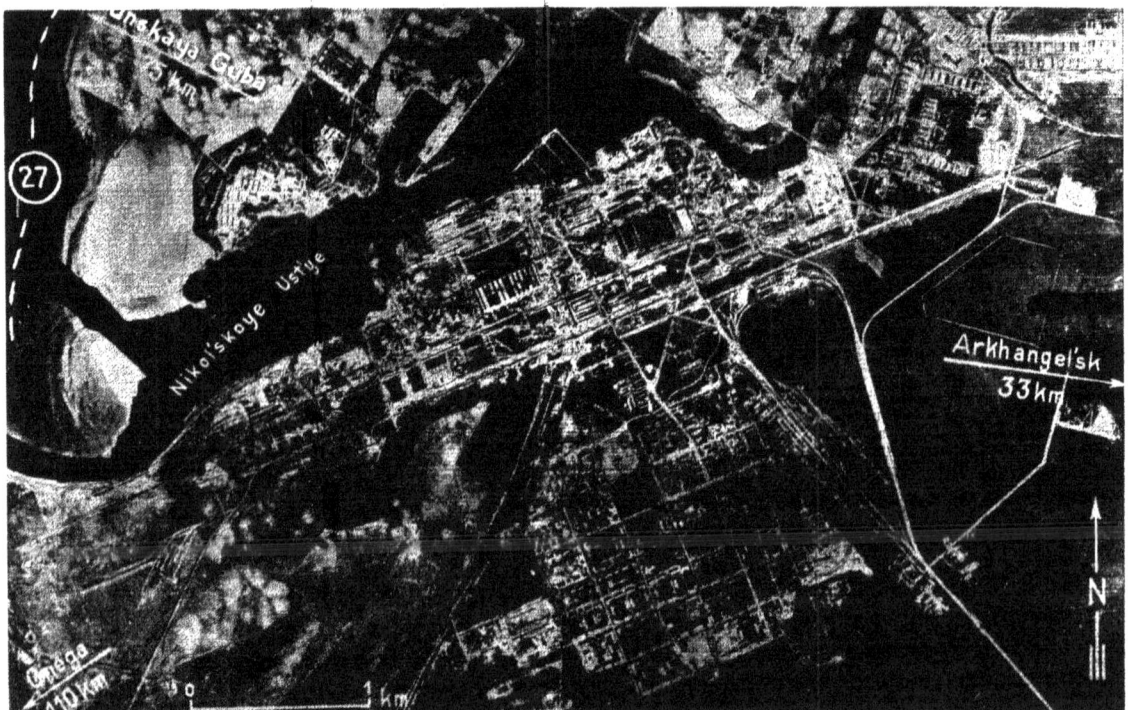

FIGURE IV-13. *Dvinskaya Guba, Molotovsk. Beach area (27).*
Nikolski mouth of river Dvina, between Ostrov Yagry and the mainland. Clear beach approaches at left. Prior to 1943. Approximate position 64°35'N, 39°55'E; B. A. Chart 2273.

FIGURE IV-14. *Letni Coast, Krasnogorskoye. Beach area (27).* Looking eastward along dunes back of beach at west end of beach area. Approximate position 64°45′N, 38°40′E; B. A. Chart 2273.

19 miles where it becomes moderately high and sandy for about 18 miles northwestward to Lekniy Navolok, (formerly Durakovo) (beach area (28)). Rocky coast extends for a distance of 2 miles northwestward of Letniy Navolok. The coast westward for about 5 miles to Mys Ukht-Navolok (FIGURE IV-15) is low sand and clay, strewn with boulders and occasional granite bluffs. Ostrov Zhizhginskiy lies 2.4 miles northward of Mys Ukht-Navolok. Sandbanks lie between the cape and the island and extend 2 miles northward of the island. The island is about 1.5 miles long and 0.8 mile wide with steep shores of sand and rock 50 feet high. At the center of the island is a hill 90 feet high.

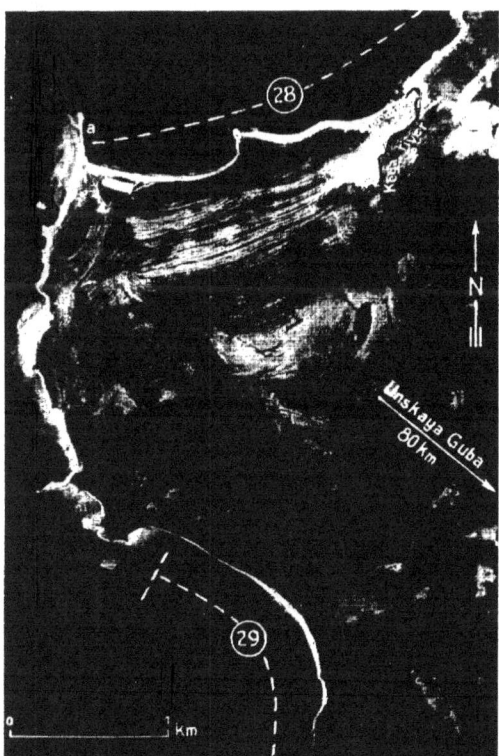

FIGURE IV-15. *White Sea, Mys Ukht-Navolok. Beach areas (28) and (29).*
Aerial view of cape (a), sparsely wooded terrain, beaches backed by sandbanks, and shoal water. Prior to 1943. Approximate position 65°09′N, 36°50′E; B. A. Chart 2274.

Mys Ukht-Navolok is the eastern entrance point of Onezhskaya Guba (the Gulf of Onega). The eastern shore of the gulf (B.A. Chart 2275) is generally composed of sand and clay and covered with earth interrupted by granite crags and smooth boulders (beach areas (29) to (32)). The terrain slopes upward moderately to hills of about 300-foot elevation a short distance inland. The approaches to this shore are poor. The 10-fathom curve is 2 to 6 miles offshore. Rocks and shoals lie along the entire coast inside the 10-fathom curve. The bays and rivers are shallow. The best route to Onega lies off this eastern coast. Onega is 95 miles by sea southward of Mys Ukht-Navolok. Heavy tides flow in the channel along this coast. Alluvial deposits make the head of the gulf shallow; the 5-fathom curve is about 12 miles outside the mouth of the Onega. Of two channels extending to the Onega, the best affords passage to vessels of not more than 7.5-foot draft. Although the river banks are steep, and hills lie to northeastward and westward of the river, the terrain inland is generally level plateau along the Onega river. There are excellent air facilities at Onega and a railroad connects this port with the lateral connection between the Arkhangel'sk and Murmansk railways. The river itself is an important communication route. West of Onega the high, level, marshy plateau terminates in steep sandbanks along the coast (beach area (33); FIGURE IV-16).

The western shores of Onezhskaya Guba are very irregular, with many inlets and bays. Islands, rocks, and shoals lie along the coast extending about 15 miles offshore. The coastal terrain is steep along the shores, leveling off inland to gently sloping marshy land covered with woods and meadows. The road and railroad from Onega westward pass along the coast to Belomorsk. Here railroads, highways, and the Stalin White Sea – Baltic Canal

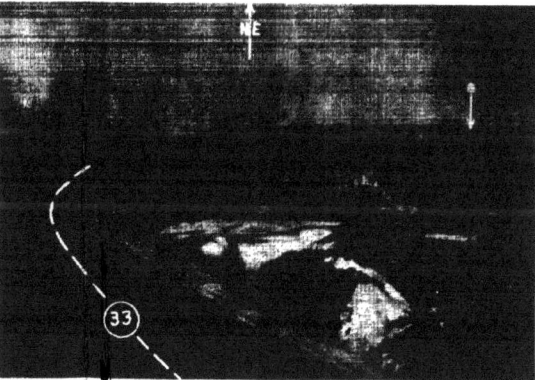

FIGURE IV-16. *Onezhskaya Guba, Mys Vorzogorskiy. Beach area (33).*
Aerial view northeastward across Yakovlevskaya, toward the mouth of river Onega (a). Prior to 1943. Approximate location 63°53′N, 37°40′E; B. A. Chart 2275.

pass southward, giving access to continental communication routes. Vessels of 15-foot draft can reach Belomorsk, but the approaches are precarious. The port of Kem' (Chapter VI) lies 26 miles northward of Belomorsk and can be reached by vessels 23 feet in draft. A mass of islands lie at the entrance, and the channel is a narrow passage between the mainland to northward and the islands (FIGURE IV-17). The shores are steep and rocky. The Murmansk railroad serves Kem', and a good highway extends inland to join Baltic routes. Kem' has a seaplane station. A group of islands, Solovetskiye Ostrova, lie in the mouth of Onezhskaya Guba, about 20 miles northeastward of Kem'. They extend 20 miles farther eastward with a channel between the principal islands (B.A. Chart 2276). The island shores are low and rocky (beach area (34)). One hill on Ostrov Solovetskiy, the larger island, reaches 240 feet in elevation, but the island terrain is mostly low and marshy, with many boulders. Small lakes cover a large proportion of the islands' surface (FIGURE IV-18). There is a seaplane station and landing ground on the islands and also an important agricultural experiment station.

The mainland coast between Kem' and Kandalaksha is steep and rugged. The coastal terrain is a wide belt of low, undulating coastal plain with extensive wooded marshes (beach areas (35) and (36)). The irregularity of the coast with islets, rocks, and shoals persists along the entire western coast of the White Sea. On Kandalakshskaya Guba (B.A. Chart 2277) the coast becomes higher, and lakes and inlets cause the railroad to trend inland before reaching the town (FIGURE IV-19). The head of the gulf is marked by hills 2,000 feet high. A railroad extends from the Murmansk railroad westward into Finland from a point 13 miles southward of Kandalaksha. Branches of the railroad serve the mining districts northward. The roads northward and westward are good. Unimproved roads extend southeastward along the coast to Mys Orlov. Kandalaksha has a landing ground and a seaplane station. Wire communication follows along the entire coast of the peninsula to Murmansk.

The highest coast of the White Sea lies eastward of Kandalaksha and the coast southeastward for 25 miles consists of hills 1,900 feet high. The northeastern shores of the gulf are high and rocky, with patches of woods (FIGURE IV-20). Approaches to this coast are good, since the irregularities consist of small inlets rather than promontories, as are found on the southwestern shores of the gulf. The depths in the gulf are the greatest in the White Sea, reaching 180 fathoms off Mys Turiy (Cape Turi).

From Kandalaksha to Mys Turiy 70 miles southeastward, the coastline is abrupt and rocky but regular, with clear approaches. There are few promontories, and only one prominent fjord, the Guba Kolvitsa, which is the outlet for Kolvitskoye Ozero. Immediately behind the coast the steep slopes are covered, near the bottom, with low arctic vegetation and wooded on higher areas.

Southeastward from Mys Turiy to Kuzomen' the coast is smooth and regular with stretches of narrow sand and shingle beach (beach area (37)). All but the last 10 miles of this coastline is fronted by flats extending from 0.2 to 0.8 mile offshore, and consisting of sand and silt, with intermittent rocky areas. Offshore the bottom is sand and silt. Behind the coastline are low wooded sand ridges with intervening marshy areas. The 10-mile stretch of coast immediately northwest of the river at Kuzomen' is

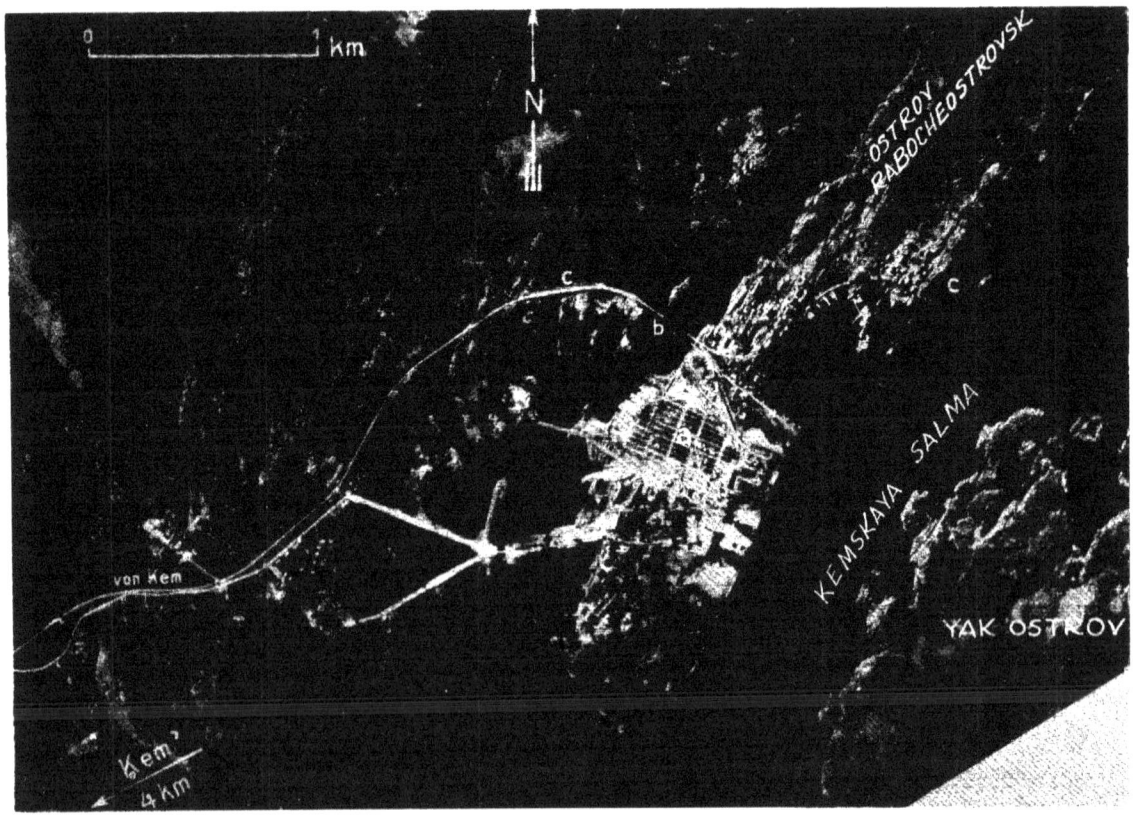

FIGURE IV-17. *White Sea, Approaches to Kem'.*
Aerial view of Ostrov Rabocheostrovsk, on Kem Strait. Note (a) sawmills, (b) rail bridge, and (c) railway from Kem'. Prior to 1943. Approximate position 64°59'N, 34°46'E; B. A. Chart 2276.

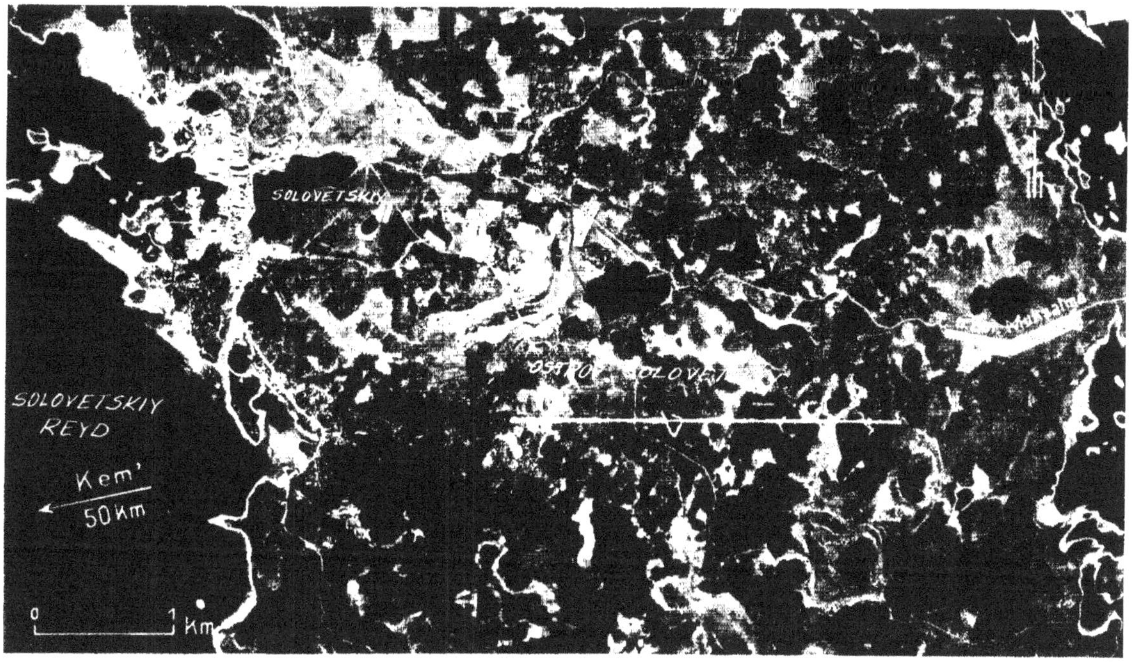

FIGURE IV-18. *Ostrov Solovetskiy.*
Aerial view of lakes, marshes, and woods at southern end of the island. Prior to 1943. Approximate position 65°01'N, 35°46'E; B. A. Chart 2276.

FIGURE IV-19. *Kandalakshskaya Guba. Beach area (36).*
Beach fronting settlement of Kandalaksha. 1915 or earlier. Approximate position 67°08'N, 32°25'E; B. A. Chart 2277.

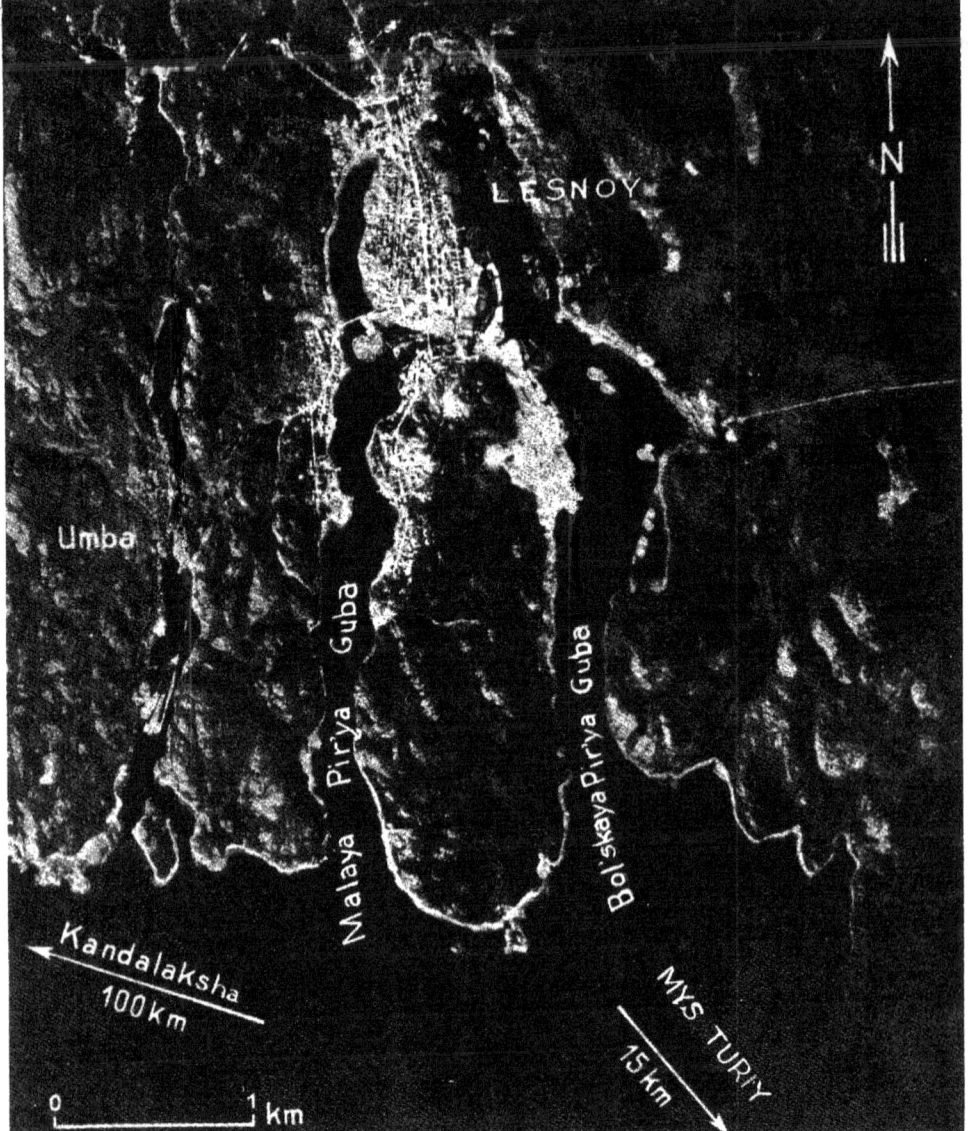

FIGURE IV-20. *Kandalakshskaya Guba, Lesnoy.*
Typical rugged terrain on the northeastern shores of the gulf. Prior to 1943. Approximate position 66°41′N, 34°19′E; B. A. Chart 2277.

fronted by a narrow sand beach (FIGURE IV-21; B. A. Chart 2274) backed in the northwestern half by an extensive marshy plain and in the southeastern half by low sand dunes.

Southeastward of Kuzomen' for 15 miles is a smooth sand beach with sand-silt flats extending 0.5 mile offshore and backed by an extensive marshy plain (beach area (38)). From this point to Chapoma the shoreline is irregular with many small sand beaches and recurrent stretches of sand-silt flats offshore. Behind the coastline the terrain is generally low and marshy. About 1 mile inland lies a 30-foot-high sand-clay bluff. Vegetation is low marsh type, with low scrub.

From Chapoma, northeastward for 55 miles to Sosnovka (B. A. Chart 2272) 40-foot clay bluffs with granite projections lie in places immediately behind the coast, while elsewhere a few hundred yards of marsh intervene. The coastline continues smooth with sections of sand-shingle beach (beach area (39); FIGURE IV-22) while the silt flats offshore disappear. Inland behind the bluffs the terrain is higher and wooded, with a few lakes and marshy areas. Near Sosnovka (beach area (40)) the clay bluffs terminate and the coastline becomes irregular, with rocky slopes rising from the shore. A 500-foot conical peak rises near the coast at Sosnovka. Offshore rocks are reported between Chapoma and Sosnovka. Inland the hills reach an elevation of 350 feet.

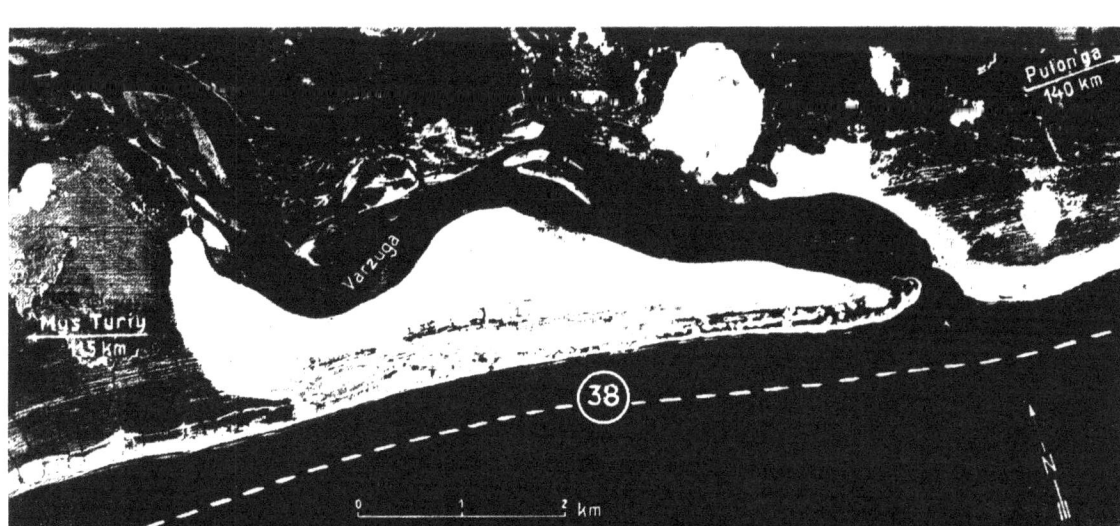

FIGURE IV-21. *White Sea, Kuzomen'. Beach area (38).*
White sandy beach at Varzuga river mouth. Prior to 1943. Approximate position 66°16'N, 36°53'E; B. A. Chart 2274.

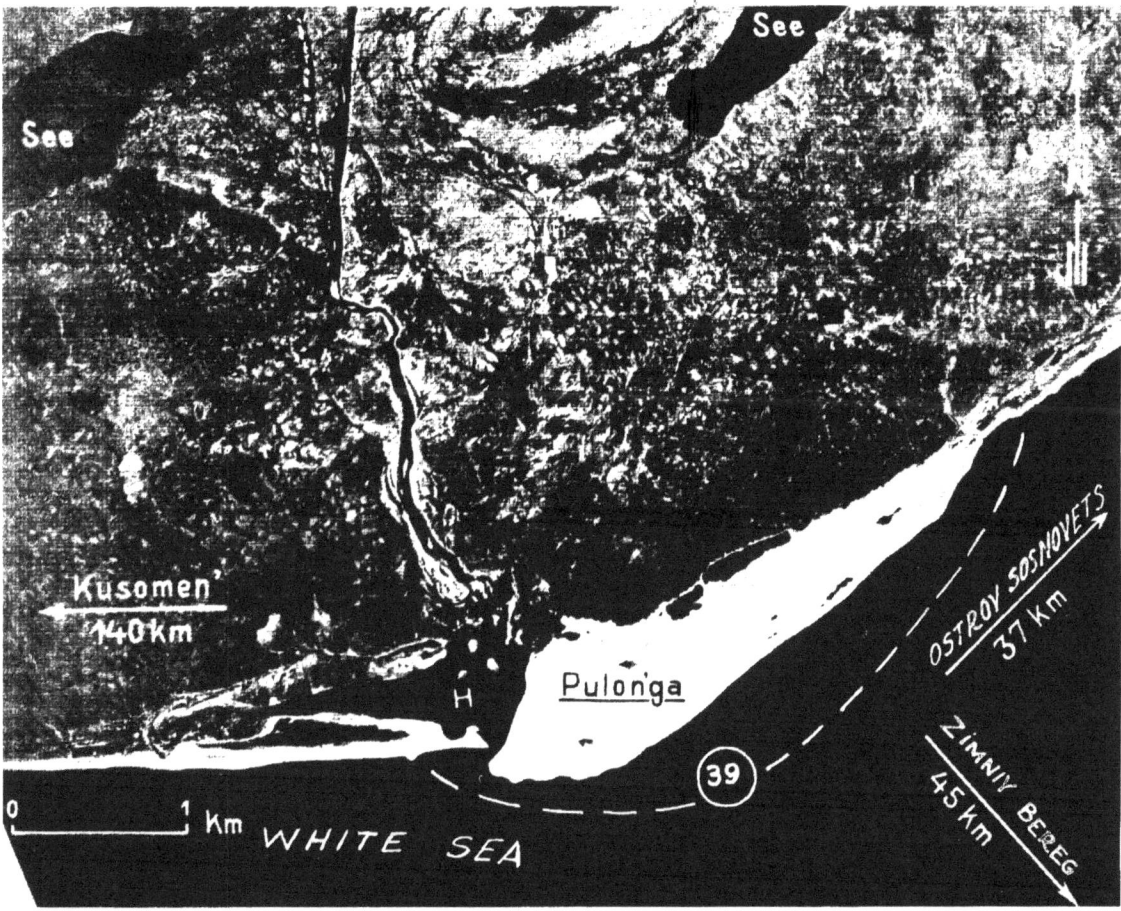

FIGURE IV-22. *White Sea, Pulon'ga. Beach area (39).*
White sandy area backed by sloping wooded terrain at eastern end of beach area. Prior to 1943. Approximate position 66°15'N, 40°01' E; B. A. Chart 2272.

Northeastward, for 50 miles to Mys Orlov (B.A. Chart 2270) the coast continues steep and rocky with hills rising inland. Offshore rocks exist for a short distance seaward and tundra-type vegetation grows on the rock slopes. About 2.5 miles north of Ponoi, on the east bank of the river there is a landing field for airplanes. Northward for 80 miles to Mys Svyatoy Nos (Cape Lenina), the coast is extremely cliffy. The rivers flow in deep ravines and granite hills 300 feet in elevation extend along the coast, with areas of tundra-type vegetation showing on the slopes. There are several small bays, the best of which is Lumbovskiy (beach areas (41) and (42)).

Mys Svyatoy Nos (FIGURE IV-23; B. A. Chart 2269), the western entrance point to the White Sea, is a narrow granite projection extending 10 miles northwestward. The cape is only 25 feet high at the point but reaches 650 feet in elevation about 7 miles southeastward. The shores are steep and cliffy.

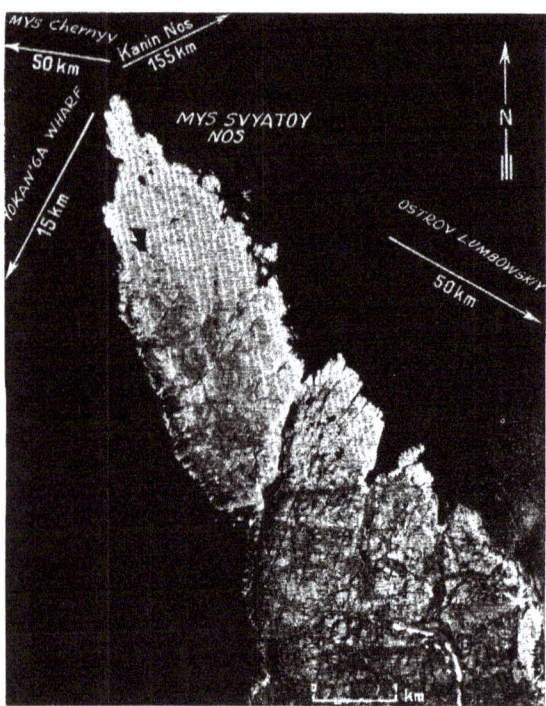

FIGURE IV-23. *Murman Coast (Murmanskiy Bereg), Mys Svyatoy Nos.*
Barren granite terrain and cliffy coast at western entrance to White Sea. Prior to 1943. Approximate position 68°09'N, 39°49'E; B. A. Chart 2284.

(2) Landing beaches

The beaches along the shores of the White Sea, (beach areas (21) to (42); TABLE IV-4), vary considerably. Along the east shore the beaches are most extensive; they are usually best developed at the small river mouths where small dune areas may lie inland. Otherwise they are backed rather generally with sand and clay cliffs. Beaches of beach areas (33) to (37), along the west shore of the White Sea, are more generally short and lie along a much indented and rocky coast; while areas (38) and (39) are long, straight, and sandy. Exit is limited to trails or winter roads through the coastal settlements.

TABLE IV - 4

LANDING BEACHES OF COASTAL SUBSECTOR 41 C

Reliability FAIR. (PLAN 12; FIGURE IV - 9)

Number and location of beach area	Nearshore	Length	Width at H.W. and L.W.	Gradient in H.W. zone	Surf and shore drift	Material and firmness	Terrain immediately behind beach	Connections inland
(21) N and S of Shoyna	Flat bottom slopes; shoals off river mouths.	Total about 35 mi., interrupted by river mouths and by steep coast near N end.	50 to 75 ft. at H.W., widest at river mouths; width at L.W. unknown.	1 on 30.	Surf light to moderate, breaks in wide belt; drift mainly to S.	Mainly sand; firm near H.W.	Sand dunes generally backed by marsh; sand-and-clay cliffs back sections near N end.	Trails to settlements may be available; details unknown.
(22) Mezenskaya Guba, E shore.	Drying banks fringe entire stretch, locally extend for about 4 mi.	Small river mouth beaches, average length 1.5 mi.; may be more continuous than shown.	50 to 100 ft. at H.W., 1 mi. to about 3 mi. at L.W.	1 on 100.	Surf moderate to heavy, intensified by tidal bore; drift varies.	Sand near H.W., grades outward to sand and mud; firm near H.W.	Sand dunes along river mouth beaches; steep sand-and-clay cliffs between, and inland is peat covered tundra.	Trails to settlements may be available; details unknown.
(23) Mezenskaya Guba, SW shore.	Very flat bottom slopes, offshore shoals, and extensive drying flats.	2 river mouth beaches, each about 1 mi.; joined at L.W. by continuous beach.	25 to 50 ft. at H.W., 300 ft. to about 1 mi. at L.W.	1 on 100.	Surf moderate to heavy, breaks in wide belt; drift mainly to E.	Sand at H.W., sand, shell, and pebbles near L.W., generally firm.	Sand and clay cliffs.	Access to settlements along river banks may be accessible; trail or winter road runs SE and W from Koyda.

COASTS AND LANDING BEACHES

TABLE IV - 4 (Continued)

Number and location of beach area	Nearshore	Length	Width at H.W. and L.W.	Gradient in H.W. zone	Surf and shore drift	Material and firmness	Terrain immediately behind beach	Connections inland
(24) NE and SW of Intsy (Fig. IV - 11.)	Bottom slopes *flat*, slightly steeper to SW; shoals off N end, nearshore rocks locally along S half.	Numerous river mouth beaches, average 2 mi.; continuous very narrow beach may connect areas.	50 to 75 ft. at H.W., may range to 500 ft. at L.W.	1 on 30.	Surf moderate to heavy; drift generally to S along N half, to N along S half.	Sand; firm near H.W.	Dunes along larger river mouths; sand and clay cliffs 50 ft. high lie between.	Settlements relatively numerous; coastal trail or winter road generally accessible.
(25) S from Mys Lysunov.	Bottom slopes *gentle* at N, become *flat* at S; rock and sand bank off Mys Keretş.	About 32 mi., interrupted by river mouths and rocky points.	15 to 50 ft. at H.W., widest at rivers; may range to 300 ft. at L.W.	Average 1 on 50.	Surf generally heavy; drift probably varies.	Sand with scattered pebbles and rock, grades to muddy sand near L.W. at S end; firm near H.W.	Generally sand and clay banks, 40 ft. high; locally lower areas of grass and birch.	River bank settlements may be accessible; trail or winter road runs NE and SE.
(26) S of Mys Kuyskiy, including Ostrov Mud'yugskiy.	Bottom slopes *flat*; shifting shoals at N, drying flat along most of area.	About 18 mi., interrupted by river and by channel between spit and island.	50 to 150 ft. at H.W., narrowest at N end and along islands; ranges to 750 ft. at L.W.	1 on 50 average.	Surf moderate to heavy; drift variable, but mainly to S.	Sand with some rock and mud toward L.W.; firm near H.W.	Generally sand hills, ranging from 10 to 20 ft. high; low grassy slopes at N end.	Exit available to settlement and trail or winter road at N end.
(27) SE of Unskaya Guba. (Figs. IV - 13 and IV - 14.)	*Gentle-to-flat* bottom slopes; anchorage within 30 ft. with shelter from SW winds.	About 43 mi., may not be as continuous as shown; is best developed along river interruptions.	15 to 75 ft. at H.W., widest at river mouths may range to 400 ft. at L.W.	1 on 50 average.	Surf moderate to heavy; drift to SE.	Sand or sand and pebbles; firm near H.W.	Generally sand and clay cliffs broken by dune areas along river mouths.	Exit to settlements near river mouths and to coastal road. Railroad available at E end of beach.
(28) NW of Unskaya Guba. (Fig. IV - 15.)	*Moderate* bottom slopes to W, flatten toward E; narrow rock ledge or sand banks obstruct approach.	Total about 47 mi., may be more or less interrupted than shown.	25 to 100 ft. at H.W., narrowest portions at NW end and near center; may range locally to 500 ft. at L.W.	1 on 30 average.	Surf likely heavy, breaks in wide belt; drift mainly to SE.	Sand and rock along NW half, mainly sand to SE; generally firm.	Steep sand banks locally between flat sandy terrain.	Exit to settlements probably available; no trails are known.
(29) N and S of Letuyaya Zolotitsa. (Fig. IV-15.)	*Flat* irregular bottom slopes; rocky drying bank borders shore.	River mouth beaches average 1 mi.; bayhead area about 6 mi.	25 to 75 ft. at H.W., range to 300 ft. at L.W.	1 on 25.	Surf generally heavy; drift mainly to N.	Sand and some rock along rivermouths; rock more predominant along bay.	Gentle hill slopes with pine cover.	Minor road probably accessible from rivermouth beaches and from E side of bay.
(30) Bay at Pushlakhta and S.	Extensive shoals off bay at N; *flat* bottom slopes and drying rocky bank.	Bayhead beach about 4 mi.; river mouth area probably 0.5 mi., may extend farther both N and S.	10 to 25 ft. at H.W., may range to 300 ft. at L.W.	1 on 30.	Surf light to moderate; drift generally to N.	Sand and pebbles or rock, probably muddy near L.W., relatively soft.	Gentle hill slopes with trees and grass border bay; steep sandy cliffs to S, range to 90 ft.	Minor road parallels coast; accessible from settlement on bay and river bank.
(31) Mys Glubokiy and bay area to E.	Shoals extend 5 mi. offshore; bank dries locally from 900 ft. to 1 mi.	About 30 mi. along bayheads and river mouths, interrupted by steep shore.	50 to 100 ft. at H.W., may range to 1,000 ft. or more at L.W.	1 on 50 average.	Surf light; drift varies.	Mainly sand with scattered rock, grades to muddy sand near L.W., relatively soft.	Low sand or sand and rock banks generally.	Exit to minor road best from village back of W end; details not known.

TABLE IV - 4 (Continued)

Number and location of beach area	Nearshore	Length	Width at H.W. and L.W.	Gradient in H.W. zone	Surf and shore drift	Material and firmness	Terrain immediately behind beach	Connections inland
(32) W and S of Tamitsa.	Bars off river mouths; drying flat about 1,000 ft. wide at N and 2 mi. wide at S.	About 14 mi., interrupted by river mouths and cliffs.	75 to 150 ft. at H.W.; 1,000 ft. or more at L.W.	1 on 50 average.	Surf generally light or absent; drift varies.	Mainly sand with some rock, probably some mud near L.W., soft.	Marsh area backed by level cultivated land backs S end; more generally sand and clay terrain fronted by dunes along N. section.	Minor road lies 1 mi. or more inland at N; exit probably best from S end to Onega.
(33) (FIG. IV - 16)	Very *flat* bottom slopes; drying bank rocky along NW extends for 1 to 4 mi. offshore.	About 34 mi., broken by river mouths and rocky points; may not be as continuous as shown.	About 50 ft. at H.W., ranges to 1 mi. or more generally at L.W.	1 on 25.	Surf generally light; drift varies.	Sand and mud at E grades to pebbles and mud to W, generally soft.	Sand and clay banks averaging 25 ft. high along E; low peat and birch covered land farther W.	Road or trail 1 to 5 mi. inland; exits generally poor.
(34) Ostrov Mal. Zayatskiy and Ostrov Anzerskiy (Solovetski Islands.)	*Flat* bottom slopes; approaches obstructed by islets and numerous rocks.	Several small beaches, probably average 1 mi. or less; exact locations are also uncertain.	Probably 15 to 25 ft. at H.W., width at L.W. unknown.	Probably 1 on 15.	Surf generally light except along beach on smaller island; drift varies.	Sand, pebbles, and rock; generally firm.	Settlements directly inland; terrain is sand and rock hills, generally covered with pine and birch trees.	Unknown.
(35) Kem' to Gridino	Approaches extensively obstructed by islets, and rocks; bottom slopes generally *flat*.	Scattered beaches at river mouths or bayheads, average about 1 mile; more such areas may be present.	Probably 15 to 25 ft. at H.W. widths at L.W. unknown.	1 on 25 average.	Surf moderate to heavy along more exposed areas; drift varies.	Sand, pebbles, and rock; generally firm.	Marsh, bog, and meadow terrain, generally impassable; inland hills reach elevations of about 350 feet 20 to 40 mi. from shore.	R. R. and minor road accessible at Kem', only foot path or trail from Gridino.
(36) Kandalakshskaya Guba, inner shores. (FIG. IV - 19.)	Approach obstructed by islands and rocks; wharf along W beach on S shore and E beach on N shore.	Short beaches at settlements, usually about 0.5 mi.; more such areas may be present.	15 to 25 ft. at H.W., width at L.W. unknown.	1 on 15.	Surf light; drift varies.	Sand and pebbles with some rock; firm.	Steep hills behind settlement areas, some forested land; coasts are generally steep rock cliffs ranging to about 400 ft. high.	Minor road and railroad accessible at Kandalaksha; otherwise exits poor.
(37) NW and SE of Olenitsa.	Bottom slopes *flat*; drying partly rocky flats extend offshore for about 500 ft. along SE to about 0.5 mi. in bay at Olenitsa.	Several short beaches, average 1 mi.	25 to 50 ft. at H.W., 600 to 2,500 ft. at L.W.	1 on 30.	Moderate surf; drift varies.	Sand or rock and sand, generally firm.	Gentle slopes or small settlements; inland hills rise generally to 100 ft. and are tree covered.	Exit probably accessible to river bank settlements connected by trail or winter road.
(38) W and SE of Kuzomen'. (FIG. IV - 21.)	Drying flat 300 to 600 ft. wide off river mouth at Kuzomen, and to W; narrower to E. Anchorage E of river in 24 to 30 ft.	About 50 mi., broken by river mouths and rocky points; may not be as continuous as shown.	50 to 150 ft. at H.W., 200 to 750 ft. at L.W.; widest near Kuzomen, and to W.	Average 1 on 30.	Surf generally heavy; drift mainly to E.	Fine sand along W; sand and pebbles to E; firm near H.W.	Extensive wind-blown sand area W of Kuzomen'; sandy hills or low bank common to E backed by grass- and tree-covered hills.	Exit accessible to settlements which are connected by trail or winter road.
(39) SW and NE of Pyalitsa. (FIG. IV - 22.)	Rocks off SW end; otherwise narrow drying flat partly rocky.	About 45 mi., interrupted by river mouths and rocky points.	50 to 75 ft. at H.W., ranges to about 300 ft. at L.W.	Average 1 on 20.	Surf generally heavy; drift varies over area.	Sand with pebbles and rock near river mouths or rocky points; generally firm.	Local dune areas; more generally a low sandy bluff lies close inland backed by wooded and brush-covered hilly terrain.	Probable accessibility to settlements on high ground above shore and to winter trail.

D. Mys Svyatoy Nos to the Norwegian Boundary

(68°09′N, 39°49′E; 69°47′N, 30°50′E) (Plan 13; Figure IV-24; U.S.H.O. Chart 5784; B.A. Charts 2269, 2284, 2333, 2334, and 2966; A.M.S. Maps—North West Russia scale 1:2,000,000 G.S.G.S. No. 4464 Key No. 312625, Murmansk scale 1:500,000 G.S.G.S. No. 4312 Key No. 100236, Port-Vladimir scale 1:100,000 G.S.G.S. No. 4383 Key No. 117476, and Petsamo scale 1:100,000 G.S.G.S. No. 4383 Key No. 100177)

(1) Coast

The coast of Kola Peninsula (Poluostrov Kol'skiy) northwestward of Mys Svyatoy Nos (Cape Lenina), known as the Murman Coast (Murmanskiy Bereg), remains open to navigation throughout the year (B.A. Chart 2284). A branch of the warm North Atlantic current flows southeastward along this coast and keeps it ice-free, despite its geographical location north of the Arctic Circle. Only small amounts of land ice appear in the bays along the coast between December and April. Deep water of the Barents Sea lies off the coast, the 50-fathom curve lying generally within 3 miles of the shore. Inside the 10-fathom curve the coast is fringed by rocks and shoals. Offshore are many small, high and rocky islands. Innumerable bays and inlets indent the coast, which is steep and cliffy, and consists generally of huge rounded outcroppings of granite. Peat and white moss of the tundra cover much of the rocky surface. Coastal heights vary between 300 and 700 feet and afford excellent observation points. Isolated low points exist at the heads of the bays and are the sites of the small fishing villages along the coast (beach areas (43) to (49), and (51)). There are neither coastal roads nor exits inland; the only communications are by sea, and by wire which passes along the coast. Limited cultivation is carried on in tiny valley plots near the river mouths. The rivers generally pass through deep ravines and are not navigable because of falls and rapids. Inland about 20 miles the terrain consists of high, undulating country with many lakes, and some flat areas of interest as potential airfield sites. Dwarfed trees and bushes grow inland. Forests of the southwestern half of Kola Peninsula lie from 50 to 75 miles inland of the Murman Coast.

Yokan'ga lies 8 miles south-southwestward of Mys Svyatoy Nos and has a good harbor (Figure IV-25; B.A. Chart 2269) which has been used frequently for forming convoys (Chapter VI). The port has a small pier, a seaplane station, and a landing ground. A trail leads southwestward along the coast. Moderately sloping rocky terrain lies behind the port extending to the hills close inland. Guba Teriberskaya (B.A. Chart 2334) lies 140 miles northwestward of Mys Svyatoy Nos. It has fair anchorage facilities and is less obstructed than other bays along the coast. It extends 2 miles inland and is 3 miles wide. Although open to northwestward the bay has a southwestern reach which is well protected. This reach has low, sandy eastern shores where the town and an airfield are located (beach area (50)). Ostrov Kil'din (Kildin Island) (B.A. Chart 2333) lies 20 miles west-northwestward of Teriberka, about 1 mile off the coast. It is 10 miles long east–west, 4 miles wide, and consists of schist hills reaching 900 feet in elevation. Only the eastern part of the southern shore (beach area (52)) is low; there is located a small town, a seaplane station, and an airfield.

Kol'skiy Zaliv (Kola Inlet) (Figure IV-26; B.A. Chart 2966) lies 10 miles eastward of Ostrov Kil'din. In this inlet are located the important ports of Polyarnyy, Vayenga, Murmansk (Figure IV-27), and Kola (Chapter VI). These ports can be reached when the ports on the White

TABLE IV - 4 (Continued)

Number and location of beach area	Length	Nearshore	Width at H.W. and L.W.	Gradient in H.W. zone	Surf and shore drift	Material and firmness	Terrain immediately behind beach	Connections inland
(40) Sosnovka	About 0.5 mi. at river mouth.	Approach obstructed by offshore island and drying shoal 1 mi. from shore.	10 to 25 ft. at H.W., 1,000 ft. L.W.	1 on 15.	Surf generally light; drift probably varies.	Pebbles and sand with scattered rock; firm.	Steep river banks back beach; settlement lies on plateau above shore.	Exit into settlement available; inland communication limited to trail or winter road.
(41)	Probably totals 0.5 mi. along shore of small bay.	Depth in bay entrance is 20 ft.; shore bordered by rocky drying bank.	Probably 10 ft. H.W., 100 ft. L.W.	1 on 10.	Surf generally heavy; drift probably negligible.	Rock and sand; firm.	Steep cliffs.	Path to lighthouse probably available.
(42) Zaliv Lumbovskiy	Total about 10 mi., may not be continuous as shown.	Rocky drying flat extends from 3,000 ft. to 2.5 mi. from shore except off Chernaya river; islands obstruct bay entrances.	10 ft. at H.W., 100 ft to 2.5 mi. at L.W.	1 on 15.	Heavy surf with N winds; drift probably varies.	Rock, sand, and mud; relatively soft.	Narrow belt of relatively low land backed by steep hills.	Settlement at SE corner of bay lies on route of trail or winter road.

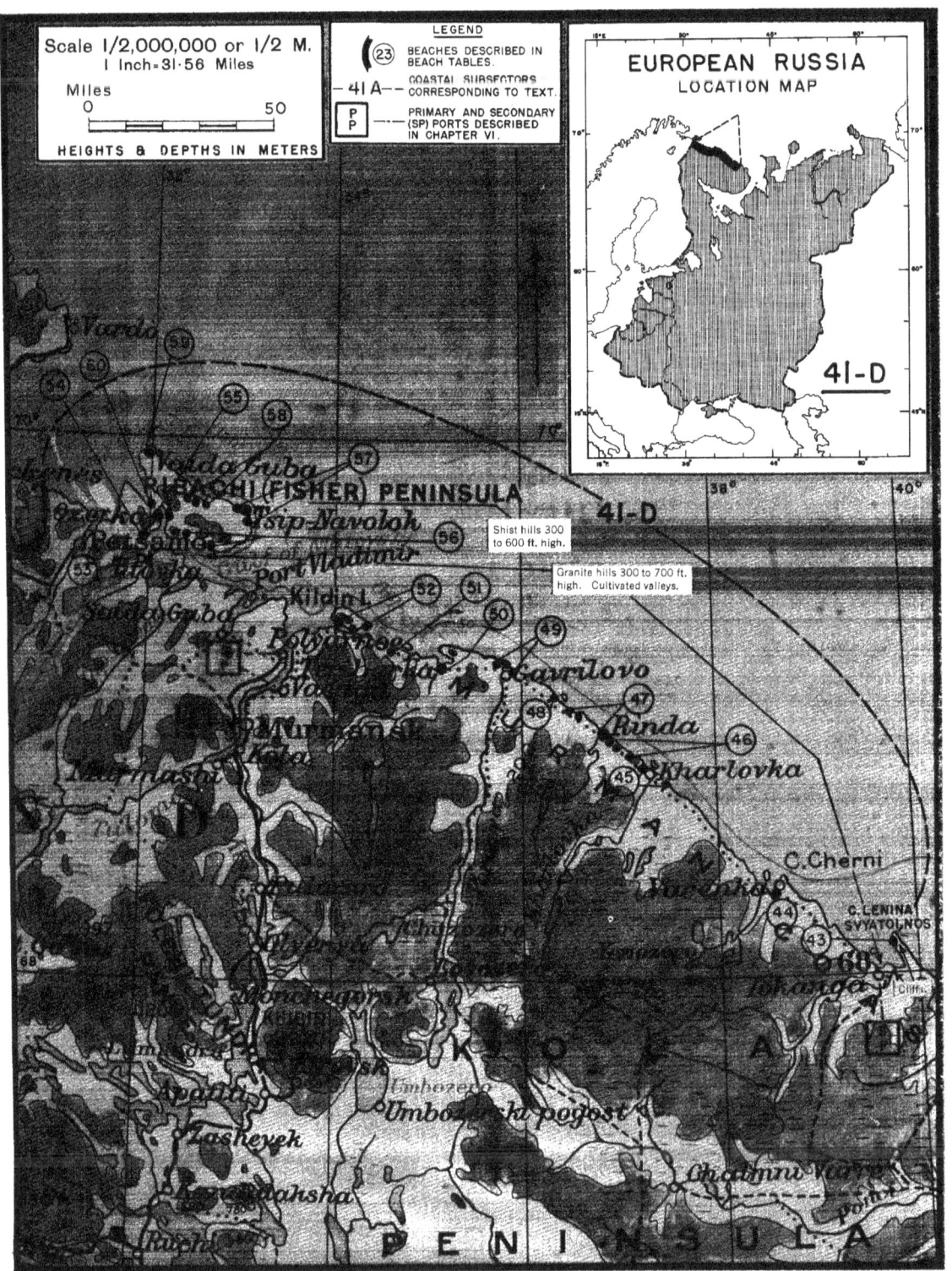

FIGURE IV-24. *Coastal subsector 41 D.*

FIGURE IV-25. *Murman Coast (Murmanskiy Bereg), Yokan'ga.*
Typical rugged granite terrain along the Arctic coast of Kola Peninsula. Prior to 1943. Approximate position 68°04′N, 39°32′E; B. A. Chart 2269.

FIGURE IV-26. *Kol'skiy Zaliv, Guba Tyuva.*
View southwestward across mouth of bay to Tyuvagubski lighthouse from watering place in the northern shore of the bay. 1936 or earlier. Approximate position 69°12′N, 33°35′E; B. A. Chart 2966.

FIGURE IV-27. *Kol'skiy Zaliv, Murmansk.*
View southwestward across harbor. Note barren, gently sloping terrain of town site and low hills across inlet. No date. Approximate position 68°58'N, 33°05'E; B. A. Chart 2966.

Sea and the Baltic are icebound. Some ice forms in the inlet in December and January, but it is easily kept open by ice breakers. The inlet is between 1 and 2 miles wide and from 10 to 140 fathoms deep, and it is bound by steep granite hills southward 26 miles to Murmansk. At Murmansk gently sloping terrain affords a site for the town and a number of airfields. The Murmansk railroad southward connects this arctic port with the Leningrad area.

Westward of Kol'skiy Zaliv (FIGURE IV-28) lies Motovskiy Zaliv (B.A. Chart 2333) which is 3 to 6 miles wide and extends westward about 30 miles to Poluostrov Sredniy. It is bounded to the northward by Poluostrov Rybachiy (Ribachi Peninsula). The southern shore of the inlet is indented by several long narrow bays which extend south-southwestward. Between them lie steep granite hills with many lakes scattered between them. The bays are deep, some reaching 145 fathoms, but they are in general between 30 and 40 fathoms deep. They are of particular interest because their heads are low, sandy areas backed by river valleys which extend to the lake country inland. A trail from Polyarnyy roughly parallels the coast 10 to 15 miles inland, passing through the fishing villages at the heads of the bays. Guba Ura lies 6 miles westward of Kol'skiy Zaliv and extends 14 miles inland; it is 1 to 5 miles wide. Ostrov Shalim lies in the mouth of the bay where the small fishing village of Port-Vladimir is situated. The town Ura-Guba, which has an airfield, lies at the head of the bay. Guba Ara, 3 miles farther westward, and Guba Vichany, 6 miles west of Guba Ara, are smaller bays connected by trail to Ura-Guba. Guba Zapadnaya Litsa lies 17 miles westward of Ura-Guba and extends 14 miles southwestward. The streams entering the bay along the southeastern shores are wooded for about 10 miles southward. Such a wooded area in the tundra region is referred to as a forest island. Guba Titovka (beach area (53)) lies 12 miles northwestward. It extends about 5 miles inland and is over 1 mile in width and varies from 14 to 50 fathoms in depth. The town of Titovka at the head of the bay has an airfield. The trail from Polyarnyy forks west of Titovka and extends westward to Pechenga (Petsamo) and northward to Poluostrov Rybachiy. Northwestward 4 miles lies the bay Guba Kutovaya, the western end of Motovskiy Zaliv. At its head is the narrow isthmus joining Poluostrov Sredniy and

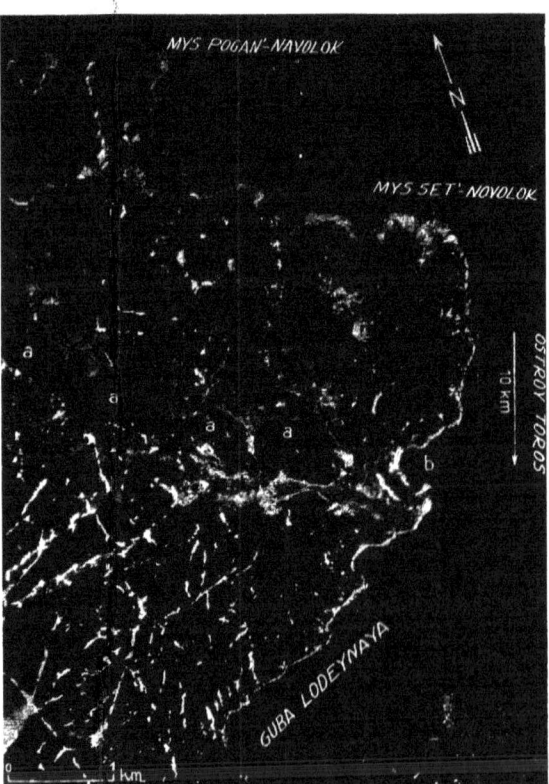

FIGURE IV-28. *Murman Coast (Murmanskiy Bereg), Mys Pogan'-Navolok.*
Western entrance to Kol'skiy Zaliv. Note lakes (a), and tiny beach (b). Prior to 1943. Approximate position 69°25'N, 33°29'E; B. A. Chart 2333.

the mainland (beach area (54)). The isthmus is a narrow, marshy valley between the granite hills on the mainland and the high schist hills of Poluostrov Sredniy. The peninsula is about 15 miles long and 8 miles wide. Its terrain is high and rocky and mostly between 800 and 1,200 feet in elevation. The trail northward lies along the eastern shores. Guba Bol'shaya Motka and its shallow northern reach, Bukhta Ozerko (beach area (55)), separate Poluostrov Sredniy and Poluostrov Rybachiy on the east. At the head of the bay is the marshy isthmus joining the peninsulas. The isthmus terrain is undulating, with one hill to the west reaching 344 feet; to northward lie the highest hills of Poluostrov Rybachiy which are about 800 feet in elevation. The shores of the bay are mostly steep and cliffy but are low for about 1 mile southward of Ozerka, a small village located on the eastern shore where the two bays join. This low coastal area is backed by moderately sloping marshy meadows. Poluostrov Rybachiy is about 35 miles long and 13 miles wide. The southern shores, which lie on Motovskiy Zaliv, and the southeastern shores are steep and cliffy; the only low point is at the head of Guba Yeyna, 6 miles eastward of Guba Bol'shaya Motka (beach area (56)). The northeastern shores of the peninsula are moderately high, with scattered cliffs. The bays Guba Laush, Guba Zubovskaya, Guba Skorbeyevskaya, and Guba Vayda (FIGURE IV-29), offer good harbors and fair landing areas backed by moderately sloping terrain (beach areas (57), (58) and (59)). Guba Zubovskaya offers the best landing conditions and has an airfield. A trail joining Guba Zubovskaya, Guba Vayda, and Guba Yeyna is connected to the trail southward across the isthmus to the mainland trail. The terrain of Poluostrov Rybachiy is undulating and has a large number of lakes, streams, and marshy localities. Slaty or shaly schist is scattered about the peninsula, and there are some meadows and bushes. The hills on each side of Guba Bol'shaya Volokovaya (beach area (60)) are covered with peat and moss and slope toward the sea, presenting bare schist rocks, especially on the northeast side of the bay. The west coast of Poluostrov Sredniy is high and steep, but not cliffy. Soil is stiff clay and the top is covered with peat and moss. The southern shore of Guba Maly Volokovaya is high and steep, being part of a ridge of hills crossing the isthmus from Motovskiy Zaliv. High granite hills continue to the entrance of Petsamon-vuono (Pechenga Gulf), which extends 9 miles southwestward from the entrance and has four reaches. Small settlements, the largest of which is Pechenga (Petsamo), are located along the gulf. The terrain westward to the river Vorema continues bold and of moderate height, indented by small coves and narrow inlets.

(2) Landing beaches

The beaches of subsector 41 D are described briefly in TABLE IV-5. The known beaches are very scattered; most of them lie at the heads of relatively shallow bays and are fronted by rocky or sandy flats. The coast between is steep and irregular.

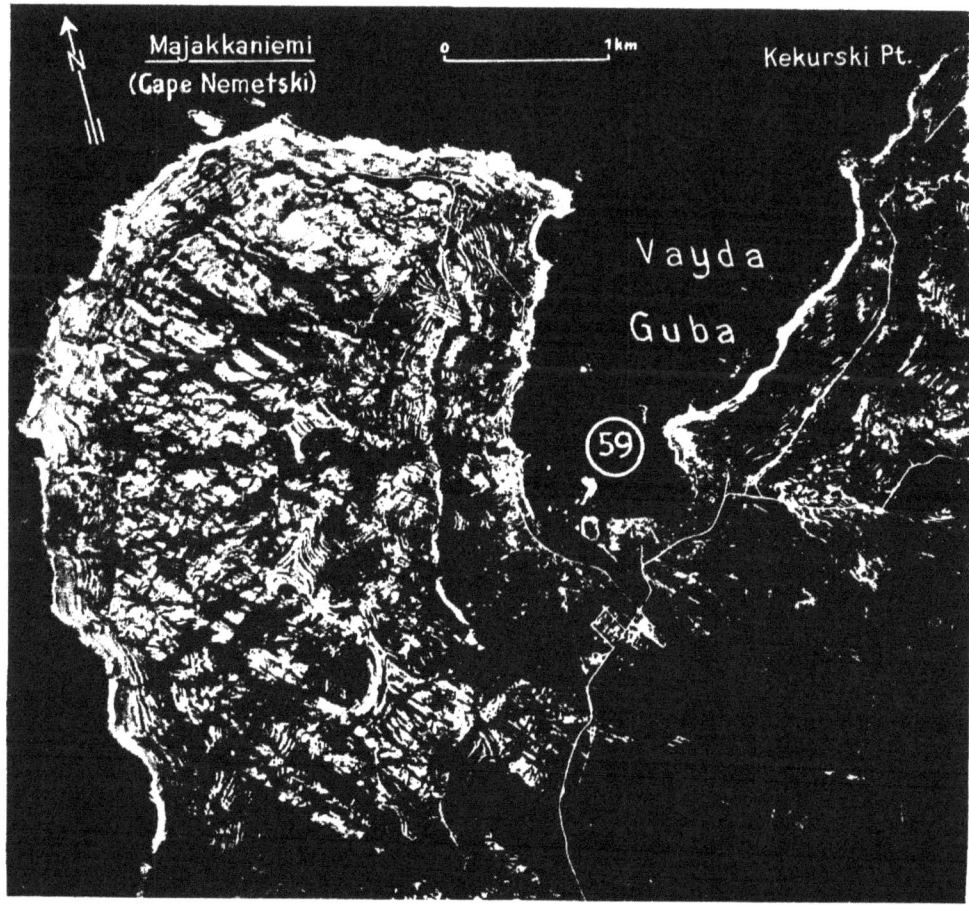

FIGURE IV-29. *Poluostrov Rybachiy, Guba Vayda. Beach area (59).*
Note fishing village and road net at head of bay. Prior to 1943. Approximate position 69°56′N, 32°E; B. A. Chart 2333.

Original

TABLE IV - 5
LANDING BEACHES OF COASTAL SUBSECTOR 41 D (PLAN 13)
Reliability POOR.

Number and location of beach area	Nearshore	Length	Width at H.W. and L.W.	Gradient in H.W. zone	Surf and shore drift	Material and firmness	Terrain immediately behind beach	Connections inland
(43) Lopskoe cove	*Moderate* bottom slopes outside rocky mud bank.	Probably 0.5 mi.	10 to 25 ft. at H.W., probably 500 ft. at L.W.	1 on 15.	Surf moderate; breaks on bank near time of L.W.	Pebbles, grade to mud and rock at L.W.; firm near H.W.	Grass-covered narrow ravine runs inland from head of cove; steep cliffs border N and S shores.	Access probably available to lighthouse and to opposite shore of promontory.
(44) Ivanovka	Approach obstructed by islands and rocky banks.	Probably 1,000 ft. at river mouth.	15 to 25 ft. at H.W., width at L.W. unknown.	1 on 25.	Surf negligible.	Sand, pebbles, and mud; relatively firm.	High river banks inland; generally steep rocky shore to either side.	Unknown.
(45) Kharlovka and SE	*Flat* bottom slopes; drying flat about 1,000 ft. wide, may be rocky.	2 areas fronting settlements at river mouths, probably about 0.3 mi. each.	25 ft. at H.W, 1,000 ft. at L.W.	1 on 25.	Surf moderate; drift varies.	Sand and pebbles; firm.	Settlements close inland on river banks; backed by low stony terraces.	Only trail or winter road.
(46) Guba Zolotaya and NW.	Bay entrances partially obstructed by islets or rocks; afford anchorage for small boats.	3 bayhead beaches, average length 1,000 ft.	50 to 75 ft. at H.W., L.W. width unknown.	1 on 30.	Surf heavy with NE or E winds; drift probably varies.	Sand; firm.	Bordered generally by rocky shore; hill slopes lie inland. Settlement at head of Guba Zolotaya.	Poor.
(47) Guba Rynda and NW.	Approach to Rynda obstructed by islets and drying bank; NW bays bordered by flats 600 ft. wide.	3 bayhead beaches, average 500 ft.	25 ft. at H.W., probably 700 average at L.W.	1 on 25.	Surf heavy with onshore winds.	Mainly sand; firm.	Settlement and terraced slopes at Rynda; rocky shores in NW bays.	Only trails.
(48) Porchnikha	Approach through long narrow cove; drying bank extends off S entrance point.	About 500 ft.	Probably 25 ft. at H.W., width at L.W. unknown.	1 on 30.	No surf except with heavy E winds; drift negligible.	Sand; firm.	Generally rocky moderate-to-steep shores; fishing huts and pier on N shore E of beach.	Poor; only trail is accessible.
(49)	Bottom slopes *mild* to *flat*; center bay dries; E and W areas fronted by flats 500 ft. wide.	3 bayhead beach areas; E and center about 500 ft., W area widest; range to about 1 mi.	25 to 75 ft. at H.W., W area widest; range to about 600 ft. at L.W.	1 on 30.	Moderate-to-heavy surf with onshore winds; drift probably varies, is to E along W area.	Mainly firm.	Large settlement backs center area; 4 piers along rocky shores near E areas; sand dunes backed by terraced bluffs behind W area.	Only trail or winter road is available from settled areas.
(50) Teriberka	Bottom slopes *gentle* to *flat*; drying flat 600 ft. wide fronts beach.	About 1.5 mi. along shore E of river at bayhead.	25 to 50 ft. at H.W., 650 ft. at L.W.	1 on 30.	Generally moderate swell; weak drift.	Sand; firm.	High grass and brush-covered plain beyond terrace backing beach; large settlement lies along river bank.	Only trail.
(51)	Shelter for small boats; details of nearshore not known.	Probably 500 ft.	Probably 15 to 25 ft. at H.W., width at L.W. not known.	1 on 20.	Surf generally light even with E winds; drift negligible.	Sand or sand and pebbles; relatively firm.	Low stony terrace backs beach; steep rocky slopes border area.	Unknown.

TABLE IV - 5 (Continued)

Number and location of beach area	Nearshore	Length	Width at H.W. and L.W.	Gradient in H.W. zone	Surf and shore drift	Material and firmness	Terrain immediately behind beach	Connections inland
(52) Ostrov Kil'din S shore.	Narrow partly rocky flat; other details not known.	E area about 2,000 ft., to W totals about 3.5 mi.	10 to 15 ft. at H.W., width at L.W. not known.	1 on 15.	Surf negligible; drift varies.	Sand and pebbles at E, pebbles and rock to W; firm.	Small settlement on E, pebble and rock terrace to W.	Unknown.
(53) Titovka.	Fronted by drying bank 4,500 ft. wide.	Total 0.5 mi. E of river mouth at bayhead.	25 to 50 ft. at H.W., over 4,500 ft. at L.W.	1 on 50.	Surf light or absent; drift soft.	Sand; probably soft.	Sand and rock terraces to E; partly wooded level land and some huts behind beach.	Only trail.
(54) Kutovaya.	Gentle bottom slopes; drying flat 1,000 ft. wide and rocks off beach.	Probably 1 mi. along N shore and head of bay.	Average 25 ft. at H.W.; over 1,000 ft. at L.W.	1 on 25.	Heavy surf with E winds; drift weak.	Probable sand with some rock; relatively firm.	Settlement backed by low partly marsh land of narrow isthmus.	Trail is available.
(55)	Fronted by drying bank of mud, sand, and rock ranging to about 1 mi. wide.	About 3 mi. on each shore of bay, interrupted by rocky point on E, lies along spit at center of W shore.	Probably 15 to 25 ft. at H.W., ranges to 1 mi. along inner W shore at L.W.	1 on 50 average.	Surf negligible; drift weak.	Sand and rock grading to mud and rock along inner shores; relatively soft.	Grassy moderate slopes with thick cover of birch; low marshy ground borders beaches to N.	Trail along E shore.
(56)	Drying bank averaging 1,000 ft. wide in W bay; gentle bottom slopes in E bay.	2 bayhead beaches, each 1,000 to 2,000 ft. long.	10 to 15 ft. wide at H.W., W area ranges to 1,000 ft. at L.W.	1 on 30.	Surf light; drift probably weak and variable.	Sand and pebbles probably with scattered rock; relatively firm at H.W.	Small temporary settlements backed by low partly wooded river valley behind W beach, by steeper valley slopes behind E beach.	None are known.
(57)	Probably mild to flat bottom slopes; small islets in approach to S bay.	3 bayhead beaches, average 1 mi. long.	Probably 25 ft. at H.W., width at L.W. unknown.	1 on 30.	Surf moderate to heavy; drift varies.	Sand or sand and pebbles; firm near H.W.	Small settlement backs S bay, fronts low, partly marshy area extending NW to center bay.	Trails across lowland between S bay and center bay.
(58)	Islets and rocks obstruct entrance to bay area; drying flat 600 ft. wide off W areas.	3 beaches at small river mouths; E beach 1,000 ft. W areas about 1.5 mi. each.	Probably 25 ft. at H.W., range to about 600 ft. at L.W.	1 on 30.	Surf moderate; drift probably varies.	Mainly sand; relatively soft.	Settlement backs E area, sandy grass land backs areas to W.	Trail runs from settlement along S bay of beach area (57).
(59) Guba Vayda. (Fig. IV - 29.)	Drying flat about 1,000 ft. wide fronts beach.	Probably about 0.5 mi. fronting fishing village.	15 to 25 ft. at H.W., 1,000 ft. at L.W.	1 on 15.	Surf moderate; drift weak.	Sand and pebbles grading to muddy sand at L.W.; firm near H.W.	Settlement and low land back of bayhead; moderate slopes border beach.	Only trails.
(60) Guba Bol'shaya Volokovaya.	Rocks in entrance to inlet; drying flat fronts beach.	About 0.5 mi. at head of narrow inlet.	50 to 75 ft.	1 on 30	Surf moderate; drift probably negligible.	Sand; firm near H.W. line.	Low, partly marshy, land of narrow isthmus behind beach; bay shores are generally rocky hills partly covered with moss and peat.	None are known.

(Text continued following Figure IV-30)

42. WEST COASTAL SECTOR—MYS KRYUSERORT (RISTNIEMI) TO SZTUTOWO (STUTTHOF)

(60°31′N, 28°15′E; 54°20′N, 19°09′E) (Plans 14 to 16; Figures IV-117 and IV-119; U.S.H.O. Chart 4845; B.A. Charts 2191, 2282, and 2842B; A.M.S. Maps scale 1:2,000,000 G.S.G.S. No. 4464—Central Europe Key No. 173153, Scandinavia Key No. 312330, and North West Russia Key No. 312625)

The Gulf of Finland extends in an easterly direction for 210 miles from Osmussar island to Leningrad (B.A. Chart 2191). It is 40 miles wide at the entrance between Pöösospää Neem (Pöösaspea) and Hangöudd, increasing gradually to 65 miles at Narva Laht, thence decreasing to 10 miles at Petrograd Bay. Deep water prevails throughout the central part. The bottom is mostly mud in the greater depths, alternating with rock and sand in the more shallow areas. The Gulf of Riga, 92 miles long and 55 miles wide, is connected with the Gulf of Finland by Vormsi Väin (Wormsö Sound) and Muhu Väin (Moon Sound) on the north, and with the Baltic Sea by Irbeni Väin on the west. The bottom at the middle of the gulf northward of Ruhnu is mostly mud, occasionally mixed with sand; toward the Estonian shore, sand and stone; and toward the Latvian coast, mostly coarse sand. The southern part of this sector runs approximately to the middle of Danzig Bay. The western sector thus describes the Baltic coast from the Finnish border on the Gulf of Finland to the former free state of Danzig, and includes the entire coastlines of the Estonian, Latvian, and Lithuanian SSR's.

Winds from west through south prevail in the western part of this sector, while to the east the prevailing winds are westerly. There is some tendency toward the development of land and sea breezes along these coastal areas during the summer months, but more generally westerly winds prevail throughout the year.

The currents of the Baltic Sea are generally to the south and west; their direction, however, varies greatly in different localities and may change with changes in wind direction and atmospheric pressure. For example, under ordinary conditions, the current in the Gulf of Finland is to the west and is strongest in the early spring. However, with westerly gales a current sets eastward along the gulf shore south of the island of Kronshtadt and to the west along the north shore, north of that island.

The variation in water level along the coast in this sector is due to the varying factors of river outflow, wind direction, and atmospheric pressure, and not to tidal influences. For this reason, the beach widths given in the following descriptive tables are average widths. For this same reason, the gradients given are an average water line. The usual water level fluctuations range from 1.5 to 3 feet; the variations are greater in the bays and narrow channels than on the open coast. In general, the fluctuations caused by wind direction are felt over a wide area and are greatest during the winter months when storms are most frequent. Fluctuations due to changes in atmospheric pressures are felt more locally; they are observed during all seasons, but most frequently in the fall and winter.

Ice forms a definite obstruction to navigation and landings during a relatively short winter period (Chapter III, Figures III-12 to III-23); the period, however, varies considerably with the severity of the weather. In the southern part of the sector, and in the northern entrance to the Gulf of Riga, ice begins to form in the inner and sheltered channels in December. Fixed or solid ice in the open sea is exceptional, although floating ice is common, especially during the early spring. Solid ice forms in the northern part of the Gulf of Riga and between the islands fringing this coast in early January; by February the whole of the gulf is generally frozen, although the larger harbors along the gulf can usually be approached with the aid of ice breakers. By the end of April, the whole of the gulf is generally free of ice. The Gulf of Finland generally does not freeze solid until early January. Even then, the ice may be quickly broken up by heavy storm winds and form large fields of drifting ice or be heaped up along the shore. Drifting ice fields are particularly dangerous in this area during the spring and may not entirely disappear until late May.

The beaches in the northern half of this sector generally are present in isolated and scattered areas and are interrupted by river mouths and rocky shores or points; they are fronted or flanked by rocky shoals on generally *flat* bottom slopes. The southern half of the sector is almost completely lined with sandy beaches with clear approaches over *mild-to-flat* bottom slopes.

A. Mys Kryuserort (Ristniemi) to Rooslepa

(60°31′N, 28°15′E; 59°10′N, 23°32′E) (Plans 14 and 15; Figure IV-30; B.A. Charts 2215, 2217, 2227, 2239, 2241, 2245, to 2247, 2279, 2826, and 3479)

(1) Coast

Mys Kryuserort (Ristniemi) lies on the northern coast of the Gulf of Finland at the western entrance to the Vyborgskiy Zaliv (Gulf of Viipuri), a large inlet which extends 19 miles northeastward to Vyborg (Viipuri) (B.A. Charts 2247, 2826, and 3479). The inner part of the inlet is obstructed by shoals and cut up into sections by several peninsulas and islands (beach area (61)). The shoreline is rocky and covered with pine forests.

The city of Vyborg, located at the head of the gulf, is on the Finnish railroad system which extends to Leningrad. A primary road parallels the coast from Vyborg south to Koyvisto (Koivisto), where it joins with a secondary road extending to Mys Inonemi. Numerous trails leading from the coast connect with a primary road about 10 miles inland. Vyborg is an excellent port with many good harbor facilities and installations (Chapter VI) and a seaplane station. In 1941 the population was 70,000. Abundant water and marshy terrain make movement inland difficult everywhere except along the dry Salpausel'ka (Sisempi Salpausselka) ridge of hills which extends along the USSR - Finland frontier in a straight east - west direction. The ridge is covered in places with forest growth and flanked by parallel sand and gravel ridges.

Proliv Koyviston Salmi, the eastern approach to Vyborg, lies between the mainland and the islands of Koyvisto (Koivista) and Piysaari (Piisaari). It is about 14 miles in length and varies in width from 0.8 to 2.3 miles. The mainland shore rises gradually to a chain of hills, 200 to 300 feet in height, on the slopes of which are numerous houses and villages. The general depths of water vary from 6 to 18 fathoms. Koyvisto (Koivisto) is hilly on the west side and covered with forests. At the middle of Torsaari, a small island to the northwest, is a conspicuous hill.

The coast between Proliv Koyviston Salmi and Mys Styursudd (included in beach area (61)), 15 miles to the southeastward, is cut up into several shallow bays with shoal water extending up to 1.5 miles offshore (B.A. Chart 2279).

Original

Petrograd Bay is 12 miles wide at its entrance between Mys Styursudd on the north and Ostrov Karavalday on the south, and extends 25 miles eastward. There are depths of 14 to 20 fathoms in the entrance, decreasing gradually to 5 and 6 fathoms at the head, with shoal water extending from the shores.

From Mys Styursudd, the north shore of Petrograd Bay trends eastward for 12.5 miles to Mys Inonemi and is backed by a steplike formation consisting of three levels. This formation is not noticeable from seaward but has the appearance of a high coast with stretches of sandy beach (beach area (62)). Sparse forests of fir trees line the shore. There are a number of villages along the beach.

From Mys Inonemi the shore extends eastward (beach area (63); FIGURES IV-31 and IV-32) for 14 miles farther and then southward for 8 miles to Mys Lisiy Nos. The shore is wooded, and between Mys Dubovskiy and Mys Lisiy Nos there are alder and birch trees.

FIGURE IV-31. *Gulf of Finland, Terioki. Beach area (63).*
Looking northward at west end of Terioki beach area. No date. Approximate position 60°10'N, 29°33'E; B. A. Chart 2279.

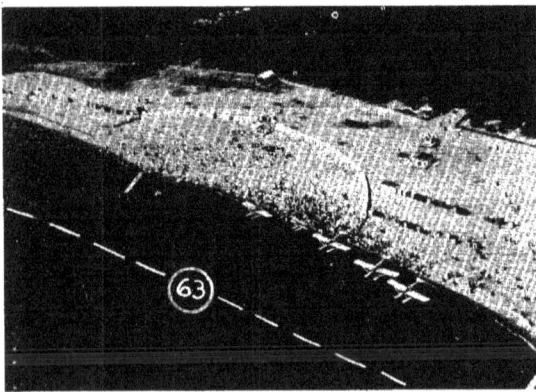

FIGURE IV-32. *Gulf of Finland Terioki. Beach area (63).*
Aerial view of center section of beach area. No date. Approximate position 60°10'N, 29°40'E; B. A. Chart 2279.

A number of rivers discharge along this coast (beach area (64)); principal of these are the Inoioki, Chernaya, and Sestra. The shore bank to the 5-fathom curve extends from 0.5 mile to 2 miles offshore as far as Mys Dubovskiy. From here to the southward it is up to 4 miles in width, joining the bank surrounding Ostrov Kotlin.

Mys Lisiy Nos marks the northern entrance point of Nevskaya Guba, the eastern part of Petrograd Bay lying between Kronshtadt and the mouths of the river Neva. The shores are low and wooded, and reefs on the northern and southern sides are strewn with rocks. The area east of Kronshtadt has a depth of 3.5 fathoms, thence gradually shoaling toward shore. The bottom is fine sand with occasional patches of mud. Oraniyenbaum and Petrodvorets, on the southern side of Nevskaya Guba opposite Kronshtadt, afford the best anchorage with docking facilities and good connections with the interior by railroad and highways (Chapter VI). Oraniyenbaum has a seaplane station.

The port of Leningrad (B.A. Chart 2239), at the eastern extremity of the Gulf of Finland, is approached through the Morskoy Kanal which leads in an east-southeasterly direction across Nevskaya Guba. The channel, with an average width of 350 feet and a minimum depth of 31 feet, joins with the river Neva at Leningrad.

The harbor of Leningrad (Chapter VI), includes Morskoy Kanal with its quays and docks as well as the lower part of the river Neva and its branches. The city of Leningrad, one of the principal commercial ports of the USSR, has telegraph and railroad communications with all parts of Europe. Several operational airfields are located at and near the city. Leningrad is exposed to floods usually twice a year in the spring and fall, as a result of backwash during the period of heavy winds. The marshy Neva delta, encompassing the city limits, is very difficult to approach whether at normal water level or at high water level. Dismemberment of the center of the city into many islands and the separation of the parts of the city through the arms of the river and deep canals makes movement difficult (FIGURE IV-33).

FIGURE IV-33. *Leningrad.*
Looking southwestward across Petropavlovskaya Krepost'. Branches of river Neva in background. Approximate position 59°58'N, 30°15'E; B. A. Chart 2239.

The river Neva is the only outlet for the various large lakes and smaller basins which empty into it. After entering Leningrad the river breaks into several deltaic branches. The greater part of the main channel of the river within the harbor limits has a depth of more than 5.5 fathoms over coarse sand bottom.

Ostrov Kotlin (B.A. Chart 2215), 5 miles northwest of Oraniyenbaum on the southern shore of Nevskaya Guba, is about 6 miles in length and 1 mile wide. It is surrounded by shoal flats which extend to the shores that lie to the east and south. The 5-fathom curve, at the western end of the flats, lies 3.8 miles from the island.

Kronshtadt harbor, a strongly fortified seaport, is situated at the eastern end of Ostrov Kotlin at the entrance of Nevskaya Guba. On its southern side are four basins with depths ranging from 9 to 35 feet. Kronshtadt harbor and port facilities are covered in detail in Chapter VI. There is an airfield and seaplane station on the island.

A broad coastal plain reaches from Leningrad to Luzhskaya Guba at the southern edge of which is a precipitous bluff separating the flat coastland from the hills of the land elevation between Peipus and Il'men lakes. The coastal plain consists of two main regions, the coastal foreland in the north and the coastal plain in the south, divided by terrace-forming slopes. The foreland is a very marshy depression intersected by beach ridges and dune stretches covered with rock detritus. Inland a gently ascending highland, from 6 to 9 miles and in some places 20 miles wide, stretches out toward the next incline. Short, shallow rivers, flowing in a northerly direction have carved channels in the bedrock. Many flat sandy beaches alternate with meadows along the coast (beach areas (65) and (66)). The shoreline is thus broken into small portions by alder groves, dunes, and beach mounds. With the exception of the eastern shore of Luzhskaya Guba, precipitous cliffs rarely edge the sea. There the coast becomes more swampy. Near the coast vegetation consists of bushy meadows and marshy forests, while higher up on the elevated plains are dry pine forests and pastures.

From Krasnaya Gorka to Ostrov Karavalday (B.A. Chart 2279), the shore is bordered by a range of hills. Mys Krasnaya Gorka is characterized by a reddish sandy slope and low sand hills. Reefs and shoal water extend offshore as far as Tolboukin Island.

Ostrov Karavalday is low and covered with bushes. From here the coast trends southwestward for 5.5 miles to Mys Ust'inskiy. Batareynaya Bukhta, to the south of the island, affords anchorage in 3.5 fathoms.

Koporskaya Guba lies between Mys Ust'inskiy and Mys Kolganpya 14 miles southwestward. The shores of the bight are low (beach area (67)), mostly rocky and wooded, with a few scattered meadows and swamps. A shore bank of varying width, with detached shoals and patches of reef, fronts the coastline. The Sista and the Kovashi are the largest of the several rivers which discharge into the bight. Mys Kolganpya, the western entrance point (B.A. Chart 2245), has shoal water extending a distance of 1.3 miles with a depth of only 3 to 7 feet at the northern entrance.

Luzhskaya Guba, between Mys Kolganpya and Mys Kurgal'skiy, is 14 miles wide at the entrance, with a number of reefs and shoals occupying the middle part. The western shore is thickly wooded. On the eastern side, hills range in elevation from 309 feet in the south to 470 feet at Gora Soykina to the northward. The slopes of the range are partly wooded, with some cultivated fields. At the head of the bay lie the Luga and Vyb'ya rivers, 1.8 miles apart. Dunes extend between the river mouths, paralleling the shore (beach area (68)). The bay has a landing ground and seaplane station.

The eastern approach to Narva Laht is obstructed by numerous small islands and rocky shoals extending within a 14-mile radius north and east of Mys Kurgal'skiy, which is the northern tip of the peninsula between Narva Laht and Luzhskaya Guba. Depths range from 0.3 fathom at Banka Namsi to 3.3 fathoms at Kurgal'skiy Rif. Lavensaari (Lavansaari), a small island 14 miles northwest of Mys Kurgal'skiy, is 3 miles long and surrounded by reefs. It is low and covered with thick pine forests.

Between the southern shore of Narva Laht and Peipus Lake, 14 miles southward, the land is level in general and is divided into three parts: 1) the coastal area with its sand dunes (beach area (69); FIGURE IV-34), 2) the Narva valley and the actual lake hollow, and 3) the cliffs where the river approaches the coast.

FIGURE IV-34. *Estonian SSR, Narva-Jõesuu. Beach area (69).* Looking northward from river mouth near Narva-Jõesuu, at south end of beach area. Approximate position 59°29'N, 28°03'E; B. A. Chart 2245.

The river Narva rises in Peipus lake and is about 42 miles in length. From the town of Narva to the entrance, the river is 7.5 miles in length, flowing in a northwesterly direction. The banks are clayey and steep, rising at places to 50 feet, and becoming low and sandy at the entrance. The lower part of the river is from 180 to 580 yards wide. The entrance, which is 110 yards wide, is fronted by a bar which silts in the spring leaving a depth of 4 to 5 feet. Narva, an important manufacturing town close to the steplike rapids of the river, has an excellent harbor and a small landing ground.

The western approach to Narva Laht is obstructed by numerous shoals and small rocky islands extending within a 26-mile radius seaward from Ledipaa Nina, with depths ranging from 1.5 to 5 fathoms. Sur-Sari (Suursaari), an island situated 30 miles northeast of Ledipaa Nina, is 6 miles long and about 1.5 miles wide. It is high and rocky with an elevation of 525 feet at its southern end. Many of the valleys and slopes are covered with pine trees. The island is steep-to and has depths of 10 to 28 fathoms over sand and mud bottom, within 0.5 mile of the western side. Vaivara Mägi (Gora Vayvara), consisting of three wooded hills 307 feet in height, lies 7.5 miles southwest of the river Narva entrance. Gora Lina-Megi, 14 miles to the north, is a sand hill 80 feet in height.

From Narva Laht to Mereküla, 5 miles southwestward, the coast is flat and sandy (beach area (70); FIGURES IV-35 to IV-37) with no visible offshore obstructions. Behind the beach lies level woodland and cultivated fields. A coastal road lies a few hundred yards inland. From Mereküla to Kalvi, a point 3 miles past Aseri, the coast

FIGURE IV-35. *Estonian SSR, Narva-Jõessu. Beach area (70).* Looking northward along beach area south of river mouth near Narva-Jõesuu. Approximate position 59°28'N, 28°00'E; B. A. Chart 2245.

Original

FIGURE IV-36. *Estonian SSR, Narva-Jõesuu. Beach area (70).* Looking southward along beach area south of river mouth near Narva-Jõesuu. For approximate location refer to FIGURE IV-35.

consists generally of a narrow sand strip with clear approaches from seaward (beach area (71); FIGURES IV-38 to IV-45). The coastline is backed by steep clay or shale bluffs varying from 10 feet to 60 feet in height. Behind the bluffs lies a raised plain with areas of both cultivated and wooded land (FIGURES IV-40, IV-42, and IV-45); extensive swamps occur farther inland. A good coastal road net exists behind the bluff line. At several points along the coast, the bluff line is broken by broad low valleys which run inland and act as main drainage channels for the area.

West of this area the coastal bluff disappears, and from Kalvi to Ledipaa Nina the coast is relatively level with occasional sand and gravel beaches lying between flat rocky points (beach area (72)). The bottom near the shore is shoal, with scattered rocks breaking the surface.

From Ledipaa Nina 20 miles to Altja the coast is low and flat, with broad sandy beaches (beach area (73); B. A. Chart 2246). The gradient immediately offshore is *flat*

FIGURE IV-37. *Estonian SSR, Narva-Jõesuu. Beach area (70).* Aerial view southeastward across beach area. Main coastal road parallels shore. 1943. For approximate location refer to FIGURE IV-35.

FIGURE IV-38. *Estonian SSR. Beach area (71).* Looking southwestward along beach from east end of beach area. Approximate position 59°24'N, 27°56'E; B. A. Chart 2245.

FIGURE IV-39. *Estonian SSR. Beach area (71).* Looking eastward toward section shown in Figure IV-38. August 1925. Approximate position 59°24'N, 27°53'E; B. A. Chart 2245.

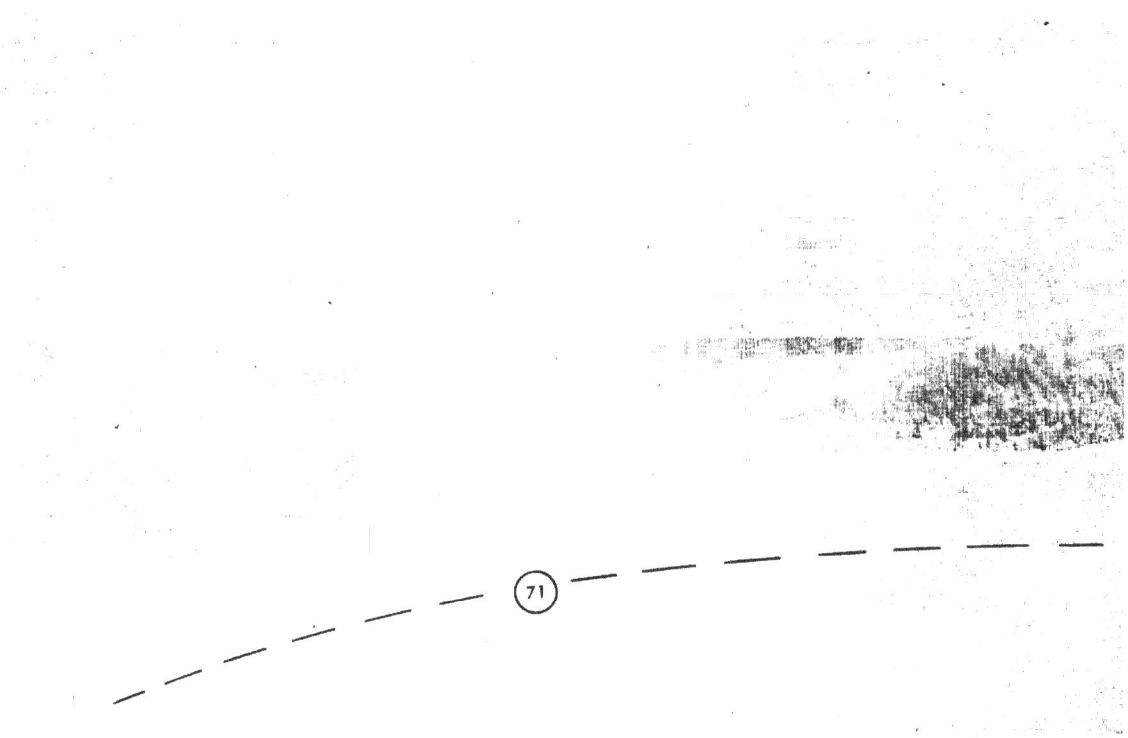

FIGURE IV-40. *Estonian SSR. Beach area (71).*
Aerial view southward across eastern end of beach area. Behind sandy beach a shelf of level grassland runs inland for 0.2 to 0.5 mile, terminating in 60-foot bluffs. 1943. For approximate location refer to FIGURE IV-39.

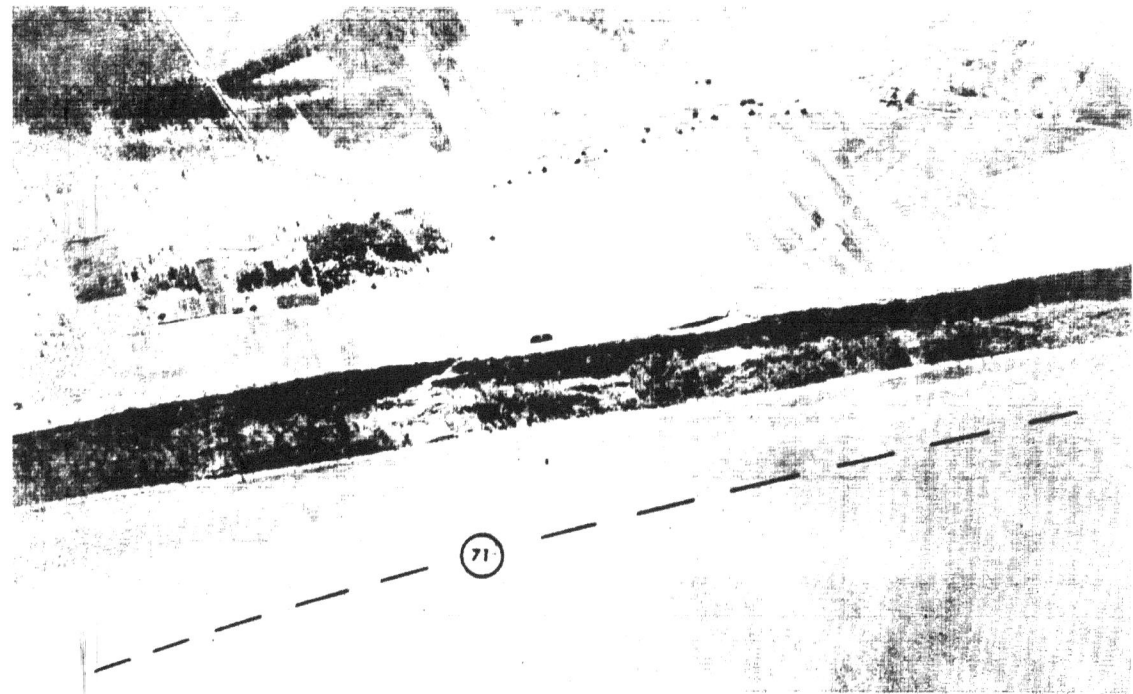

FIGURE IV-41. *Estonian SSR. Beach area (71).*
Aerial view southward across western end of beach area. High bluffs immediately behind beach. 1943. Approximate position 59°26'N, 27°08'E; B. A. Chart 2245.

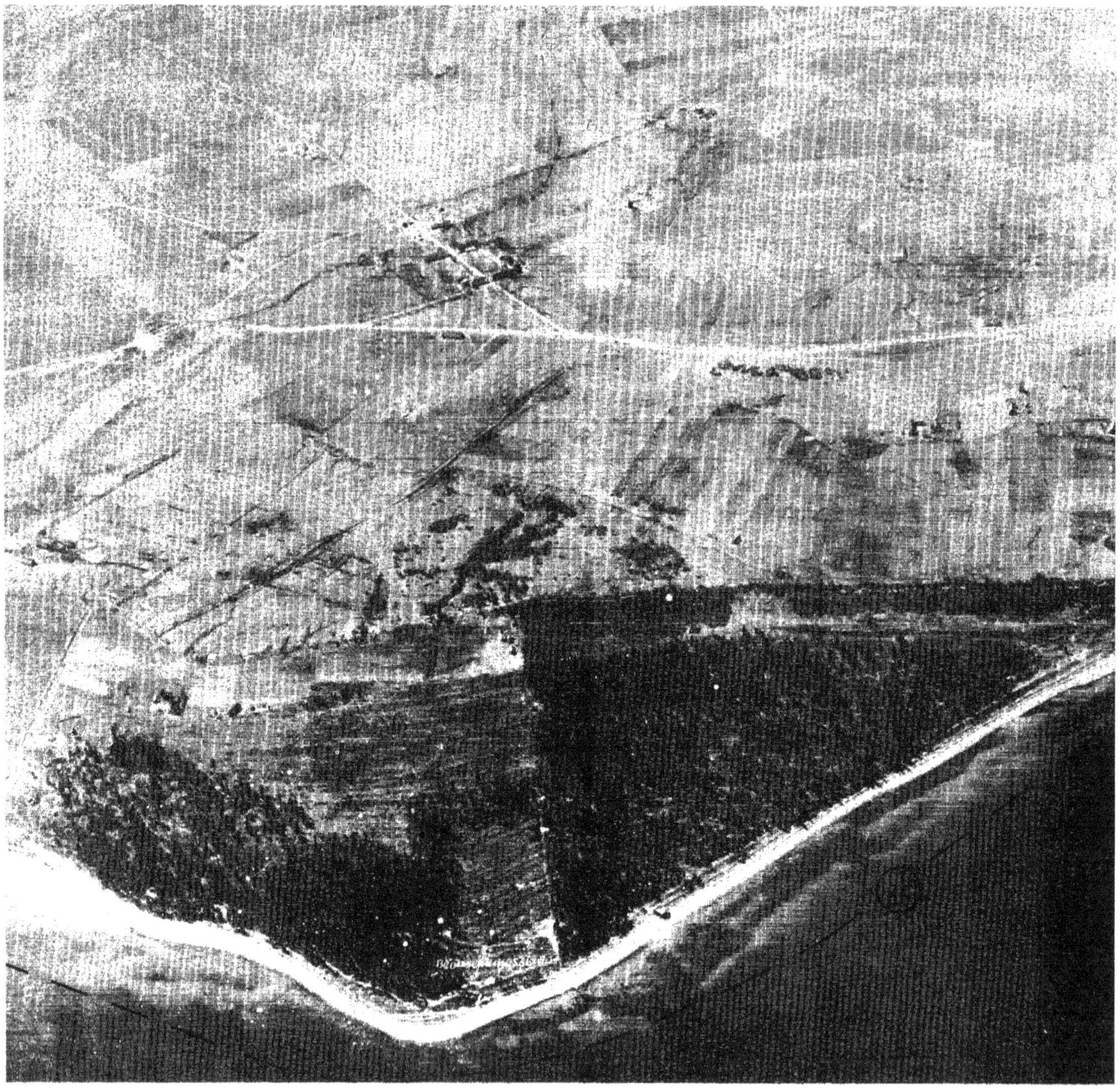

FIGURE IV-42. *Estonian SSR, Pattenina Point. Beach area (71).*
Aerial view southward across beach area at Pattenina point, 7 miles westward of Mereküla. 1943. Approximate position 59°25′N, 27°44′N; B. A. Chart 2245.

FIGURE IV-43. *Estonian SSR, Toila. Beach area (71).*
Looking eastward along beach area east of Toila. July 1924.
Approximate position 59°25′N, 27°33′E; B. A. Chart 2245.

FIGURE IV-44. *Estonian SSR, Toila. Beach area (71).*
Looking eastward along shingle beach near Toila. August 1925.
Approximate position 59°26′N, 27°30′E; B. A. Chart 2245.

FIGURE IV-30
COASTAL SUBSECTOR 42-A
JANIS 40

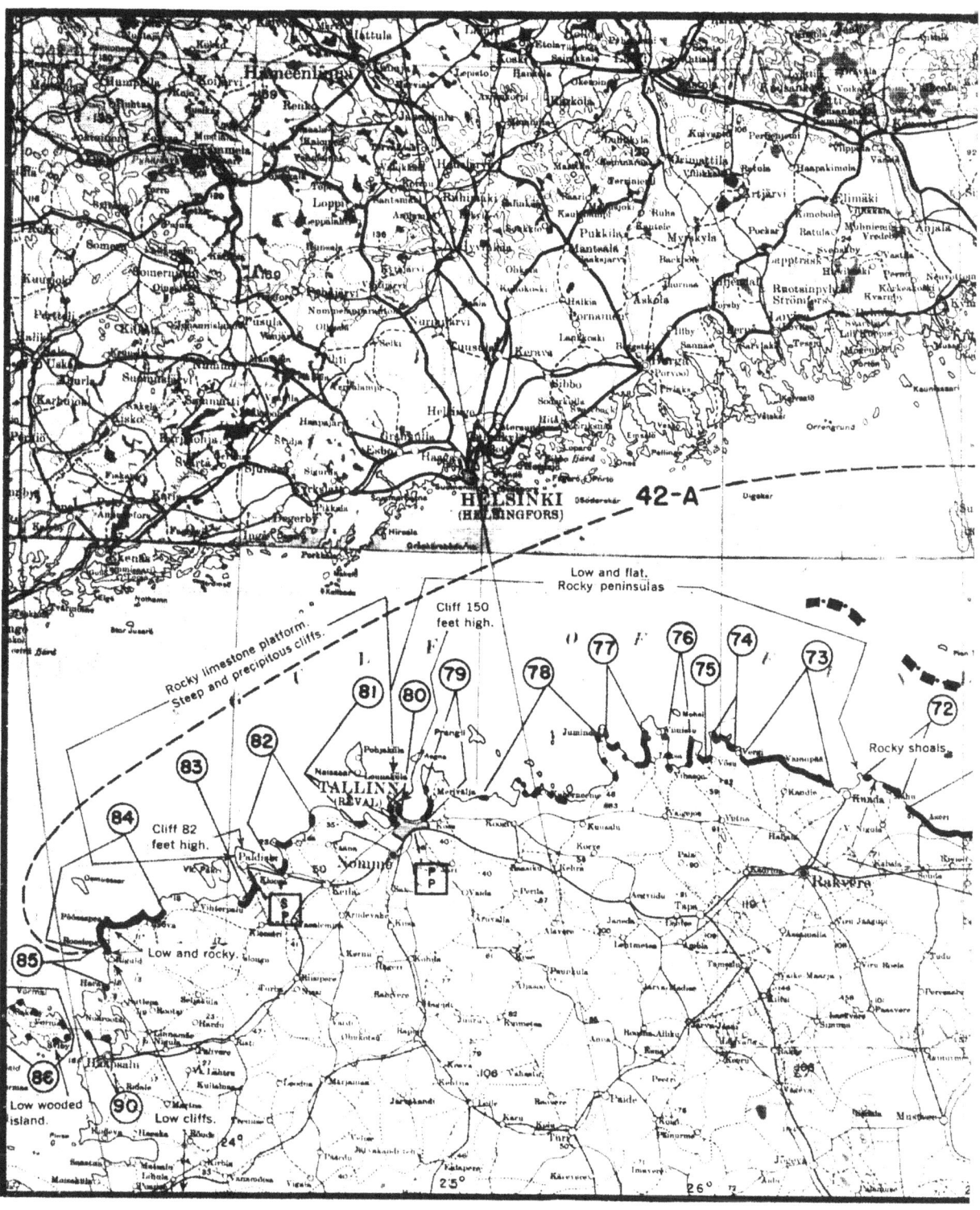

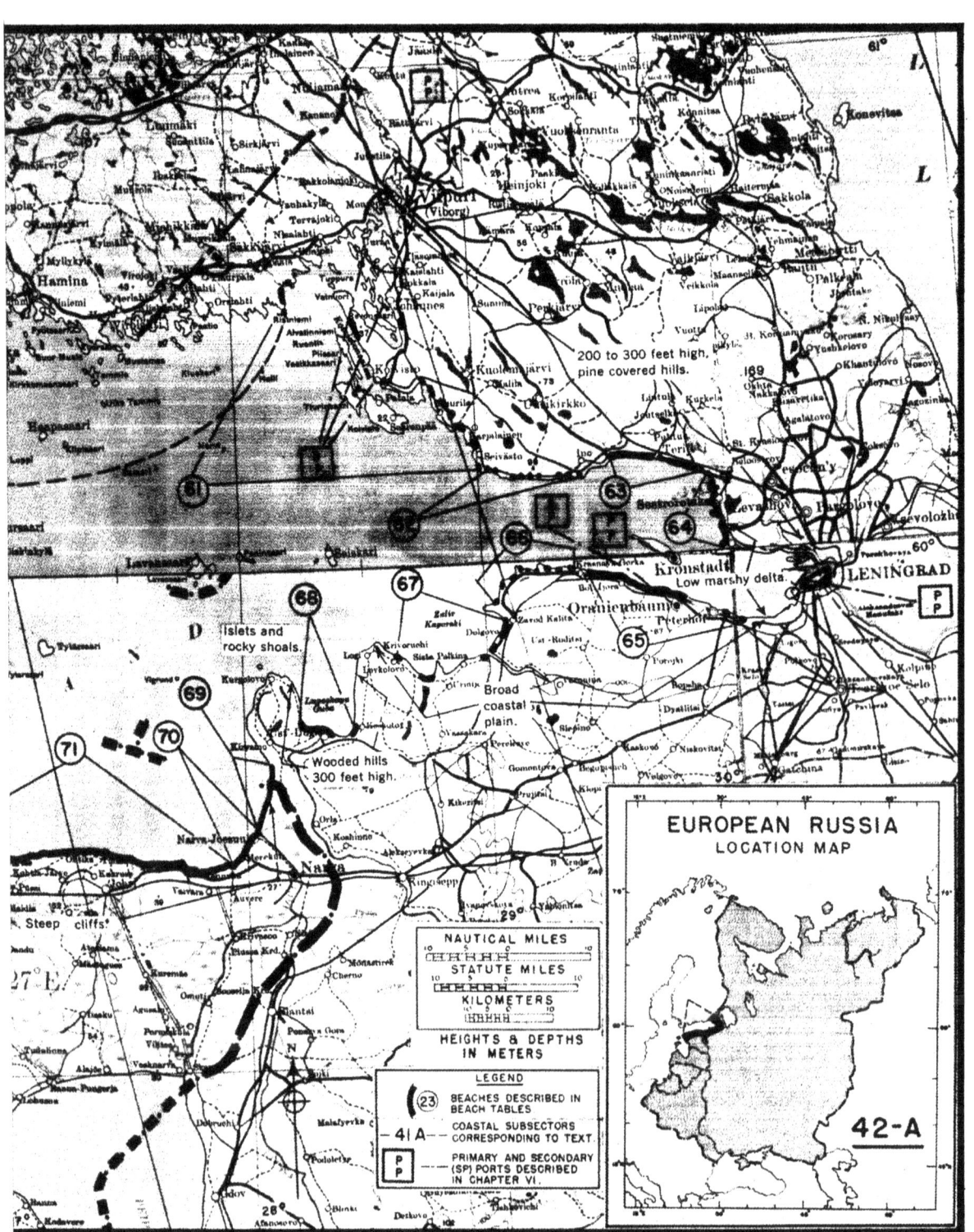

Kunda Laht is 3.3 miles wide between Toolse Neem and Ledipaa Nina, the eastern entrance point. The eastern and southern shores are low and rocky, consisting of tree-covered areas, meadows, and swamps with a range of hills extending farther inland. The river Kunda empties into the middle of the bay. A rocky reef extends from 0.5 to 1.8 miles offshore, with rocky shoals scattered throughout the middle of the bay. A main highway runs inland from Kunda 12 miles to connect with the main coastal road at Rakvere.

From Altja, westward to Tallinn, the coast consists of a series of bays, separated by low sand-and-rock peninsulas. Sand or silt banks extend seaward from the beaches, with scattered rocks breaking the surface. Approaches are obstructed by numerous offshore shoals and by islands, generally flat, sandy, and wooded. The coastline continues level but is irregular in outline with many sand-silt beaches lying between small projecting shoals and headlands (beach areas (74) to (81)). The land behind the coast is about equally occupied by woodland and cultivated fields. Large stretches of the coastal area are marshy, particularly at the base of the peninsulas. A 12- to 16-foot paved coastal road runs behind much of the coast, touching the beach at each of the small towns scattered along the coastline.

Käsmu Laht (Zaliv Kyasmu-Lakht) extends 3.5 miles southward from Lobi Neem, the eastern point. Depths in

FIGURE IV-45. *Estonian SSR. Beach area (71).*
Looking westward along beach area toward point shown in FIGURE IV-42. August 1925. Approximate position 59°24'N, 27°46'E; B. A. Chart 2245.

with a sand bottom and numerous scattered rocks breaking the surface. Behind the beach the land is level, extending inland without break in terrain. Woodland predominates, with some cultivated areas interspersed. Streams reaching the coast are broad and meandering. Farther inland are extensive swampy areas. A few roads run inland from towns on the coast.

FIGURE IV-46. *Estonian SSR. Eru Laht (Monk Bay). Beach area (76).*
Aerial view westward across the wooded and partially cultivated shore of Eru Laht at Viinistu. 1943. Approximate position 59°38'N, 25°48'E; B. A. Chart 2246.

Original

the bay range from 4 to 13 fathoms. The shores are flat and wooded, with a sandy beach (beach area (75)) and some cultivated areas at the head of the bay. Võsu, a lumbering village, is located at the bay head. Lobi Neem is bare and rocky and has a reef extending 1.5 miles northward with a depth of 4 fathoms at the outer end. On the western side of the bay entrance is a chain of islets and rocks awash.

Eru Laht extends 7.5 miles in a southerly direction from the northern end of Mehni (Ekholm), a small narrow island 1.5 miles in length. The coast (beach area (76)) is sandy with rocks in the water offshore. The land behind the western shore of the bay consists largely of cultivated fields with patches of woodland farther from the coast (FIGURE IV-46). The eastern shore is predominately woodland, while the head of the bay (to the south) is low and partly wooded.

Hara Laht (Zaliv Kara-Lakht), which extends 6 miles west-southwest between Purikari Neem the western entrance point of Eru Laht and Juminda Nina, has a depth of 30 to 40 fathoms in the entrance, decreasing gradually toward the head. The beach is sand and shingle with rocks in the water offshore. The eastern shore is predominantly forest land (FIGURE IV-47). On the western side is a range of hills, uniform in height, which are steep and thickly wooded, sloping gradually toward the coves. The southeast shore at Loksa is low (beach area (77)), but thence to Odakivi Nina it rises gradually. From Purikari Neem a reef extends 1.8 miles to the northwestward with detached shoals continuing for a mile farther westward.

Kolga Laht (beach area (78)) is 9 miles wide between Juminda Nina and Rammusaar island and extends about 8 miles to the southeastward, with general depths from 6 to 50 fathoms. In the middle of the entrance lie the Malos islets, forming a chain 1.3 miles in length, extending north-south. Pedassaar and Rohusaar, two thickly wooded islets in the southern part of the bay, are joined to the mainland by a reef covered with 2 feet of water. Juminda Nina has a reef of sand and stone extending 0.8 mile north-northwestward with the 5-fathom shoal 2 miles west of the point.

Kaberneeme Laht, to the westward of Kolga Laht, has depths of 6 to 33 fathoms over mud bottom. From Kaber Neem, a point 3.8 miles east of Ihasalu Nina, a reef with least depth of 3 feet extends 1.3 miles west-northwestward.

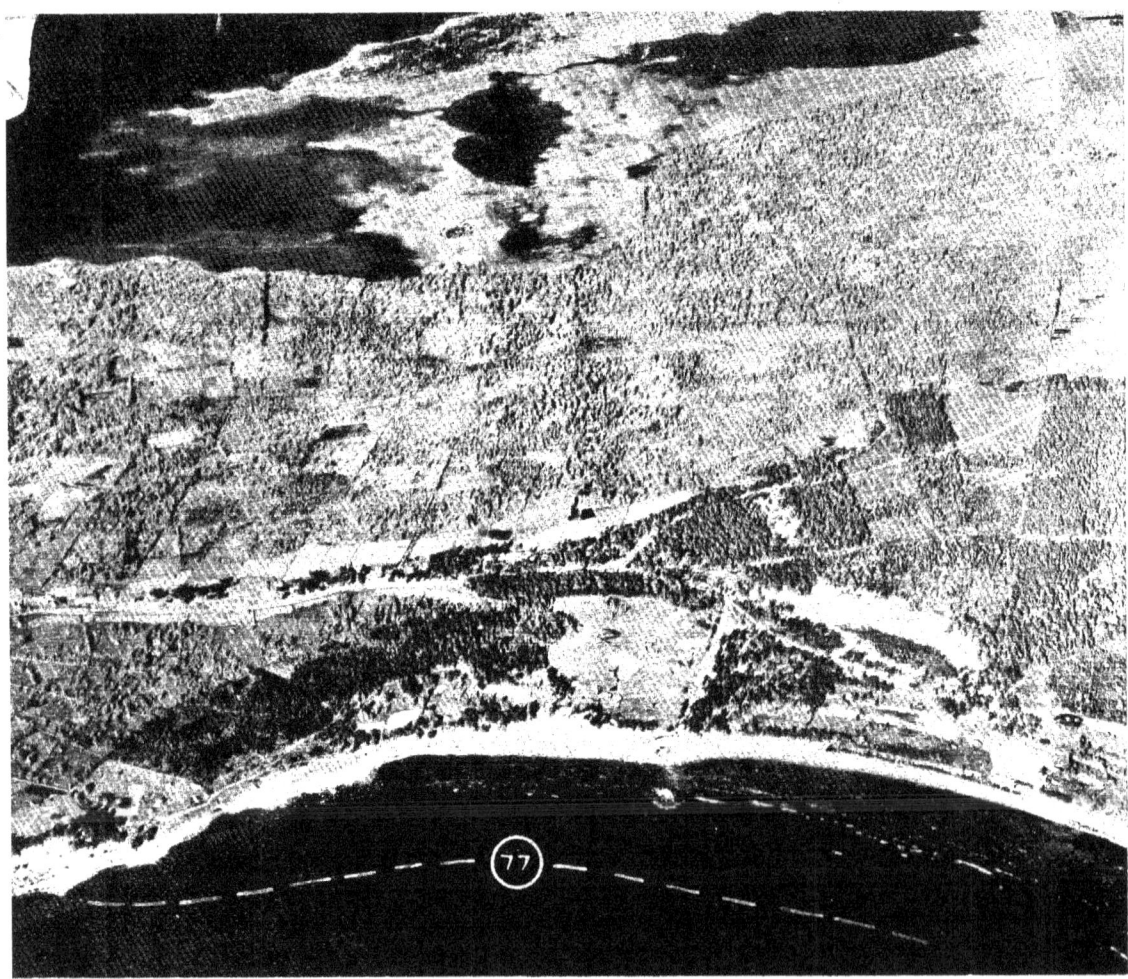

FIGURE IV-47. *Estonian SSR, Hara Laht (Papon Bay). Beach area (77).*
Aerial view eastward across northern extremity of peninsula separating Hara Laht from Eru Laht. Shoreline of Eru Laht, at top, lies about 1 mile north of area shown in FIGURE IV-46. 1943. Approximate position 59°39'N, 25°43'E; B. A. Chart 2246.

Another reef, on which lie Koibsesaar and Rammusaar islands, extends 4.3 miles north-northwestward from the same point. The former island is high and bare, while the latter is low and sandy.

Ihasalu Laht, between Ihasalu Nina and Minde Neem, is 2 miles wide and recedes 2.5 miles to the southeastward. In the middle of the bay there is anchorage with good holding ground of mud in depths of 7 to 16 fathoms. Rocks above water are scattered along the shore fronted by a reef extending 0.5 mile to seaward.

From Minde Neem, on the southern shore of Ihasalu Laht the coast trends westward for several miles thence northwestward for nearly 8 miles to Rohu Neem, the northwestern extremity of the Viimsi peninsula. About midway between these two points the shore trends more to the southward, forming a bay 2.8 miles wide between the entrance points. The 5-fathom curve lies 1 mile offshore. Approaches to Ihasalu Laht are obstructed by several low wooded islands and numerous detached reefs which extend about 10 miles offshore.

Tallinna Laht (B.A. Chart 2227), between Aegna island and Suurupi, is partly sheltered by Naissaar island. From Aegna the shore trends southward for 8 miles, thence westward for 13 miles to Suurupi. Along the southern shore are three smaller bays with generally low and wooded coasts.

Tallinna Reid, the southeastern part of the bight (beach area (79); FIGURES IV-48 to IV-50), is open to the northwest and subject to heavy seas and wind. Approaches to Tallinna Reid are obstructed by reefs and small islets between Naissaar and Aegna islands. There is a depth of 25 fathoms at the entrance over mud bottom. Toward the

FIGURE IV-50. *Estonian SSR, Tallinna Laht. Beach area (79).* Looking southward along beach area south of Pirita river mouth. Note rocky approach offshore. No date. Approximate position 59°27'N, 24°49'E; B. A. Chart 2227.

shore the bottom consists of mud and sand with scattered patches of rock. The town of Tallinn with its churches, factories and other buildings is visible well out at sea (FIGURE IV-51). The harbor is described in detail in Chapter VI.

Tallinn in the principal port of Estonia. The upper part of the town is located on the rocky heights of Zilie Kalni, while commercial and manufacturing sections occupy the more extensive lower section. Railroads connect Tallinn with all parts of Europe. Several airfields and seaplane bases are located in the vicinity of the city.

From Tallinn westward to Paldiski, the northern coast of Estonia is based on a rocky platform with many steep and precipitous cliffs (FIGURE IV-52) edging the sea. In-

FIGURE IV-51. *Estonian SSR, Tallinna Laht. Beach area (79).* Looking southwestward toward Tallinn along south end of beach area. No date. Approximate position 59°27'N, 24°48'N; B. A. Chart 2227.

FIGURE IV-48. *Estonian SSR, Tallinna Laht. Beach area (79).* Looking northward along beach north of Pirita river mouth. No date. Approximate position 59°28'N, 24°50'E; B. A. Chart 2227.

FIGURE IV-49. *Estonian SSR, Tallinna Laht. Beach area (79).* Aerial view of beach area at Pirita river mouth. No date. For approximate location refer to FIGURE IV-48.

FIGURE IV-52. *Estonian SSR, Tallinna Laht.* Rocky platform of coast near Tallinn, terminating in precipitous cliffs which edge the sea. Foreshore strewn with rocks and boulders. Specific location unknown.

land the cliff-top surfaces drop gently southward to a lower second step, at the foot of which are shallow lakes and extensive swamps. This section is traversed by many small northerly flowing streams, which descend slightly as they approach the cliffs. In their lower courses they form larger valleys by cutting deep into the limestone formation. At Tallinn the coastal cliffs rise in height to 150 feet and at Paldiski attain an elevation of 82 feet (FIGURE IV-53). The shoreline is indented by several bays with sandy beaches and marshy or wooded shores (beach areas (80) to (82)). The steep slopes are broken in places, affording exits inland, however, best communications with the interior are through the ports of Tallinn and Paldiski. Movement in the natural countryside is hampered by many swampy areas and the lack of up-to-date highways.

FIGURE IV-53. *Estonian SSR, Paldiski Laht.*
Looking northward along Paldiski coast. Cliffs show level stratification. Approximate position between 59°21′N, 24°04′E, and 59°23′N, 24°02′E; B. A. Chart 2217.

Teliskopli Laht, between Teliskopli Neem and Kakumäe Neem, is open to the northwest and has good holding ground of soft mud during southwest and west winds. The shore bank is strewn with rocks. A reef extends 0.8 mile northward and 0.5 mile westward from Teliskopli Neem.

Kakumäe Laht, the westernmost of the three bays, can only be used as an anchorage during southwest winds. Near the middle there is a depth of 11 fathoms over sand bottom. The rocky shores are fronted by a bank. A reef extends about 0.8 mile from Kakumäe Keem, the eastern entrance point.

Naissaar island, 5 miles northwest of Aegna, is 4.3 miles long and 2 miles wide. It is for the most part wooded; the east side is hilly and sandy, with clay hills rising to a height of 49 feet at the northern end. At the highest point of the island the tops of the trees are about 100 feet above sea level. Villages are situated on the east, west, and south sides. Hülgekari Ots, the southeastern extremity, is low and sandy.

Suurupi (Cape Sourop), the western extremity of Tallinna Laht, is mostly wooded and serves as a landmark for vessels bound for Tallinn. The 5-fathom curve lies about 0.5 mile off the cape. From rocky cliffs south of Suurupi, elevations decrease gradually southward, increasing again in height at Lohusalu Nina, which is surrounded by a rocky shoal. There is a hill on the point with a village and white sand cliffs to the eastward.

Lohusalu Nina divides the 11-mile coast which trends southwestward from Suurupi to Paker Ort into two bays. Lahepere Laht, the western bay, has depths of 6 to 16 fathoms with shallow water at its head and along the eastern shore.

The town of Paldiski, which lies 2 miles south of Pakri Neem (B.A. Chart 2217), is connected by railroad to Tallinn and Leningrad and is an important seaport of Estonia. A seaplane station is located there. The harbor is formed by two jetties with a 69-foot wide entrance between their heads. It has a depth of 21 feet but is very limited in area. Paldiski is very rarely blocked by ice and is therefore used as a winter harbor for Tallinn (Chapter VI).

Paldiski Laht lies between Väike Pakri (Vk. Pakri) island and the mainland. It has a depth of 25 fathoms at the entrance, decreasing gradually toward its head. The bottom consists of mud with sand along the shore (beach area (83)). The eastern shore rises gradually, terminating in high perpendicular cliffs at Pakri Neem

FIGURE IV-54. *Estonian SSR, Pakri Neem (Paker Ort).*
Looking southward along high, rocky west coast of Pakri Neem. Sandspit, 1,300 yards south of Pakri Neem light, in center. No date. Approximate position 59°23′N, 24°02′E; B. A. Chart 2217.

FIGURE IV-55. *Estonian SSR, Pakri Neem.*
Looking north-northeastward toward Pakri Neem light and the old light tower, to seaward. Precipitous limestone cliffs characteristic of northern half of Pakri Neem peninsula. No date. For approximate location refer to FIGURE IV-54.

(FIGURES IV-54 and IV-55). The shore bank here extends from 200 to 500 yards off to the 3-fathom curve.

Suur Pakri and Väike Pakri (Vk. Pakri) are two small islands lying in the bight between Pakri Neem and Risti Nina. Both are about 3.5 miles long and 1.5 miles wide, separated by a narrow channel. The islands are high and steep-to on the northern side with scattered woodlands. The coastal reef, with a least depth of 3 feet, extends 1.5 miles westward from the western coast of Suur Pakri (B.A. Chart 2241).

Keibu Laht, between Risti Nina and Tooma Nina, is nearly 2 miles long and affords anchorage near the middle in 15 feet of water over sand bottom. From abreast of Keibu village, on the rocky eastern shore, a reef extends 0.8 mile westward. The southern shore of the bay is low (beach area (84)). Risti Nina is recognized by a wood between it and the village with occasional cliffs to the eastward. Westward to Pöösaspää Neem (Pôôsaspea), for approximately 8 miles, the coast consists of sand hills lined with fir trees.

Osmussaar, a moderately high island 4 miles northwest of Pöösaspää Neem is 2.5 miles long and 0.8 mile wide. At its northern end are overhanging cliffs of sandstone 33 feet in height; on the western side several prominent hills, and on the southern shore a sandy beach with boulders.

Pöösaspää Neem, the northwestern point of Estonian SSR, is a low forest-covered sandy point. The 5-fathom curve lies 0.3 mile north of the point and 2 miles westward. The shore bank within the 5-fathom curve extends in the form of a spit 2.3 miles southeastward from the southern end of Osmussaar island. Southward from Pöösaspää Neem to Rooslepa the coast is low and rocky.

(2) Landing beaches

Subsector 42 A includes beach areas (61) to (84), (TABLE IV-6). With the exception of beaches (69) to (71), which form an almost unbroken stretch about 57 miles long, the beaches are scattered and range generally to about 3 miles in length. The nearshore area throughout the subsector is prevailingly *flat* and rocks obstruct the approaches to most of the beaches.

TABLE IV - 6
LANDING BEACHES OF COASTAL SUBSECTOR 42 A
Reliability FAIR. (Plans 14 and 15)

Number and location of beach area	Nearshore	Length	Width	Gradient	Surf and shore drift	Material and firmness	Terrain immediately behind beach	Connections inland
(61) W and S of Vyborg	Irregular bottom slopes; approaches obstructed by islands and rocky shoals.	Scattered beaches ranging to about 3 mi.	Probably range from 15 to 100 ft., widest beach at river mouth N of Ristniemi.	Average 1 on 15.	Surf light or negligible, may be heavy along beaches at SE end; drift varies.	Pebbles with some sand; firm.	Generally a wooded bluff or cliff, averaging 15 ft. high.	Secondary roads generally parallel coast but lie along bluff above beach.
(62) W from Ino	Bottom slopes *mild*, clear off E half, rocky off W half.	Scattered beaches in vicinity of stream mouths along 13-mi. stretch; may be more continuous than shown.	Probably range to 150 ft. near river mouths and along sandy points.	Average 1 on 15.	Light surf with SW wind; drift to W.	Sand, scattered rock along W half.	Generally a high wooded bluff rising in 3 steps to 60 ft. close inland; generally wooded.	Main road parallels coast along terrace of bluff; numerous trails and secondary roads run inland from beach R. R. connection at Ino.
(63) E and W of Terioki (Terijoki). (Figs. IV-31 and IV-32).	Clear approach; *mild* to *flat* bottom slopes.	Total about 13 mi. interrupted by wooded bank and by numerous stream mouths.	Varies from about 50 ft. to about 300 ft. along Terioki.	1 on 15 to 1 on 30.	Surf usually light or negligible; no predominant drift.	Mainly sand with pebbles and boulders along narrow sections; relatively soft.	Fishing and resort villages mainly with wooded bank and some dunes between.	Main road close behind beach, railroad parallels coast about 7 mi. inland.
(64) N and S of Sestroretsk.	30-ft. depth about 3 mi. offshore; bottom slopes steepen only slightly toward both ends; nearshore rocks off center.	Total 10 mi., interrupted by river mouths.	100 to 300 ft.	1 on 30.	Light surf with W winds along N section; drift weak and variable.	Mainly sand with some mud near stream mouths, soft.	Low wooded plain with some dunes at N, some marsh at S; town directly backs center area.	Good exits generally into town areas; exits locally hindered by marsh.
(65) E and W of Oraniyenbaum.	Generally obstructed by shoal water; 18-ft. depth lies as much as 3 mi. offshore near Oraniyenbaum.	Small bathing beaches along E; W beach totals 14 mi. interrupted by stream or river mouths.	75 to 150 ft.	1 on 25.	Surf negligible; drift varies but is probably mainly to E.	Sand; firm near water line.	E sections front towns and probably bulkhead or seawall; dunes generally back W section with local areas of marsh.	Road and R.R. lie within 0.2 mi.; exit from beach hindered by sand dunes.
(66)	Rocky foul ground for about 2 mi. offshore.	Numerous pocket beaches, range up to about 3,000 ft. long.	15 to 50 ft.	1 on 15.	Surf heavy with W winds along W part of area; drift varies.	Mainly pebbles to W, more sandy to E, all with scattered rock; relatively firm.	Backed by low land rising gently to E, meadow or tree-covered.	Exits by trails behind beaches leading to main road within 0.5 mi. inland.
(67) Kaporskaya Guba (Zaliv Kaporski.)	*Flat* bottom slopes with fringe of rocks nearshore.	Several beaches near stream mouths, range to 3 mi. long.	Probably 15 to 50 ft.	1 on 25.	Light to moderate surf with N winds; drift mainly to W around bay.	Sand mixed with mud and some rock; soft.	Low partly marsh and wooded land; lake lies close inland at bayhead.	Exit by trails to road within 0.5 mi. inland.
(68) Luzhskaya Guba (Luposkaya Guba.)	*Flat* bottom slopes; obstructed by rocky shoals.	6 mi. interrupted by river mouths and marshy shore.	150 to 200 ft.	1 on 25.	Heavy surf only with N winds, more generally light or negligible; drift varies.	Sand mixed with mud near river mouths; soft.	W half backed by sand dunes; borders marsh at bayhead; low tree-covered land partly marshy backs E section.	Exits generally poor; main road lies from 0.2 to 1 mi. inland.

COASTS AND LANDING BEACHES
Page IV-43

TABLE IV - 6 (Continued)

Number and location of beach area	Nearshore	Length	Width	Gradient	Surf and shore drift	Material and firmness	Terrain immediately behind beach	Connections inland
(69) N of Narva-Jõesuu. (Fig. IV - 34.)	Clear except for shoals off N end, bottom slopes *flat*.	10 mi.	75 to 150 ft., generally widens to S.	1 on 15 ft., to 1 on 20.	Moderate surf; drift to S.	Mainly sand; firm at water line.	Generally a steep wooded sandy bluff which probably lowers toward N end.	Exit laterally along beach or up bluff to trail paralleling coast.
(70) Narva-Jõesuu and SW. (Figs. IV - 35 to IV - 37.)	*Flat* bottom slopes; rocks nearshore off SW end.	5 mi.	200 to 250 ft., narrows slightly toward SW end.	1 on 30.	Heavy surf with W to N winds; main drift to NE.	Sand; firm near water line, backshore soft.	Resort areas, or sand dunes with pine cover.	Exits are good; main road parallels shore.
(71) E and W of Toila. (Figs. IV - 38 to IV - 45.)	*Flat* bottom slopes; W portion obstructed by rocky shoals.	40 mi. interrupted by river mouths and for short stretches by rocky points.	Varies from 6 to 50 ft. at base of cliffs to about 150 ft. along river-mouth areas.	1 on 10 to 1 on 25, steepest fronting cliffs.	Heavy surf with N winds; main drift to E.	Mainly sand along river mouths; pebbles and boulders at base of cliffs.	Steep cliffs of varying height except for low areas near river mouths where cliff line runs inland along valleys.	Exits are generally poor; road lies above cliff but may be accessible from river mouth areas.
(72) NW and SE of Mahu.	Bottom slopes *flat*; fringed with rocks and shoals for 1 mi. offshore.	About 6 mi., interrupted by long stretch of rocky shore, E section interrupted by small port.	25 to 75 ft.	1 on 20.	Surf heavy with N winds; drift varies.	Sand and pebbles with scattered rock; relatively firm.	SE section backed by low land and small town; NW section by low tree-covered bluff.	Exits good into town at SE end; to road above bluff at NW.
(73) E from Vergi	*Mild* bottom slopes; generally fringed with rock.	Total about 14 mi., interrupted by river mouths and possibly by short rocky stretches.	25 to 100 ft., widest near river mouths.	1 on 20.	Surf heavy with N winds; drift mainly to W.	Mainly sand; relatively firm.	Generally sandy hills or low bluff with forest cover; several town areas immediately inland.	Exits generally poor except into towns along river mouths; road parallels coast along bluff.
(74) NW of Vergi	Fringed with rock; *flat* bottom slopes.	Total about 4 mi., probably more interrupted by rocky points than shown.	Probably about 50 ft.	1 on 15.	Surf heavy with N winds; drift probably weak and variable.	Sand with scattered rock; relatively firm.	Low bank locally.	Exits generally poor.
(75) W of Vosu	*Mild* to *flat* bottom slopes; direct approach clear with rock fringe along flanks.	2.5 mi., interrupted by stream mouths.	25 to 75 ft. probably widest toward E end.	1 on 20.	Surf heavy with N winds; main drift to E.	Sand, somewhat muddy toward W end; relatively soft.	Backed by low marshy land at W; by low bank and town at E; and by rising wooded ground in center.	Road embankment directly backs W end; roads easily accessible from town at E end.
(76) Bay at Vihasoo and at Viinistu. (Fig. IV - 46.)	Numerous rocky shoals; bottom slopes *mild* off sides of bay, *flat* off head.	Total about 5 mi. on E shore; scattered beaches average 0.7 mi. each on W shore, may be more continuous than shown.	Probably average 50 ft.	1 on 15 to 1 on 20.	Surf probably moderate with N winds; drift negligible.	Mainly sand on E; sand, mud and some rock on W; W shore soft.	Low marshy land on W shore and along bayhead; slightly higher wooded land backs E shore.	Exits generally poor; good road closest to beach on W shore.
(77) Bay at Loksa. (Fig. IV - 47.)	Generally *mild* bottom slopes; nearly continuous rocky fringe.	Total about 12.5 mi., interrupted by river mouth and small port at Loksa and by marsh on W shore. May be more or less continuous than shown.	Average about 50 ft.	1 on 20.	Surf moderate with NW to N winds; drift varies.	Sand, probably with some mud along river mouth on E shore and along parts of W shore; soft.	Lowland, partly marshy between higher wooded areas; settlements line much of bay shore.	Secondary road generally within 1,000 ft. inland along E shore and bayhead.

Original

TABLE IV - 6 (Continued)

Number and location of beach area	Nearshore	Length	Width	Gradient	Surf and shore drift	Material and firmness	Terrain immediately behind beach	Connections inland
(78) Bay shore W from Juminda.	Generally obstructed by rocky shoals and islands; bottom slopes generally *mild*.	Scattered beaches, ranging up to about 1.8 mi. long.	Each beach probably varies from 25 to 100 ft.	1 on 20.	Surf probably moderate with N wind; drift mainly to E.	Sand, probably with some mud; soft.	Low marsh land, partly tree-covered; small villages back or flank beach areas.	Exits by trails; probably poor.
(79) NE of Tallinn. (Figs. IV - 48 to IV - 51.)	*Flat* bottom slopes; rocky approach to N beach and to S half of S beach near bayhead.	2 beaches: N beach 0.7 mi., S beach 3.5 mi.; interrupted by river mouth.	S beach 50 to 100 ft., widest near river mouth at center; N beach narrower.	About 1 on 20 near center of S beach; other portions generally steeper.	Surf moderate with W winds; drift probably weak and variable.	Sand, N beach may be pebbly; firm at water line.	S beach backed generally by park or resort area and low sand hills; N beach backed by low land and small village or resort.	Exit directly to road from S half of S beach; exits otherwise easy also to road close inland.
(80) NW of Tallinn	Fringe of rocks along shore; approach obstructed by islands and shoals; bottom slopes vary from *gentle* to *flat*.	2 beaches along E and W shores of narrow peninsula; E beach about 1.6 mi., ends in narrow point; W beach in bay about 1 mi. long.	W beaches about 100 ft., E beach about 50 ft.	1 on 50.	Moderate to heavy surf with N to W winds; drift varies.	Sand; relatively soft.	Embankment or dike backs S end of E beach, extends to wharf near center of beach; whole peninsula is low and partly marshy.	Exits probably best near wharf at center of E beach; otherwise poor.
(81)	*Flat* bottom slopes; approach clear.	2 bayhead beaches, each about 1.2 mi.	75 to 100 ft.	1 on 50.	Moderate surf with W to NW winds; drift probably weak and variable.	Sand and mud; soft.	Low marsh land.	Main road about 0.5 mi. inland; exits to it are not known.
(82) N and NE of Klooga.	Direct approach clear except to S beach in bay; bottom slopes *mild* to *flat*.	3 beaches, totaling 5.5 mi., separated by high shores and interrupted by river mouths.	Probably 60 to 150 ft., widest along river mouth at NE beach.	1 on 30.	Generally light to moderate surf, may be heavy with NW to N winds; drift to S along NE beach and probably to W otherwise.	Sand; firm at water line.	Low spit backs NE beach; otherwise bluffs generally with some low partly marshy land back of bayhead.	Secondary road available from NE beach; main road along bluff above center beach; main road generally accessible from S beach.
(83) Bay S of Paldiski	*Flat* bottom slopes otherwise clear.	4 mi. along bayhead.	25 ft.	1 on 50.	Surf light or negligible; drift weak.	Sand and mud; soft.	Low marsh land.	Poor exits except near both ends where road lies close inland.
(84) E and W of Nova	Generally *flat* bottom slopes; rocky shoals nearshore.	15 mi., interrupted by river mouths and possibly by short rocky stretches.	50 to 200 ft., E bayhead sections are widest.	1 on 30 average.	Surf light to moderate; drift varies.	Sand and pebbles, may be some rock; all relatively firm.	Sand hills, tree covered inland; low bluffs locally and low land along rivers.	Exit by trails to main road generally 1 to 2 mi. inland.

FIGURE IV-56
COASTAL SUBSECTOR 42-B
JANIS 40

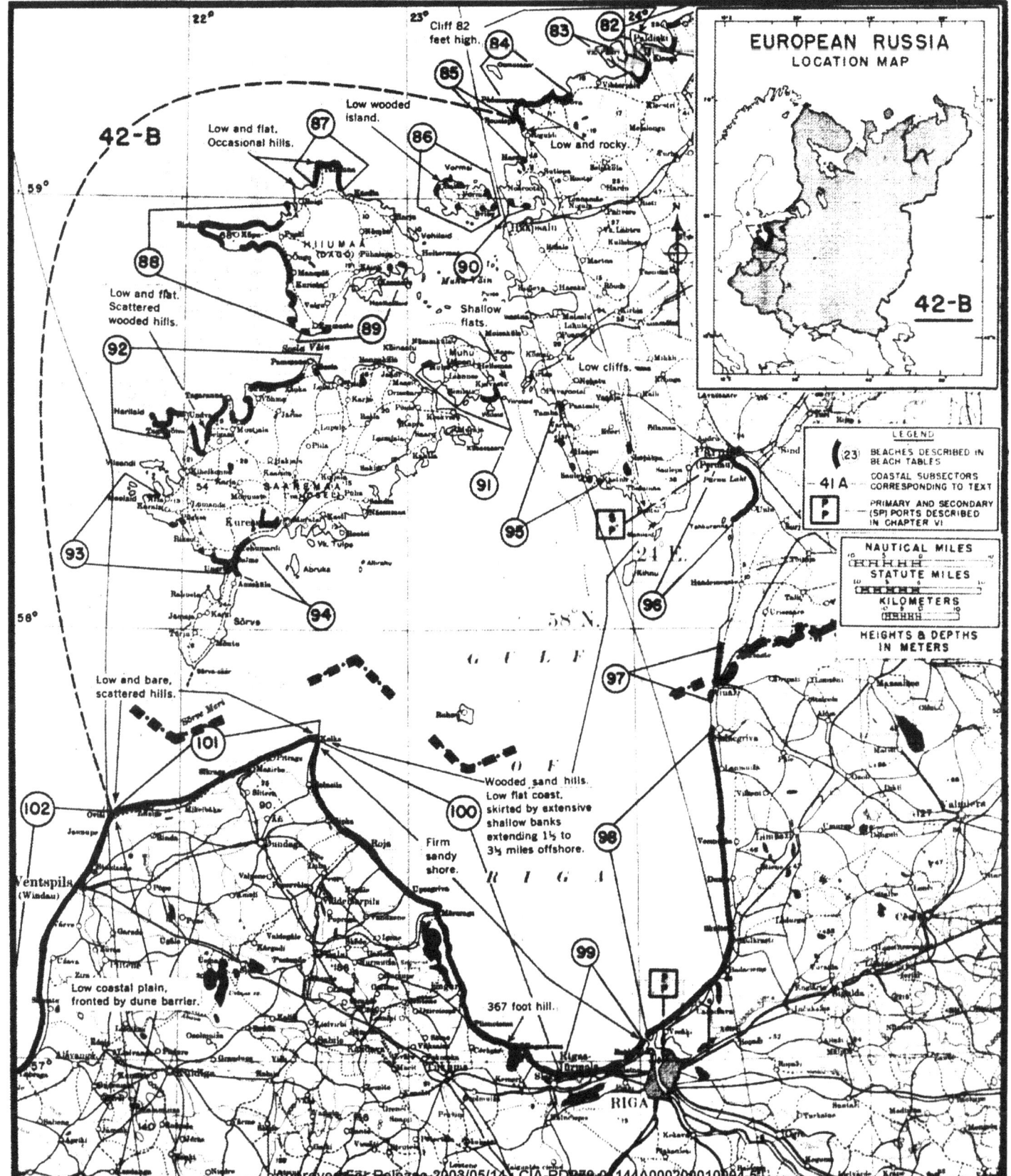

B. Rooslepa to Oviši

(59°10′N, 23°32′E; 57°34′N, 21°43′E) (PLAN 15; FIGURE IV-56; U.S.H.O. Chart 4880; B.A. Charts 870, 2271, 2256, 2263, and 2842B)

(1) Coast

The principal northern approach to the Gulf of Riga (U.S.H.O. Chart 4880) is by Vormsi Väin (Wormsö Sound) and Muhu Väin (Moon Sound). Vormsi Väin (B.A. Chart 870), between Vormsi and Hiiumaa (Dago) islands, is 2 to 3.5 miles wide, with a least depth of 5.5 fathoms in the channel. Vormsi, situated between Hiiumaa and the mainland, is 8 miles long and 4.5 miles wide. It is low, wooded, and surrounded by reefs (beach area (86); TABLE IV-7) Hiiumaa is 30 miles long, east–west, and 24 miles wide (beach areas (87), (88), and (89); B.A. Chart 2241). The interior is flat and marshy, rising gradually to a height of 88 feet on the northeastern coast. The northwestern coast is lower and less wooded. The shore is rocky with scattered stretches of sand. Andresemägi (Mount Andrew), on the thickly wooded Kõpu Poolsaar (Dager Ort peninsula), is 223 feet high while the southwestern coast is low and slightly above sea level. The island is entirely surrounded by reefs and shoal water extending from 1 to 7 miles seaward. There is a landing strip at Käina on the southeastern coast. Kassaare Laht (bay), connected with the Baltic by Soela Väin (Sele Sound) and enclosed by the islands Hiiumaa (Dago), Muhu (Moon), and Saaremaa (Ösel), has general depths of 4 fathoms over mud bottom. Muhu Väin has a very narrow channel, with a depth of 2.8 fathoms, between Muhu and the mainland coast of Estonian SSR. Muhu (beach area (91)) is 11 miles long and 8 miles wide with a highest elevation of 79 feet, and is surrounded by a narrow coastal reef.

Saaremaa is 50 miles long, northeast–southwest, and 30 miles wide. Its southern tip borders Irbeni Väin, the western entrance to the Gulf of Riga. The island is composed chiefly of limestone and is thickly wooded. The coasts (beach areas (92), (93) and (94)) are broken and indented by numerous bays, between which are peninsulas; most prominent of these are Sõrre in the south and Tagamõisa in the northwest. Coasts are low (FIGURE IV-57), except for high, rocky slopes in the north and on the east shore of Tagamõisa. Inland the island is in general low and flat with a few wooded hills in the middle and northern parts. The highest elevation is a 65-foot hill in the northwestern section. A few small islets lie off the south and west coasts while the remainder of the island is surrounded by scattered reefs and shoal water. The island has a fully equipped seaplane base and five landing grounds.

The mainland coast from Rooslepa for 5.5 miles southward to Noarootsi peninsula (B.A. Chart 2241) is low and rocky (beach area (85)), fronted by outlying reef patches and shoal water. The peninsula forms the northern shore of Haapsalu Laht (B.A. Chart 2842B), a shallow inlet filled with banks and shoals (beach area (90)). The inner bay, east of the town of Haapsalu on the southern shore, is entirely shoal. The ragged coastline trends southward for 11 miles to Matsalu Laht, which extends 12 miles inland, with depths of 8 to 10 feet in the outer half; thence the coast trends southward for 16 miles to Tamba, on the eastern shore of Muhu Väin. The shoreline between the point Pika Nina, at the southern entrance of Matsalu Laht, and Tamba consists of low cliffs with numerous reef patches extending between it and Muhu (Moon Island), 5 miles westward.

From Tamba the coast trends southward 10.5 miles to Sõmeri Poolsaar, and consists of low cliffs, rocks, and sand, with a few off-lying shoals (beach area (95)). The shoreline for a distance of 13 miles southeastward to Kiriku Nina the western point of Pärnu Laht (Pernau Bight) is broken by several bays and sharp promontories. The last 5.5 miles of this coast is fronted by a number of small islets and shoals.

Pärnu Laht (beach area (96); FIGURE IV-58) is 8 miles long, northeast–southwest, and 6.5 miles wide at its entrance between the points Kiriku Nina and Tahku Nina, with a depth of 4.5 fathoms gradually decreasing to 2.5 fathoms at the mouth of the river Pärnu. Approaches are obstructed by shoals and small islands, the largest of which is Kihnu, 4 miles in length and covered with low pine forests. Pärnu Reid, at the inner part of the bight, affords secure anchorage in 18 feet of water over mud and

FIGURE IV-57. *Estonian SSR, Saaremaa (Ösel)*.
Vilsandi lighthouse, at the end of a chain of small islands of the western coast of Saaremaa island. Approximate position 58°23′N, 21°50′E; B. A. Chart 2263.

FIGURE IV-58. *Estonian SSR, Pärnu. Beach area (96).*
Looking northwestward along beach area southeast of Pärnu. No date. Approximate position 58°23'N, 24°30'E; U. S. H. O. Chart 4880.

sand bottom. The harbor (Chapter VI), at the mouth of the river, consists of the harbor proper, the dredged channel, and the mouth of the river Sauga. The middle of the harbor is blocked by ice from December to April. The river is navigable only for a short distance above its entrance. Pärnu, situated on the south bank of the river Pärnu, is an important shipping center connected by rail with the Riga-Leningrad line. All-weather two-lane roads lead inland from the port. A small operational landing field is located at Pärnu.

The coast from Pärnu Laht trends southerly for almost 80 miles to the mouth of the river Daugava (Zapadnaya Dvina). The flat, even coast line is skirted by shallows from 1.5 to 3.5 miles offshore. Numerous villages line the entire coast and many small rivers and streams empty into the gulf, their mouths fronted by sandbanks. The river beds are shallow and swampy, and subject to spring floods. The resulting bog areas and flooded meadows, as well as the forests, impede movement inland. At the head of the gulf the Daugava and Gauja rivers have deeply cut courses, exposing the rock structure in their steep banks.

From Tahku Nina, the swampy eastern entrance point of Pärnu Laht, to the cape Sarre Nina, 9 miles southward, the coast is low with foul ground extending from it for a distance of nearly 3 miles. At Sarre Nina the coast increases in height and is partly wooded. Pihinurme Mäed, a wooded range 130 feet high, lies inland 1.5 miles north of Sarre Nina. Woods extend to the beach between Orajõe (Orrenhof) and Treimani (Dreimansdorf), where the coast decreases in elevation. From Ainaži (Gainish) to the river Salaca (Salaces Upe) the shore is low and rocky, fronted by shoal water and detached reefs extending 7 miles southwestward of Ainaži (beach area (97)). From Ainaži to Sophien Ruh Farm, 24 miles southward, the shore is low and sandy (beach area (98); FIGURE IV-59) with a few mounds about 20 feet high a short distance inland. Moderately high sand hills extend from Sophien Ruh

FIGURE IV-59. *Latvian SSR, Gulf of Riga. Beach area (98).*
Typical section of beach area. Breakers on flat, gently sloping beach; backed by sand dunes about 30 feet high and fringed with pine woods. No date.

southward to Peterupe; thence to the Daugava the coast continues low and sandy.

The Daugava (Zapadnaya Dvina), before entering the sea, separates into two arms forming low, marshy islands. Daugavgrīvas Sala (Dunamond Island) on the western side of the river entrance, is formed by the Bullupe (Mukha) river (FIGURE IV-60). The valley through which the Daugava flows is composed partly of sand hills and partly of meadows and swamps. Within the river are several low islands and sandbanks partly covered with grass. The bar of the Daugava extends over a mile from shore. The least depth at the entrance of the river was 25 feet in 1927.

Daugavgrīva harbor, on the southwestern side of the river entrance, with a depth of 22 feet, is the outer port of Riga. Riga harbor (B.A. Chart 2256), about 7 miles above the entrance, consists of a river channel with a number of basins and quays (Chapter VI). Riga, the capital and one of the principal ports of Latvia, has railroad connections with other ports as well as the interior. An airfield, seven landing grounds, and two seaplane stations are located near the town.

Many small lakes lie inland several miles from the southern shore of the gulf (beach area (99); FIGURES IV-61 to IV-66). The river Bullupe, which flows parallel with the coast eastward of Ragaciems, terminates at the mouth of the Daugava. Milzukalns, a 367-foot hill, 9.5 miles westward of Ragaciems point, is visible for a distance of 20 miles at sea.

From the mouth of the Daugava the coast trends in a westerly and northwesterly direction for 73 miles to Kolkasrags. It is low and wooded, with occasional hills. The shore is of firm sand with a bank extending from 1.5 to 3.5 miles offshore (beach area (100); U.S.H.O. Chart 4880).

The island Ruhnu, 19.5 miles eastward of Kolkasrags, is 3 miles long and 2 miles wide. It is low and sandy with scattered pine forests.

Irbeni Väin, the main entrance to the Gulf of Riga, is bounded on the south by the coast from Kolkasrags to Oviši (Lyser Ort) and by shoals extending south and southwest from Saaremaa (Ösel) on the north (B.A. Chart 2263). The western end is divided into two channels by Michailovo Sēklis, 7.5 miles northward of Ouiši. The southern channel is 3.5 miles wide with a least depth of 5 fathoms; the northern is about 2 miles wide and much deeper.

From Kolkasrags, the northernmost point of Latvian SSR, to Oviši the coast is generally low and bare with only a few scattered hills (beach area (101)). Kolkasrags is moderately high, with a reef and shoal water extending 3.3 miles northward. Zilie Kalni, 18.5 miles eastward of Oviši, is a range of hills 164 to 197 feet high.

Oviši, a low sandy point, gives a whitish appearance from seaward. The coast is foul close to shore with scattered shoals and banks lying to the northward across the entrance of the Gulf of Finland.

(2) Landing beaches

Subsector 42 B (beach areas (85) to (101); TABLE IV-7), includes all shores of the Gulf of Riga, the mainland, and the islands lying just north of the gulf. The island beach areas vary considerably but are all approached through shallow narrow channels which are obstructed by rocks and small islets. This is equally true of the few known beaches on the mainland fronted by islands. Beaches (98) to (101), on the other hand, are fronted by shallow, but generally clear, near-shore areas. These beaches form almost a continuous stretch around the gulf and along the southern side of Irbeni Väin. Exits to roads are best from beach (99); otherwise trails are available close inshore but usually lie behind dune or bluff areas.

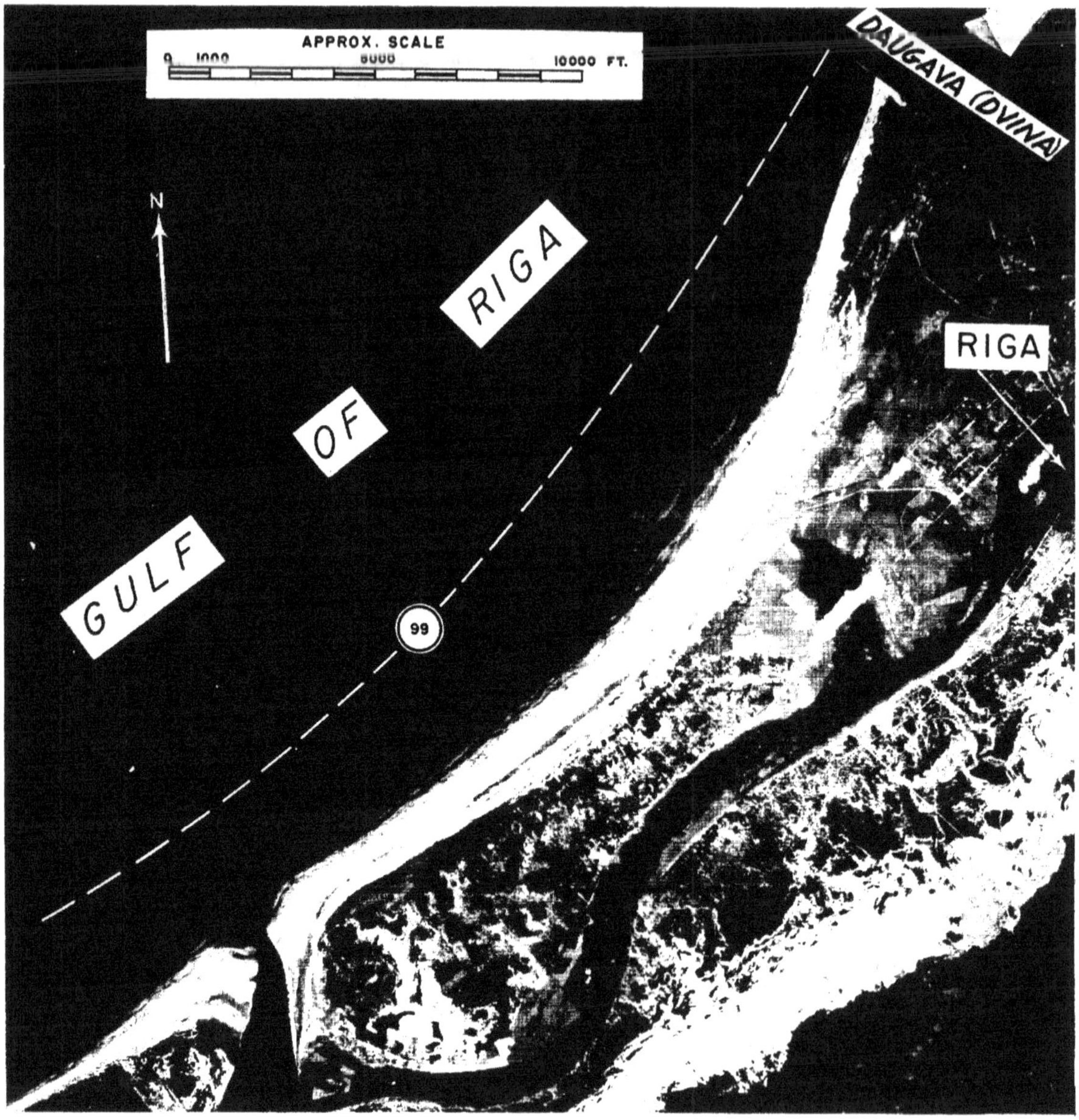

FIGURE IV-60. *Latvian SSR, Gulf of Riga. Beach area (99).*
Vertical aerial view of Daugavgrīvas Sala at east end of beach area. July 1944. Approximate position 57°02′N, 23°58′E; U. S. H. O. Chart 4880.

FIGURE IV-61. *Latvian SSR, Gulf of Riga. Beach area (99).* Looking eastward along beach area east of Rīgas Jūrmala. No date. Approximate position 56°58′N, 23°45′E; U. S. H. O. Chart 4880.

FIGURE IV-62. *Latvian SSR, Gulf of Riga. Beach area (99).* Looking eastward along beach area at Rīgas Jūrmala. No date. Approximate position 56°58′N, 23°44′E; U. S. H. O. Chart 4880.

Original

FIGURE IV-63. *Latvian SSR, Gulf of Riga Beach area (99).*
Aerial view looking east-northeastward across Majori toward area shown in FIGURE IV-60. Sharp bend of Lielupe river in center. 1941. Approximate position 56°58′N, 23°45′E; U. S. H. O. Chart 4880.

FIGURE IV-64. *Latvian SSR, Gulf of Riga. Beach area (99).* Looking eastward along beach area at Rīgas Jūrmala. Note automobile on beach. No date. For approximate location refer to FIGURE IV-62.

FIGURE IV-65. *Latvian SSR, Gulf of Riga. Beach area (99).* Looking westward along beach area at Rīgas Jūrmala. No date. For approximate location refer to FIGURE IV-62.

FIGURE IV-66. *Latvian SSR, Gulf of Riga. Beach area (99).* Looking eastward along beach area west of Rīgas Jūrmala. No date. Approximate position 56°58′N, 23°43′E; U. S. H. O. Chart 4880.

TABLE IV - 7

LANDING BEACHES OF COASTAL SUBSECTOR 42 B

Reliability FAIR. (Plan 15)

Number and location of beach area	Nearshore	Length	Width	Gradient	Surf and shore drift	Material and firmness	Terrain immediately behind beach	Connections inland
(85) Hara and shore to N.	Flat bottom slopes with rocks nearshore.	2 beaches: N beach about 2.5 mi.; S beach at river mouth about 0.6 mi.	75 to 150 ft.	1 on 20.	Surf light to moderate; drift varies.	Sand and pebbles, probably with some rocks along S beach; relatively firm.	Narrow area of sandy hillocks and locally a low bluff heavily wooded back of N beach; low land partly marshy with village close inland back of S beach.	Exit from N beach by trails to main road about 0.5 mi. inland; exit through village or road 1 to 2 mi. inland.
(86) Vormsi (island).	Approach obstructed by very shallow depths, shoals, islets, and nearshore rocks.	Several scattered beaches, longest areas lie on E point and NW point of island; each is about 1.5 mi. long.	Probably 25 to 100 ft., widest along most extensive beaches.	1 on 30 to 1 on 50.	Surf light or negligible along E and S shores; drift varies.	Generally sand or sand and pebbles, S shore beaches may be muddy; S shore beaches most soft.	Low bluffs along N shore locally; more generally low land wooded or partly marshy.	Exits generally only by trail; are probably best from NW beach where minor road and trail are directly accessible.
(87) Hiiumaa (island), N shore.	Flat bottom slopes with rock shoals off W end, nearshore rocks off N and E ends.	About 11 mi. along 3 sides of square peninsula.	25 to 50 ft.	1 on 15 to 1 on 20.	Surf usually moderate to heavy; drift varies.	Sand and pebbles with some rock; probably soft toward E and W ends.	Hilly wooded country with low bluff locally along N shore of peninsula; marsh land flanks beach at both ends.	Exit by trail only; easiest from E shore of peninsula.
(88) Hiiumaa, NW and W shores.	Bottom slopes are very irregular and flat; nearshore rocks front most of areas.	Generally extensive beaches, longest is about 20 mi.	75 to 150 ft.	1 on 20 average.	Moderate surf; drift probably varies from beach to beach and with winds.	Mainly sand, with some scattered rock; relatively firm at N, softer toward S end.	Low wooded bank or wooded sand hills back N sections; low sandy ground with some swamp toward S.	Exit by trails running inland; road lies closest to tip of narrow peninsula and to center of W coast.
(89) Hiiumaa, S and SE shores.	Approach through narrow, shallow, and rocky channels with islets off SE shore.	4 beach areas, longest area about 2 mi.	Probably average about 50 ft.	1 on 50.	Surf negligible; drift may be mainly to E along S shore; otherwise variable.	Sand, probably with mud; soft.	Low wet meadow land or wooded swamp.	Exits by trail; probably best from W beach on S shore.
(90) N of Haapsalu.	Approach obstructed by very shallow depths and rocks.	Total 2.2 mi. interrupted by low, probably marshy, shore.	100 ft.	1 on 50.	No surf; drift negligible.	Sand; soft.	E section backed by flat land, partly swampy; W section backed by more sandy land rising to the N.	Exit may be possible to small village and to trails from W section; best exit from E section to main road running inland from center.
(91) Muhu (island).	Approach very shallow and rocky.	2 beaches: SE beach about 6 mi., may be interrupted by marsh; W beach about 1 mi.; NE and N shores probably lined with narrow beach at foot of bluff.	About 50 to 75 ft.	1 on 30 to 1 on 50.	Surf light or negligible; drift is probably generally to S in both cases.	Sand with scattered rock and with some mud along SE beach; generally soft.	Low bluff line backing marsh or partly tree-covered meadow back of SE beach; similar, but perhaps more sandy, land backs W beach.	Exits by trail except at N end of SE beach where road runs to small town and pier.

TABLE IV - 7 (Continued)

Number and location of beach area	Nearshore	Length	Width	Gradient	Surf and shore drift	Material and firmness	Terrain immediately behind beach	Connections inland
(92) Saaremaa (island), N and NW shores.	Bottom slopes are irregularly flat but generally flat; rocks are present locally.	About 50 mi. of beach, interrupted by river and stream mouths and by stretches of swampy or rocky coast.	Probably varies from 25 to 150 ft.; narrowest portions generally lie to the W, widest portions along deep bays.	1 on 25 to 1 on 50.	Surf may be moderate, will be lightest along W shores of bays or headlands; drift varies.	Sand and pebbles generally bay shores partly mud; most generally firm to E.	Generally, low marsh or tree-covered land along E shores of bays and at bayheads; higher wooded land frequently bluffed along W bay shores and on open coast; W end backed by extensive sandy neck which becomes marshy toward E end.	Best exits to roads from E end of area or from bay shores.
(93) Saaremaa, W shore.	Flat bottom slopes with numerous shoals and nearshore rocks.	Scattered beaches generally average 1 mi.; longest areas at S is 4 mi.	Generally 50 to 100 ft.	1 on 50 generally, long beach at S may be slightly steeper.	Surf probably moderate; drift varies, is probably to S and E along long beach.	Mainly sand; firm near water line, backshore soft.	Low meadow or marsh land along W beaches; road directly inland of S beaches fronting rolling meadow and wooded land.	Direct access to road from 2 beaches at S; otherwise best exits are from 2 beaches at NW end.
(94) Saaremaa, E shore.	Flat shoal bottom slopes; otherwise clear.	About 7.5 mi. interrupted by small stream near center.	75 to 100 ft.	1 on 30.	Surf light or negligible; main drift to N and E.	Sand; relatively soft.	Low but gently rising sand plain or wooded hills; low broken bluff along center.	Good road lies within 0.2 mi.; is easily accessible generally.
(95) Paaisalu and shore S.	Obstructed generally by rock shoals and islands; bottom slopes flat.	5 beaches, average about 1 mi. each; other such areas may occur.	Probably average 50 ft.	1 on 30 to 1 on 50.	Surf light or absent; drift weak.	Sand, probably with some mud; soft.	Land is flat or rises gently; meadow cover common, with some swamp and forest.	Exit is generally by trails; may be difficult because of swamps.
(96) W and S of Pärnu. (Fig. IV - 58.)	Flat bottom slopes; rocks along S end; dredged channel leads to harbor entrance.	15 mi., interrupted by jettied entrance to harbor near head of bay.	25 to 150 ft., widest portions along town at bayhead.	1 on 50.	Surf light or absent; drift probably weak and variable.	Sand with some mud and probably some rock along S end; generally soft.	Low, partly swampy land at W end; town directly inland along bayhead; to S land is low swampy or tree-covered.	Best exits into town or to main road which parallels E bay shore about 0.5 mi. inland for about 3 mi. S of Pärnu.
(97) N and S of Ainaži.	Bottom slopes flat with rocky shoals.	Total about 6.5 mi., interrupted by harbor structures at Ainaži and marshy shore.	N stretch 50 ft., S stretch may range to 100 ft.	1 on 30.	Surf generally moderate; drift mainly to N.	Mainly sand; firm along water line.	Partly wooded sand hills or low bluff lie back of beach or close inland.	Main road lies from 0.2 to 0.5 mi. inland; runs locally along top of low bluff.
(98) NE of Riga. (Fig. IV - 59.)	Flat bottom slopes; clear approach.	Total about 56 mi., interrupted by numerous stream mouths and by Gauja River near S end.	50 to 300 ft., widest along Gauja river and along jetty at SW end.	1 on 30 to 1 on 50; flattest toward SW end of beach.	Light to moderate surf; heavy along SW end with N winds; main drift to S and W.	Sand; firm near water line.	Wooded sand hills or low bluff; dune area is extensive near mouth of Gauja river; villages or resort areas common along E shore of bay.	Exits generally hindered by dunes or bluff; road lies within 0.5 mi. inland at N, more generally 1 to 2 mi.

C. Oviši to Klaipėda (Memel)

(57°34′N, 21°43′E; 55°43′N, 21°08′E) (Plan 15; Figure IV-67; U.S.H.O. Chart 4878; B.A. Charts 1770 and 2370)

(1) Coast

The western coastal area of Latvian SSR presents a narrow plain bordering the shores of the Gulf of Riga and those of the Baltic Sea. The coast lacks articulation and is flat, except for a closed dune barrier separating the coastal plain from the sea. Numerous small coastal rivers spend themselves behind the dune embankment, forming swamps and small ponds which greatly hinder movement inland south of the Gulf of Riga. Most of the harbors along this coast are oriented diagonally to the sea. Railroads avoid the swampy coastal plain, being laid out along the dune wall roughly parallel to the coast. The narrow coastal stretch of Lithuanian SSR, adjoining that of Latvian SSR, is also flat and separated from the interior by a dune hill barrier and a fairly wide stretch of swamp. The coasts are rich in vegetation and lined with groves of fir trees.

From Oviši the coast trends south-southwestward for 50 miles to Akmeņrags (Stein Ort), a point about 5 miles southwestward of Pāvilosta, thence southward for 66 miles to Klaipėda (Memel). The coast is low to moderately high and wooded in sections. The bottom, east of the 20-fathom curve, is composed of sand with general depths of 7 or 8 fathoms at a distance of 2 miles seaward.

From Oviši to Ventspils, 11 miles southeastward, the coast is mostly wooded, with sand dunes along the beach (U.S.H.O. Chart 4878). Ventspils Osta (B.A. Chart 1770) consists of an outer and an inner harbor. The outer harbor is formed by two jetties and has a width of 350 yards at the entrance and a channel dredged to 23 feet. The inner harbor, formed by the channel of the river Venta, has a minimum depth of 22 feet (Chapter VI). The town of Ventspils lies on the southern side of the river entrance. Railroads connect with nearby ports and the interior, and steamship lines run to Rīga and Liepāja (Libau). There are two landing fields and a seaplane base at Ventspils.

From Ventspils southward for 54 miles to Liepāja (U.S.H.O. Chart 4878) the coast is sandy (beach area (102); Table IV-8), backed by partially wooded sand hills which attain a height of 60 feet near Strante, near Pāvilosta. The port of Liepāja, extending for 2.3 miles along the coast, is situated on the shore end of Liepāja Bank (B.A. Chart 1770). It is formed and sheltered by four breakwaters and has depths ranging from 22 to 32 feet (Chapter VI). The roadstead, outside of the breakwaters, is entirely unprotected and is not favorable as an anchorage. The important commercial city of Liepāja lies at the outlet of the lake Liepājas Ezers on the narrow strip of land between the lake and the Baltic Sea. Its exports are principally lumber, grain, and oil. There are railroad connections with Rīga and the interior. There are several partially equipped airfields and a seaplane base in the vicinity.

Liepājas Ezers, which is connected with Tosmares Ezers 1.5 miles northward, is 8 miles long, 1 to 2 miles wide, and navigable for craft drawing 3 feet. Its banks are marshy, with low islands and shoals at the entrance.

From Liepāja the coast extends southward for 51 miles to Klaipėda (B.A. Chart 2370). The shoreline is low and very regular. Immediately offshore for the entire area are two well-defined sand bars which extend 70 and 200 yards seaward; otherwise the surface in the nearshore area appears to be free of obstruction. A sand beach, varying

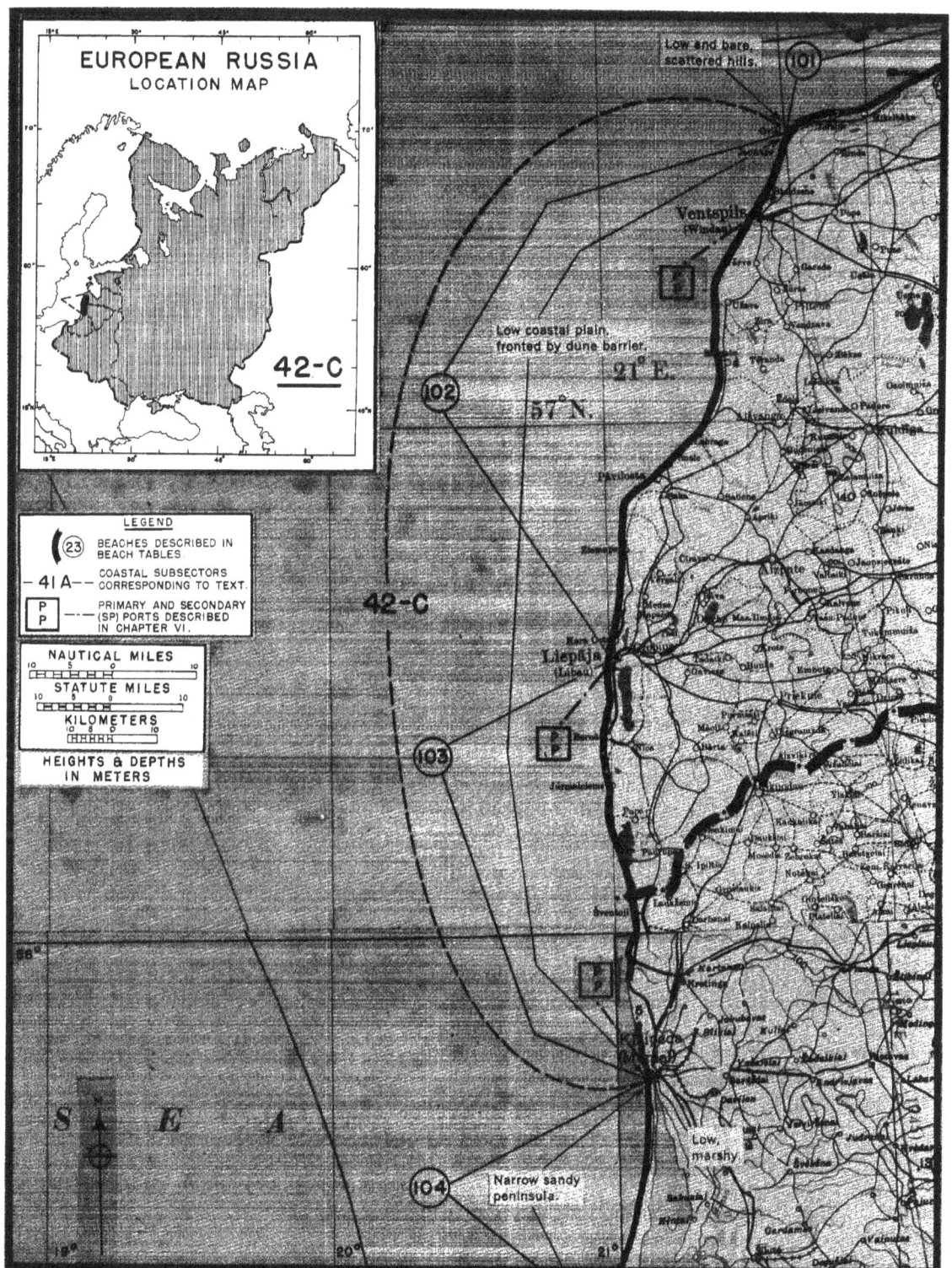

FIGURE IV-67. *Coastal subsector 42 C.*

in width from 40 feet to 200 feet, parallels the coast (beach area (103); FIGURES IV-68 and IV-69). The beach is backed by a strip of low grass- and scrub-covered sand dunes (10 to 80 feet high) extending 30 to 200 yards inland. Behind these dunes the terrain varies considerably throughout the area. For 7 miles south of Liepāja, a narrow strip of flat cultivated land behind the dunes is backed by Liepājas Ezers, behind which lies fir woodland. For a 14-mile stretch of coast south of this portion, the woods begin immediately behind the dunes on 30- to 50-foot sand hills, which give way to level woodland about 1 mile inland. For the next 11 miles of coast southward, to Šventoji, the dunes are again backed by a strip of flat cultivated ground, behind which lies an extensive marshy area, with fir woods beginning 2 to 3 miles inland. From Šventoji to Klaipėda, the dunes are backed by level cultivated fields and patches of woodland. A number of roads run inland from this last section of the shore to the 25-foot, paved Liepāja–Klaipėda coast road, which lies 0.5 to 3 miles behind the coast. Through the soft ground north of Šventoji to the coastal road behind, road exits are few.

FIGURE IV-68. *Latvian SSR, Liepāja (Libau). Beach area (103).*
Looking eastward along beach area south of Liepāja. No date.
Approximate position 56°30′N, 20°59′E; B. A. Chart 2370.

FIGURE IV-69. *Lithuanian SSR, Klaipėda (Memel). Beach area (103).*
Looking northward along south end of beach area, near Klaipėda.
No date. Approximate position 55°45′N, 21°05′E; B. A. Chart 2370.

(2) Landing beaches

The two beaches of subsector 42 C, constituting about 139 miles of almost continuous beach, are described briefly in TABLE IV-8.

TABLE IV-8
LANDING BEACHES OF COASTAL SUBSECTOR 42 C
Reliability FAIR. (PLAN 15)

Number and location of beach area	Nearshore	Length	Width	Gradient	Surf and shore drift	Material and firmness	Terrain immediately behind beach	Connections inland
(102) Ovīši to Liepāja	Flat bottom slopes; generally clear.	Total about 82 mi., interrupted by streams and by structures at Ventspils and Pāvilosta.	N half 100 to 200 ft.; S half probably ranges up to 100 ft.	1 on 25 to 1 on 50; N half flattest.	Surf moderate to heavy, heaviest along S half; drift varies, is most generally to N.	Sand; firm at water line, backshore soft.	Sandy plain or wooded sand hills back N half; sand hills are steeper and generally form a steep bluff behind S half.	Main road and R.R. lie close inland; exits from beach by trails hindered by sand hills and bluff; easiest near town areas.
(103) Liepāja to Klaipėda. (Figs. IV-68 and IV-69.)	Bottom slopes flat; shoals 2 mi. offshore at Berenati and 11 mi. N of Klaipėda; otherwise clear.	About 57 mi., interrupted by small stream mouths.	100 to 200 ft.	1 on 30 to 1 on 50.	Moderate to heavy surf; drift to S.	Fine white sand; relatively soft.	Sand bluffs, or dunes, wooded in places.	Good exits from villages or resorts; otherwise hindered by sand dunes or bluff.

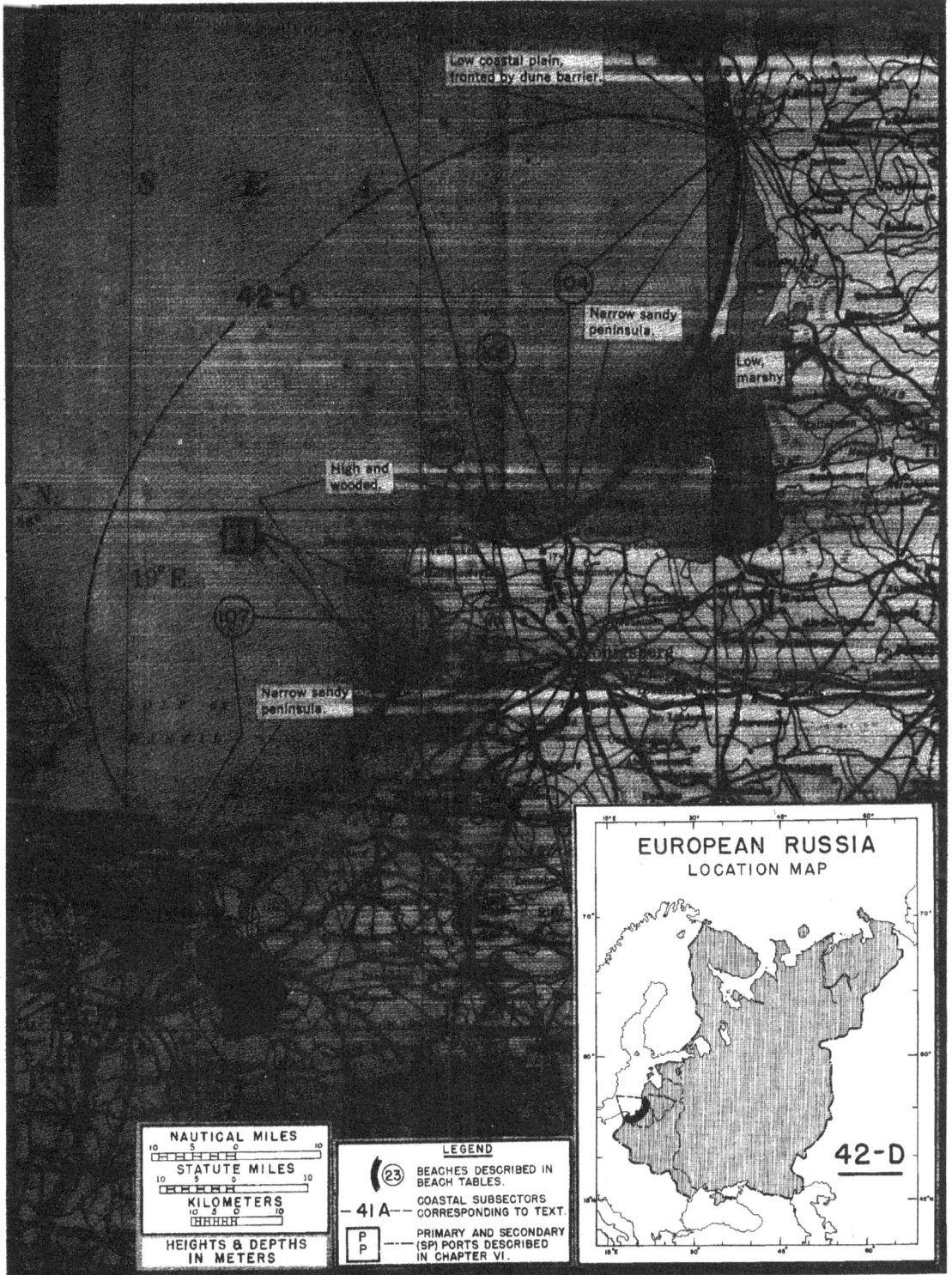

FIGURE IV-70. *Coastal subsector 42 D.*

D. Klaipėda (Memel) to Sztutowo (Stutthof)

(55°43′N, 21°08′E; 54°20′N, 19°09′E) (Plan 16; Figure IV-70; B.A. Charts 2369 and 2370)

(1) Coast

Klaipėda (Memel) harbor is formed by the Zeyetif (See Tief) which is the entrance channel to Kurisches Haff, a large body of water lying behind the coast (B.A. Chart 2370; Figure IV-71). The harbor is entered between projecting jetties 420 yards apart (Chapter VI). The Zeyetif is about 4 miles long and about 500 yards wide, with a depth of 19.5 to 26 feet. The town of Klaipėda, an important commercial port with up-to-date loading facilities, is situated on the north bank of Zeyetif with the principal part of the town on the south bank of the river Dange, which flows through the town and empties into the harbor. There are railroad connections with other ports and the interior.

Figure IV-71. *Lithuanian SSR, Klaipėda. Beach area (104).*
Aerial view northeastward to harbor entrance. Sandy beach at north end of beach area backed by embankments. 1943.
Approximate position 55°43′N, 21°07′E; B. A. Chart 2370.

Kurisches Haff, separated from the Baltic Sea by Kurische Nehrung, is the largest inland sea on the coast. The Haff is about 50 miles long north – south and 25 miles wide at the southern part, decreasing gradually in width to 0.5 mile at the southern end of Klaipéda harbor. In the northern part there are general depths from 3 to 6 feet and in the southern part depths from 2 to 3 fathoms. From the Zeyetif southward, shoal banks are overgrown with huge rushes and reeds, fringing marshes which extend a short distance inland. South of the mouths of the Nemunas river, the eastern and southern shores of Kurisches Haff are low and thickly wooded. Kurische Nehrung (beach area (104); FIGURES IV-72 to IV-75) is a narrow sandy peninsula extending in a southerly and southwesterly direction for about 50 miles from Klaipéda to Sarkau Forest, where it joins the mainland near Krants. Wooded sand hills are backed by steep barren dunes ranging from 100 to 200 feet high, lying along the eastern edge.

Kurisches Haff is separated from Frisches Haff, a similar inland body of water, by the Zamland peninsula, which rises steeply on the north and west to a height of 365 feet at Gallgarben. The center of the peninsula is covered with wide, well-cultivated fields. From Sarkau Forest, the southern part of Kurische Nehrung, the coast trends westward for 19 miles to Mys Bryusterot, a bold cliff-like point surrounded by a reef which extends 0.8 mile

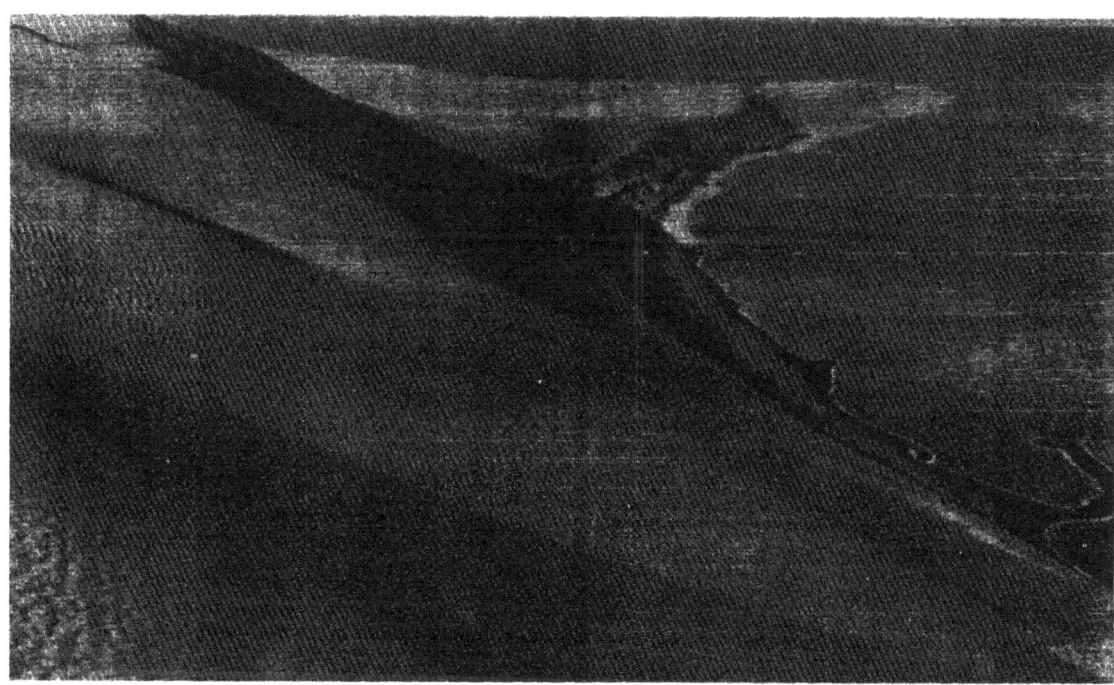

FIGURE IV-72. *Lithuanian SSR, Kurische Nehrung. Beach area (104).*
Looking northeastward along sand dunes 200 feet high back of center section of beach area. Kurisches Haff right and at top. Approximate position 55°19′N, 21°02′E; B. A. Chart 2370.

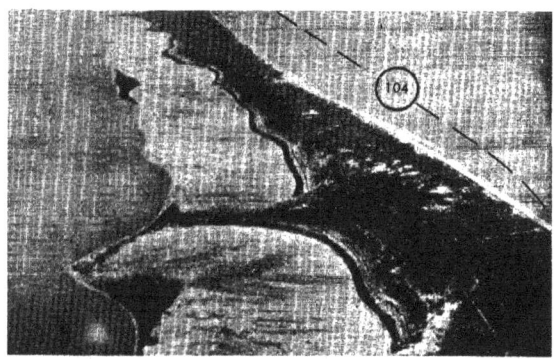

FIGURE IV-73. *Kaliningradskaya Oblast', Kurische Nehrung. Beach area (104).*
Aerial view looking southwestward along barrier separating Kurisches Haff, left, from Baltic Sea and beach area, right. Prior to 1931. Approximate position 55°10′N, 20°50′E; B. A. Chart 2370.

FIGURE IV-74. *Kaliningradskaya Oblast', Kurische Nehrung. Beach area (104).*
Looking northeastward across dunes and typical fishing village on shore of Kurisches Haff. No date. Approximate position 55°10′N, 20°50′E; B. A. Chart 2370.

FIGURE IV-75. *Kaliningradskaya Oblast', Kurische Nehrung. Beach area (104)*
Looking northeastward along southern end of beach area. No date. Approximate position 54°58'N, 20°30'E; B. A. Chart 2370.

offshore. The shores are high and wooded (beach areas (105) and (106); FIGURES IV-76 to IV-80). From this point the coast extends southward for 19 miles to Baltiysk (Pillau). Between Mys Bryusterort and Yantarnyy (formerly Pal'mnikken) (B.A. Chart 2369) the shore continues high with a yellowish appearance. Rocky shoal patches extend several miles offshore northeastward of Rotenem, a coastal village about 9 miles northward of Baltiysk. About 3 miles northeastward of Baltiysk, a forest, Lokhshtedtskiy Les, extends across the peninsula from the Baltic Sea eastward to the bay, Zaliv Fishkhauzen. Northward of the forest the shores of the bay are steep. Near Baltiysk are sandy heights fronted by trees along the shore.

FIGURE IV-76. *Kaliningradskaya Oblast', Zamland Coast. Beach area (105).*
Looking eastward along beach area from Krants. No date. Approximate position 54°58'N, 20°29'E; B. A. Chart 2370.

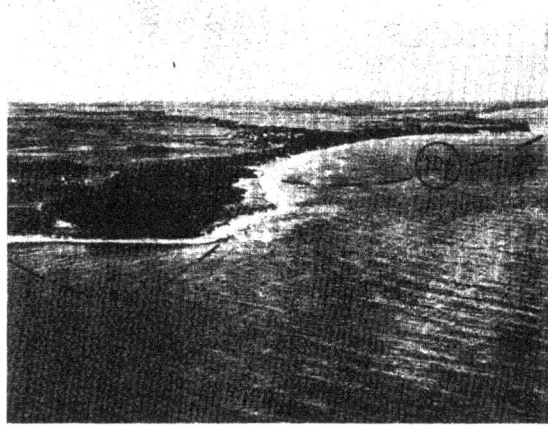

FIGURE IV-77. *Kaliningradskaya Oblast', Zamland Coast. Beach areas (105) and (106).*
Aerial view westward across Mys Rantauyer Shpittse and Neukuhren Bay showing high wooded shores with cultivated fields in the center of Zamland Peninsula. Right background is Mys Vanger Shpittse. Prior to 1931. Approximate position 54°57'N, 20°14'E; B. A. Chart 2370.

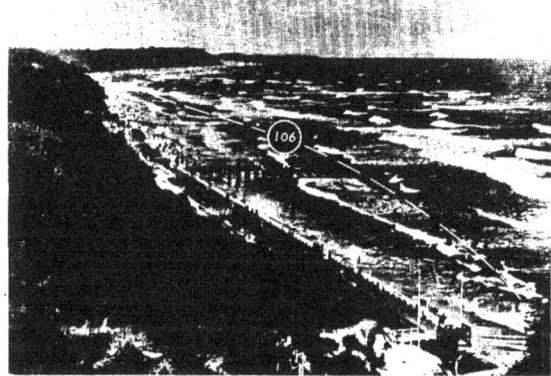

FIGURE IV-78. *Kaliningradskaya Oblast', Zamland Coast. Beach area (106).*
Looking westward from hill back of beach area at Svetlogorsk (formerly Rauschen). Compare heavy swell and water line with FIGURE IV-79. 1935. Approximate position 54°57'N, 20°08'E; B. A. Chart 2370.

FIGURE IV-79. *Kaliningradskaya Oblast', Zamland Coast. Beach area (106).*
Section of beach area shown in FIGURE IV-78, showing different surf conditions and water line. 1938.

FIGURE IV-80. *Kaliningradskaya Oblast' area, Zamland Coast. Beach area (106).*
Looking northwestward from cliff behind west end of beach area near Gross-Kuhren. 1928. Approximate position 54°'56N, 20°03'E; B. A. Chart 2370.

The only outlet from Frisches Haff to the Baltic is through the Pillau Tief, a channel lying between the northern extremity of Frische Nehrung, a narrow sandy stretch of coastline (beach area (107)) separating the Haff from the sea, and the town of Baltiysk (Pillau). Baltiysk harbor is entered by the Zeyetif (See Tief), a channel 328 yards wide and 31 feet deep dredged in the Pillau Tief (Chapter VI). This entrance seldom freezes over, due to strong currents. The Baltiysk inner harbor extends in a northeasterly direction from the eastern end of the Zeyetif and consists of several small havens with depths of from 6 to 26 feet. The town of Baltiysk has railroad communication with Kaliningrad (Königsberg) and shipping connections with Klaipėda (Memel), Danzig (Gdańsk), and Liepāja (Libau). A canal, 17.5 miles long and 21 feet deep, extends eastward to the mouth of the river Pregel', which empties into the Haff 4.5 miles from Kaliningrad.

The harbor of Kaliningrad consists of the several branches of the Pregel' and three large basins on the southern side of the river (Chapter VI). The city, capital of the former province of East Prussia, is connected by railroads with the principal towns of the country and by steamship with nearby ports.

Frisches Haff is about 50 miles long northeast–southwest, with an average width of 5 miles. The two principal rivers flowing into the Haff are the Pregel' in the northeastern part, and the eastern mouth of the Wista (Vistula) which discharges into the southwestern part. General depths in the Haff are 1.3 to 2.5 fathoms, the deepest part being southeastward of Baltiysk. The bottom consists of soft clay and mud mixed with sand. On the shores of the Haff a hard bank underlies the soft bottom, having a breadth of 1,200 to 1,600 yards, with depths of 3 to 6 feet. In some areas, banks of hard sand and shingle extend some distance from the beach. Where the shore consists of meadowland or soil deposited by rivers, reeds and rushes extend for a distance inland. The eastern shore of the Haff is well cultivated. Hills skirt the coast in places, rising gradually inland. Wooded dune hills average from 30 to 40 feet high with exceptional heights of as much as 120 feet. The northern shore is well wooded.

(2) Landing beaches

The beaches of subsector 42 D (beach areas (104) to (107); TABLE IV-9), lie along the two narrow sandy barriers which enclose the two large lagoon and harbor areas, Kurisches Haff and Frisches Haff, and for short stretches along the cliffed coast of Zamland peninsula which lies between. The long barrier beaches are rather narrow and are backed by steep dunes, so that exits are difficult or impossible. The nearshore area is generally clear, with bottom slopes varying from *gentle* to *flat*.

TABLE IV - 9

LANDING BEACHES OF COASTAL SUBSECTOR 42 D

Reliability FAIR. (Plan 16)

Number and location of beach area	Nearshore	Length	Width	Gradient	Surf and shore drift	Material and firmness	Terrain immediately behind beach	Connections inland
(104) Klaipėda to Krants. (Figs. IV - 71 to IV - 75.)	Bottom slopes *mild* to *flat*; clear.	About 60 mi.	50 to 100 ft.	1 on 20 average.	Moderate surf; drift probably varies but is mainly to S.	Sand; soft.	Narrow belt of wooded sand hills backed by steep barren dunes ranging from 100 to 200 ft. high and lying along inner edge of narrow barrier which encloses Kurisches Haff; small settlements lie between dunes on inner shore.	Trail along barrier, but movement inland hindered by high dunes and enclosed lagoon.
(105) W of Krants. (Figs. IV - 76 and IV - 77.)	*Mild* bottom slopes; clear.	8 mi., continues from end of beach (104); interrupted by small stream near center.	150 ft. near E end; narrows to W.	1 on 10 to 1 on 15.	Moderate surf; main drift to E.	Sand; firm only at water line.	Relatively low dune ridge backed by partly wooded country which rises slightly to W; resort and town area immediately inland at E end.	Main road runs inland from Krants; R.R. parallels coast about 1 mi. inland.
(106) E and W of Svetlogorsk (Rauschen). (Figs. IV - 77 to IV - 80.)	*Gentle-to-mild* bottom slopes; direct approach clear.	4 small beaches along cliffed rocky coast, each about 0.5 mi.	25 to 50 ft.	1 on 15 to 1 on 25.	Surf heavy with NE through NW winds; drift varies.	Sand and pebbles; relatively firm.	Backed immediately by promenade and resort buildings at Svetlogorsk; more generally by steep partly wooded cliffs.	Exit hindered by steep cliffs from all areas; although railroad and roads lie close inland.
(107) NE and SW of Baltiysk	*Mild* bottom slopes; generally clear.	13 mi., interrupted by channel and harbor jetties at Baltiysk, and probably by areas where old dunes lie directly inland of water's edge.	Probably 200 to 300 ft. near structures at Baltiysk; otherwise generally 25 to 75 ft. narrowing out at N end.	Generally 1 on 20.	Moderate to heavy surf with N to NW winds; main drift to S and SW.	Sand; generally firm except near harbor structures.	Generally steep wooded dunes averaging 30 to 40 ft. but ranging as high as 120 ft.; whole area lies along narrow barrier fronting Frisches Haff.	Only exit is into Baltiysk; lateral movement along shore is probably difficult or impossible.

(Text continued following Figure IV-81)

FIGURE IV-81
COASTAL SUBSECTOR 43-A
JANIS 40

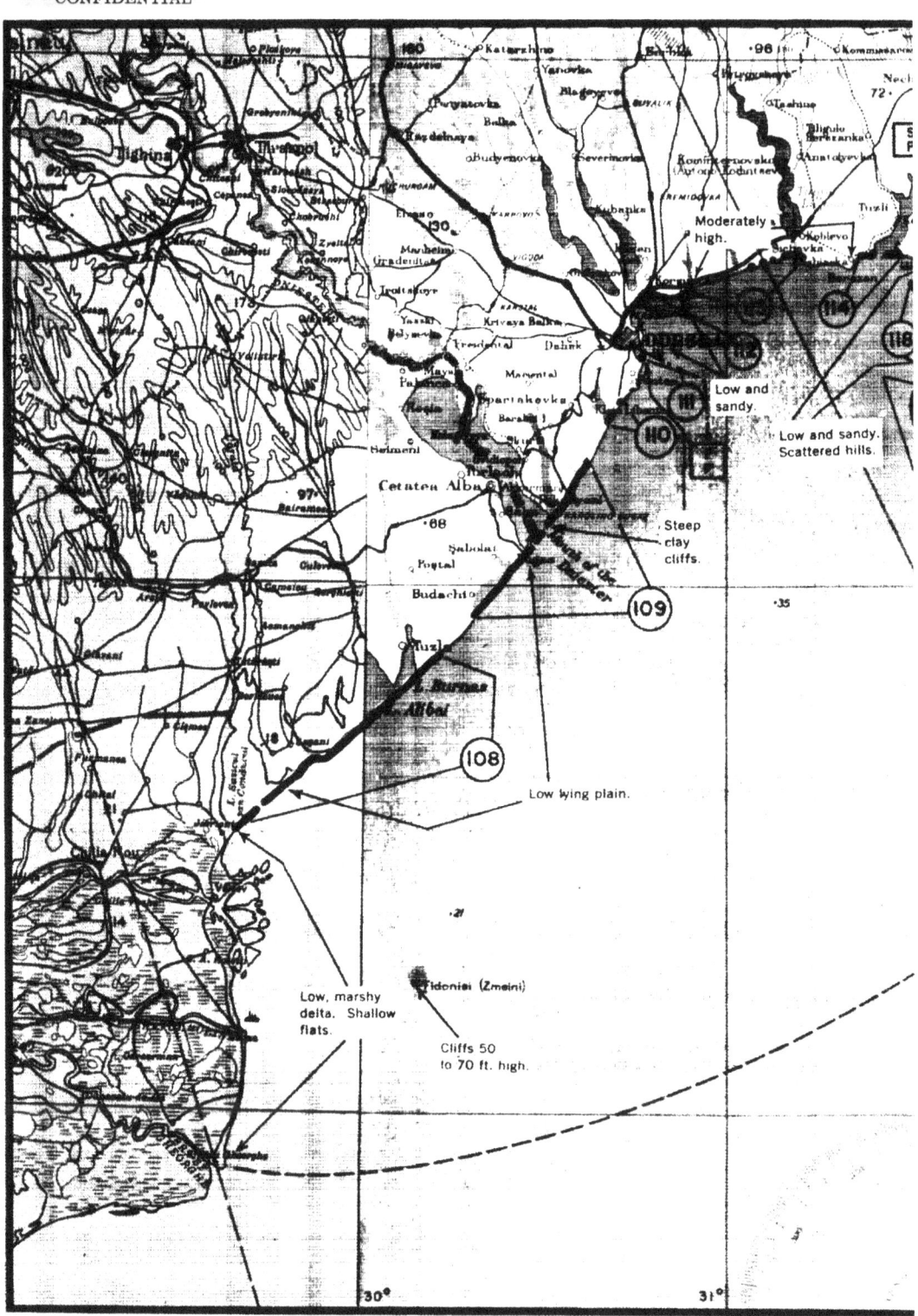

43. SOUTH COASTAL SECTOR—DANUBE RIVER MOUTH TO PORT-KATON

(44°51′N, 29°37′E; 46°53′N, 38°45′E) (Plans 17 to 19; Figure IV-118; B.A. Chart 2214; A.M.S. Maps scale 1:2,000,000 G.S.G.S. No. 4464—Central Europe Key No. 173153, and West Central Russia Key No. 316883)

The Black Sea is restricted in the center by the Crimea, a peninsula which extends southward from the northern shore. It is connected by straits to the Aegean Sea and the Sea of Azov. The bottom in the central portion consists of bluish-gray mud; near the coast it is mud, mixed with shells, and in places with sand and shingle.

Prevailing winds over the Black Sea during the winter months vary from northwest through north to northeast; their direction being modified by local topography. During the summer months, land and sea breezes regularly predominate along the northern and western coasts. Along the north coast, their prevailing direction is northwesterly. Along the south coast of the Crimea, summer land and sea breezes are irregular and long periods of calm frequently result. The intensity and direction of land and sea breezes is dependent upon the over-all wind pattern.

The water level of the Black Sea and the Sea of Azov is not subject to tidal influences, but is subject to variations caused by changes in atmospheric pressure and winds. The mean annual water level varies from year to year; but variations at different points in the area are generally the same in any one year. The mean annual change is about 2.2 inches; but reductions of the mean level by 4 to 7 inches and rises of as much as 5 to 6 inches have occurred. Seasonal variations show that the maximum water level occurs generally in June; the minimum level occurs most frequently in November. For these reasons, the tabular descriptions of the beach areas which follow show only one width for each beach. This width is an average and will vary with the unpredictable changes in water level. Likewise, the gradient given denotes an average gradient in the zone of the average water line.

Surface currents flowing out of the Sea of Azov and out of the Black Sea are almost constant, although reversals due to wind peculiarities have been noted. In addition, a general counterclockwise current flows along the shore, its rate and occurrence varying with wind variations.

Ice obstructs navigation and landings in the river Danube, the northwestern part of the Black Sea and the Sea of Azov. The Dniester estuary freezes solid in January and floating ice is encountered offshore. Although navigation to Odessa ceases only in very severe winters, Kherson is icebound during January and February. Ice which forms in Kherson Bay and in the large bays to the southeast is often blown out of the bays and encountered in offshore regions. In the Sea of Azov, ice usually appears in December, attains a thickness of 2.5 feet, and breaks up in the latter part of February or the middle of March. Ice does not form a hazard to navigation along the southern coast of the Crimea, although thin pancake ice forms in the shallower bays during severe winters. Elsewhere, except in enclosed or very shallow bays, the Black Sea is navigable throughout the year.

Extensive beach areas line more than one-half of the coast included in this sector. Shorter beaches are thickly scattered over the remainder.

A. Danube river mouth to Mys Kartkazak

(44°51′N, 29°37′E; 45°57′N, 33°37′E) (Plans 17 and 18; Figure IV 81; U.S.H.O. Charts 4202, 4204, 4206, Misc. 10,219-13, and Misc. 11,954-3; B.A. Charts 603, 2208, 2231, 2379, 2380, and 2835)

(1) Coast

The river Danube branches out near Ceatal about 40 miles from the coast, and flows into the Black Sea through Bratul Sfântul Gheorghe (Br. Sf. Gheorghe), the Bratul Sulina, and the numerous outlets of the Kilia delta (B.A. Chart 2835). The Bestepe Range, from 700 to 800 feet high, rises in the middle of the low-lying districts forming the delta, about 28 miles northwestward from Bratul Sfântul Gheorghe, the southernmost mouth of the Danube. The shores of the delta, covered with reeds and a few scattered trees, are low and only slightly above sea level. Since the Danube is normally heavily charged with sediment, shoals form frequently and depths are subject to constant change. The highest water may be expected from February to July and the lowest from August to December.

The mouth of Bratul Sfântul Gheorghe, (U.S.H.O. Chart Misc. 10,219-13) is blocked by extensive sandbanks, with general depths of from 1 to 3 feet, which extend, with depths of less than 3 fathoms, about 2.3 miles eastward from the entrance and from the coast southwestward of it. The principal channel lies northward of these banks, close to the northern side of the entrance, with depths increasing upstream from 11 to 75 feet.

Bratul Sulina, the middle entrance to the Danube, lies about 17 miles northward of Bratul Sfântul Gheorghe, and is the principal entrance used by vessels because of its greater depth. The channel across the bar has a minimum depth of 21 feet. The river extends from the sea for a distance of 43 miles to Ceatal, with a minimum depth of 4 feet and width varying from 240 to 720 yards. The shores are low, sandy, and devoid of trees. Sulina, a port of transshipment for the large bulk of grain brought down the Danube extends 3 miles upstream.

The mouths of the Bratul Chilia (Kilia Branch) of the Danube extend northward along the coast for about 18 miles. The whole of the delta is fronted by a shallow flat which extends about 3 miles off Gura Vechiu Stambul, the largest of the mouths, and about 1 mile off the others, rendering them useless for other than local small craft. The coastline, channels, and depths are constantly changing and land is barely visible in many places on the outer edge of the flat. A pine forest lies 5.5 miles northwestward of Gura Vechiu Stambul at Letea.

Ostrov Zmeinyy (Fidonisi, or Zmeini), is situated about 21.5 miles east-northeastward of Gura Vechiu Stambul, is about 130 feet high. The coastline is a continuous cliff from 50 to 70 feet in height.

From the northern side of the Kilia delta the coast trends northeastward for 50 miles to the Tsaregradskoye Girlo, mouth of the river Dniester, forming the edge of a low-lying plain which is just above sea level, in places, with occasional small hills (U.S.H.O. Chart Misc. 11,954-3). A chain of shallow salt lakes, separated from the sea by narrow necks of sand (beach area *(108)*; Table IV-10), extends from Zhebriyany (Jibrieni) to Mys Burnas, 29 miles northeastward. At Mys Burnas there is a slight rise in the sand ridge which continues for 10 miles to Budaki thence the ridge gradually decreases to the Tsaregradskoye Girlo (mouth). Budakskoye Ozero lies within the low sandy ridge. The coastal bank with depths of less than 5 fathoms extends about 0.5 to 1 mile off this stretch.

Original

Dnestrovskiy Liman (B.A. Chart 2208) consists of a large lagoon or salt lake having general depths of from 5 to 9 feet, separated from the sea by two tongues of sand which extend from either shore (beach area *(109)*). The Tsaregradskoye Girlo is a 250-foot-wide channel between these two narrow sandspits and has a depth of 9 to 12 feet over the bar fronting it, increasing to about 5 fathoms within the bar. A former shallow northern mouth, the Ochakovskoye, is now completely silted up, forming a part of the sandspit. The entrance to the river Dniester, 16 miles northwestward of Ust'ye Tsaregradskoye discharges through a low delta plain and is only navigable by small craft.

From the northern side of the Dnestrovskiy Liman the coast trends northeastward (FIGURE IV-82) for 24 miles

FIGURE IV-82. *Ukrainian SSR, Bielyaevka. Beach area (109).* Vertical aerial view near north end of beach area. April 1944. Approximate position 46°11′N, 30°35′E; B. A. Charts 2208 and 2231.

to Mys Lanzheron (B.A. Chart 2231). With the exception of several sand bars which separate two salt lakes from the sea (beach area (110)), the shores are characterized by steep clay cliffs, (FIGURE IV-83) 30 to 120 feet in height. A bank with depths of less than 5 fathoms extends about 3.5 miles offshore.

FIGURE IV-83. *Ukrainian SSR.*
Looking northward along characteristic clay cliffs south of Odessa. Approximate position between 46°09′N, 30°33′E and 46°22′N, 30°45′E; B. A. Chart 2231.

Odesskiy Zaliv (U.S.H.O. Chart 4202) lies between Mys Lanzheron and Mys Severnyy Odesskiy, 5 miles northeastward. At the southern extremity of the bay (beach area (111); FIGURE IV-84), adjacent to the former point, is a breakwater-protected harbor which extends approximately 2.5 miles along the shore. At the northern extremity of the bay, adjacent to Mys Severnyy Odesskiy, steep clay cliffs extend along the coast for a distance of approxi-

FIGURE IV-84. *Ukrainian SSR, Odessa. Beach area (111).*
Looking southward toward south end of beach area near Odessa. No date.

mately 2 miles. Between these two points there is a low-lying sand beach (beach area (112); FIGURE IV-85), approximately 3 miles long, backed by a low plain which extends inland to the shores of two large lagoons. The lagoons are separated by a ridge (FIGURE IV-86 and IV-87) which extends seaward to within 1,000 yards of the beach. The ridge, which has a height of 130 to 150 feet at its seaward edge, separates the low plain into two distinct parts. Odessa harbor has excellent holding ground of mud, sand and shells (Chapter VI). The town, with a population in 1939, of 604,223, is situated about halfway between the estuaries of the river Dniester and of the Dnepr and Bug rivers, and is one of the principal trading ports on the Black Sea. It is built on a hill which rises

FIGURE IV-85. *Ukrainian SSR, Odessa. Beach area (112).*
Looking southward across beach area north of Odessa. 1935. Approximate position 46°32′N, 30°45′E; U. S. H. O. Chart 4202.

rather steeply from the sea to a height of 120 feet. The city is connected to the general railway system which extends to the principal cities of Europe. First-class roads extend to other important inland cities. Steamship communications are maintained with the Black Sea ports. There are three airfields, four landing grounds, and two seaplane bases in the vicinity.

From Mys Severnyy Odesskiy to Mys Adzhiyask (B.A. Chart 603), about 22 miles eastward, the coast is characterized by high (approximately 150 feet) steep slopes which rise to a relatively level, extensively cultivated plain. The uniformity of the coast is broken by several salt lakes which are separated from the sea by low, narrow sand bars (beach area (113)). These salt lakes are former embayments, and lie in long, narrow, steep-sided valleys. This section of coast is fronted by a bank, with irregular depths of less than 5 fathoms extending 1.5 miles offshore. Odesskaya Banka lies about 3 miles off the coast and extends for 22 miles eastward to Kinburn Peninsula. The northern side of the bank is steep-to but the southern side is shelving. The entrance channel to the Dneprovskiy Liman lies between Odesskaya Banka and the coastal bank of the mainland.

Berezanskiy Liman extends 14 miles inland from its entrance between two low, sandy spits (beach area (114)) 3 miles northeastward of Mys Adzhiyask. The entrance is fronted by a flat with a depth of 4.5 feet.

The entrance to the Dneprovskiy Liman (Estuary of the Dnieper) (B.A. Chart 2379) lies between Kinburn Point, 4.5 miles east-southeastward of Ostrov Berezan' and Ochakovskiy Mys about 2.3 miles northeastward from Kinburn Point. About 1.7 miles westward from the tip of the latter point lies a small island bearing a lighthouse. Kinburn Peninsula is the prolongation westward of the left bank of the Dnepr, and forms the southern shore of the estuary terminating westward in Kinburn Point (B.A. Chart 2380). It is low and swampy with low scattered sand dunes and some sand scrub growth (beach area (117)). High rushes grow along the entire shore. The northern shore of the estuary (beach areas (115) and (116)), for its whole length, has an almost constant elevation of from 145 to 160 feet, consisting of dark yellow to reddish clay bluffs broken by gullies and valleys, except for 3.5 miles immediately adjacent to the mouth of the river Dnepr, where the bluffs become 30 to 40 feet in height. In the center of its length the coast is broken by the mouth of the river Bug. Adzhigiol'skaya and Mys Stanislav extend

FIGURE IV-86. *Ukrainian SSR, Odessa. Beach area (112).*
Looking southeastward from Zhevakhova hill, a high bluff north of Odessa, across flat strip separating Kuyal'nitskiy Liman, to left, from beach area on Odesskiy Zaliv, top right. Prior to 1942. Approximate position 46°34'N, 30°43'E; U. S. H. O. Chart 4202.

FIGURE IV-87. *Ukrainian SSR, Odessa.*
Looking across park northwest of Odessa, on Gadzhibeiskiy Liman. Gadzhibeiskiy Liman is separated from Kuyal'nitskiy Liman by the long ridge at top. Compare FIGURE IV-86.

southward from the northern shore and are fringed by an extensive bank. These extensions divide the estuary into three basins. The eastern shore is formed by the marshy delta of the river Dnepr which is entirely covered with reeds, bushes, and a few trees. The shore is fronted by a very shallow bank which is constantly changing and forming small islands. In the deeper parts of the estuary, and in the river Bug, the bottom consists of soft mud. The shoals off the mouth of the Dnepr are composed of hard sand. Ice forms in the winter, covering the shoal and fresh-water areas. Only the river mouths freeze completely and in the estuary itself the ice often breaks up and sometimes disappears for short periods.

The entrance to the river Bug, between Adzhigiol'skaya Kosa and Mys Bublikov, is 11 miles wide (U.S.H.O. Chart 4204). The important town of Nikolayev (Nikolaev) is situated on the eastern bank about 21 miles above the entrance. The river is winding and is from 1 to 3 miles wide. Its banks are bordered by sand flats which extend beyond the middle of the river from the eastern side. The western bank, composed of clay, is high and steep; the eastern bank consists of undulating hills with low tongues of sand. The channel generally follows the western bank, and the river is navigable for small boats for a distance of about 40 miles above Nikolayev (Nikolaev).

The town of Nikolayev, with a population in 1938 of over 100,000, covers a large area of the promontory formed between the Bug and Ingul rivers. The commercial port lies on the southern side of the town and consists of two adjacent ports (Chapter VI). Regular steamship communications are maintained with Odessa, Kherson, Nikopol', and Ochakov. First-class highways extend to Odessa, Kherson, and the interior. Nikolayev lies on the main railroad system which connects with Kherson and the important cities farther inland. Four landing fields and two seaplane bases are located in the vicinity of the town.

The river Dnepr rises at an elevation of 830 feet in the Smolenskaya Oblast' and is about 1,200 miles in length. About 2.3 miles below Kherson, which lies 13 miles east-northeastward of Mys Kizim, the river divides into two channels. These in turn are divided into many interlacing channels which form a large marshy delta. The Rvach entrance is the only one of the nine mouths, through which the river discharges, which is navigable by seagoing vessels. The town of Kherson, with a population in 1939 of 97,186, is situated on the northern bank of Koshevaya branch, at its junction with the river Dnepr (Chapter VI). It is an important trading center and the seat of local government. A railroad and main highway

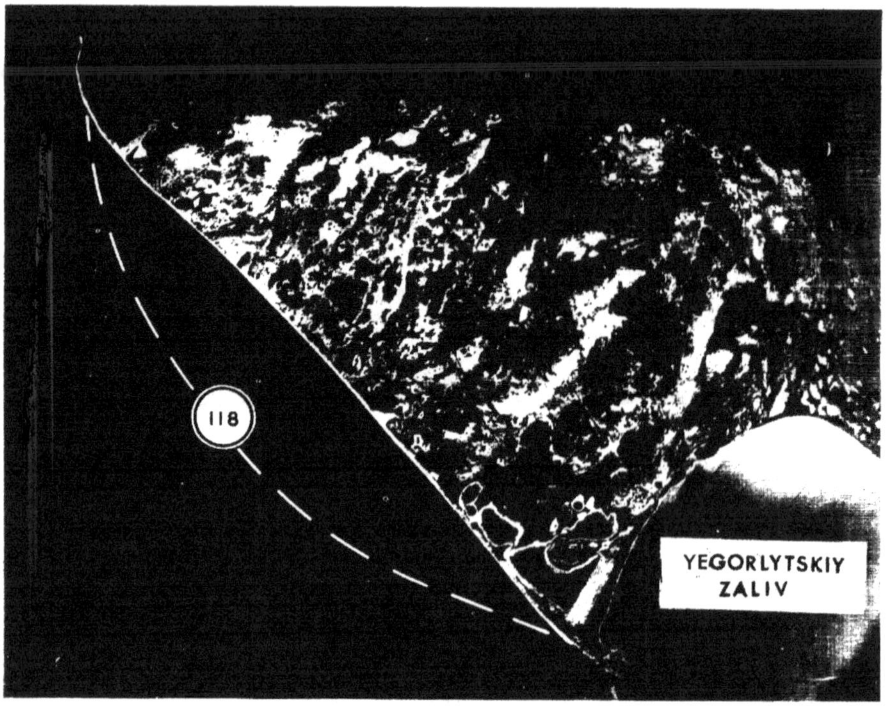

FIGURE IV-88. *Ukrainian SSR, Kinburn Peninsula. Beach area (118).*
Oblique aerial view of beach area west of Yegorlytskiy Zaliv. July 1943. Approximate position 46°30′N, 31°40′E; B. A. Chart 2380.

connect the city with Nikolayev. During the period of navigation, steamship communications are maintained with Black Sea ports and various towns on the river Dnepr (Dnieper). Two landing strips are located near Nikolayev.

From Kinburn Point the low, sandy, southwestern coast of Kinburn Peninsula (beach area (118); FIGURE IV-88) trends southeastward for about 11 miles to the northern entrance point of Yegorlytskiy Zaliv (Yagorlilski Bay). The entrance, 9 miles in width, is obstructed by two low, sandy islands which lie near the edge of the shallow flat extending southeastward. The channel, 2.5 miles wide, lies between Ostrov Dolgiy (Dolgi Island) and the southern entrance point of the gulf. The northern and western shores consist of low, sandy beaches backed by the low, sandy marsh terrain of Kinburn Peninsula. The southern and eastern shores are flat and marshy with the eastern shore fronted by a broad, shallow bank of soft ooze.

Tendrovskaya Kosa (Tyendyerovskaya Spit), a low, long, narrow, curved sandspit (beach area (119)) lies about 10 miles westward of Ostrov Dolgiy. The northern part is about 1 mile wide, trending southwest for about 4 miles, thence south-southeastward for 30 miles to the mainland. The spit is low and barren, with the exception of a few trees near the northern tip.

Tendrovskiy Zaliv lies between Tendra Point and the entrance to Yegorlyk Gulf. The eastern part of the bay is shallow and flat with a depth of 3 feet on either side of Orlov Island. Anchorage is afforded in the western part in depths of 7.5 fathoms over mud and shell bottom.

From the junction of the Tendrovskaya Kosa with the mainland the coast trends eastward for 13 miles with somewhat higher elevation (beach area (120)). Inland the area is relatively level and extensively cultivated. Another sandspit (beach area (121)) extends eastward for 22 miles forming the southern shore of Dzharylgachskiy Zaliv (beach area (122)). The western end of this strip is not more than 120 feet wide but about 10 miles from the western end it widens, forming Ostrov Dzharylgach (Dzharilgatski), which is low and marshy.

The Karkinitskiy Zaliv (Gulf of Karkinitt) is entered between the northern extremity of Tendrovskaya Kosa (Tyendyerovskaya Spit) and Mys Tarkhankut, the western extremity of the Crimea, about 73 miles southeastward. The eastern part of the Karkinitskiy Zaliv is entered between the eastern extremity of Ostrov Dzharylgach and Kyln Murun about 13 miles south-southeastward (U.S.H.O. Chart 4206). Its shores are indented by numerous shallow bays (beach area (123) Port Khorli) bordered by extensive flats which occupy about half of the area. This part of the gulf terminates northeastward in Perekopskiy Zaliv (Gulf of Perekop) which is very shallow. At the head of the bay is a narrow isthmus which joins the Crimea to the mainland and separates Perekopskiy Zaliv, a Black Sea inlet, from the Sivash lagoon on the Sea of Azov. The shores of the bay are low, backed by a slight rise to flat cultivated land, with marshlands extending along the eastern coast as far south as Mys Kartazak.

(2) Landing beaches

The beaches included in subsector 43 A (beach areas (108) to (123); TABLE IV-10) are for the most part along narrow ridges bordering salt lakes, some of very extensive size; along river estuaries or long narrow spits enclosing large bays. Beach approaches are generally flat but clear of any rock obstructions. Exits into the interior are only fair, usually involving movement along sandy spits, dunes, or marsh areas before reaching roads. Good lines of exit are available only locally and are best from the beaches near Odessa (beach areas (111) and (112)).

TABLE IV-10

LANDING BEACHES OF COASTAL SUBSECTOR 43 A

Reliability FAIR. (Plans 17 and 18)

Number and location of beach area	Nearshore	Length	Width	Gradient	Surf and shore drift	Material and firmness	Terrain immediately behind beach	Connections inland
(108)	Irregular bottom slopes, *mild* off center, *flat* toward both ends; otherwise clear.	38 mi., interrupted by inlet to salt lake and quay at Ozero Burnas; may continue N to beach (109).	Probably averages 75 ft.; narrowest toward N end.	1 on 50.	Surf light sand over broad belt except with E winds; drift varies.	Sand; relatively firm.	Generally a narrow sand neck fronting salt lakes; toward N low hills or bluff and fishing huts.	Only lateral movement possible along most of area; access to trails between villages accessible near N end.
(109) N and S of mouth of Dniester. (Fig. IV-82.)	*Gentle* bottom slopes with clear approach off S section; shoals, wrecks, and *flat* slopes off river mouth and to N.	26 mi., interrupted by 2 channels into estuary; may continue N to beach. (110).	150 to 200 ft. near center; narrows to about 15 ft. near N end.	1 on 25 to 1 on 50: steepest near N end.	Surf light except with E to SE winds; drift varies.	Sand; firm at water line.	Narrow sand ridge or plain forming barrier to salt lake, a spit, or low island; N end backed by low bank bordering cultivated land.	Road and railroad close inland from N entrance to river.
(110)	*Mild* uniform bottom slopes; clear.	S beach 2.5 mi., N beach 0.5 mi.	Average 100 ft. along S; 25 ft. along N.	1 on 30 to 1 on 20; N beach steepest.	Surf heavy with E or SE winds; drift varies.	Sand along S, probably sand and pebbles along N; N area more firm.	Narrow sand neck fronting salt lake and marsh backs S area; wooded ravine leading to village backs N area.	Exit to village about 0.5 mi. may be difficult; main road from village runs N to Odessa.
(111) S of Odessa. (Fig. IV-84.)	Generally *mild* bottom slopes, steepest off N beach, rock off S end of center beach.	About 1,000 ft. limited by rocky points.	75 ft. generally, narrows to 25 ft. at S end.	1 on 10.	Surf heavy only with E winds; drift varies but may be mainly to N.	Sand and pebbles at water line; backshore soft sand.	Sea wall about 15 ft. high or steep bank at S end, wall may extend entire length of beach; buildings and roads within wall.	Roads and tramways run N to Odessa.
(112) Bay N of Odessa. (Figs. IV-85 and IV-86.)	Depths of 30 ft., lie 1.5 mi. offshore; approach clear.	4 mi., between harbor and cliffed shore at N end of bay.	100 to 150 ft., probably widest along center.	1 on 8 at water line; flattens inland.	Surf generally light; drift may be mainly to NE.	Generally sand, pebbly and firm near water line along N; backshore soft.	Sand plain or low hills partly tree covered at N; buildings and streets along S.	Easy access into Odessa and to roads and railroads inland from city.
(113)	*Flat* irregular bottom slopes; otherwise clear.	Several beaches ranging from 1,000 ft. to 4 mi., E beach longest.	Smaller areas near center 25 ft.; others 50 to 75 ft.	Average 1 on 15.	Surf generally light; drift varies.	Sand and pebbles, E beach may be somewhat muddy and soft; others relatively firm.	Narrow sand or sand-marsh barriers, fronting small lakes; or narrow wooded ravines.	Road, locally along embankment, backs 2 beaches on W; exit otherwise up ravines or across marsh to same road.
(114) Mouth of Berezanskiy Liman.	Approach obstructed along center by island and by shoal extending N to mainland.	2 mi. on W side, about 1 mi. on E side.	Probably 100 to 150 ft.	1 on 25.	Surf light; drift generally to W.	Sand; probably soft.	Flat sandy and barren land; light structure at E end of E beach.	Probably difficult access to trail on W; railroad runs E to Ochakov from inland and E of E beach.

COASTS AND LANDING BEACHES Page IV-67

TABLE IV - 10 (Continued)

Number and location of beach area	Nearshore	Length	Width	Gradient	Surf and shore drift	Material and firmness	Terrain immediately behind beach	Connections inland
(115) W of Bugskiy Liman (Estuary of the Bug).	Depths of only 6 ft. lie 1,000 to 2,000 ft. offshore; approach except for channel is through depths of 18 ft. or less.	Probably 6 mi. on W, 2 mi. around point on E.	W beach probably 10 to 15 ft., E beach 25 to 50 ft.	Average 1 on 20.	Surf negligible; drift mainly to W.	Probably sand and mud along W beach, more sandy to E; all relatively soft.	Steep bluff with almost continuous line of villages back W beach; low sand and marshy point backs E beach.	Approach to road through villages difficult because of steep bluffs; better exit along trail to N from E beach.
(116) E of Bugskiy Liman.	Bottom slopes are flat; depths in approach are generally 14 ft. or less.	Total about 5 mi., interrupted by steep clay cliffs.	Probably averages 25 ft.	1 on 20.	Surf negligible; drift probably varies, but is mainly to W.	Sand or sand and mud; soft.	Small salt lakes or towns above bluffed slopes back E and W areas; sandy spit fronting bluffs backs center area.	Exit necessitates access to minor roads or trails above bluff.
(117)	Depths of 6 ft. lie as much as 1 mi. offshore.	Total about 10 mi. between marshy shores; beaches may be more continuous than shown.	15 to 50 ft., probably widest along spit at W.	1 on 30.	Surf negligible; drift mainly to W.	Mainly sand; soft.	Low sand plain backs most of W sections with some dunes, cultivated land, and marshy ponds; villages lie directly inland of 2 areas to E.	Access to coastal track or trail best from villages.
(118) N shore of Yegorlytskiy and to W. (Fig. IV - 88.)	Approach to bay obstructed by islands and shallow channel; slopes are flat and reeds line shore.	Total about 22 mi.	50 to 100 ft. along outer shore, averages 25 ft. within bay.	1 on 30.	Surf may be heavy along outer shore in summer; negligible in bay; drift to E in bay, in both directions from center along outer shore.	Mainly sand on outer shore, bay beach muddy; all soft.	Low sandy plain with some sand hills and numerous ponds or marsh areas along bay shore; fishing huts and clumps of trees line outer shore locally.	Access to trail along bay shore may be possible; all exits hindered by sandy or wet ground.
(119) Tendrovskaya Kosa (Tyendyerovskaya Spit.)	Bottom slopes are gentle sand flat, steepest off W end; otherwise clear.	About 48 mi., partly along inner side at W end; interrupted near E end by 2 channels.	25 to 100 ft., widest along W end.	1 on 50 average.	Surf may be moderate to heavy in summer; main drift to W.	Sand; firm along water line, back shore soft.	Narrow sandspit, much of inner shore marshy; fishing village, farm, and trees along W end.	No exits to mainland lateral movement along spit possible.
(120) E of Tendrovskaya Kosa.	Bottom slopes apparently flat; details not known.	16 mi., bordered at both ends by narrow channels between spits.	15 to 75 ft., wider areas border salt lakes.	1 on 30.	Moderate surf likely during summer; drift varies.	Sand; most firm along narrow sections bordering bank.	Low cultivated land locally inland of low bank, or brush covered sand ridges bordering salt lakes which may be partly dry; several villages lie close inland.	Best exits from near villages to tracks leading in sand.
(121) Ostrov Dzharylgach (Dzharilgatski Island).	30 ft. depths are generally 1 mi. or more offshore; shifting shoals likely.	About 25 mi., interrupted by channel near W end.	Generally 150 to 200 ft.	1 on 50.	Moderate-to-heavy surf in summer; main drift to E.	Sand; firm near water line only.	Narrow sandspit, partly brush covered or marshy along inner shore backs W half; low brush-covered sand ridges extend inland 1 mi. or more to inner shore along E half.	No exits to mainland.

Original

TABLE IV - 10 (Continued)

Number and location of beach area	Nearshore	Length	Width	Gradient	Surf and shore drift	Material and firmness	Terrain immediately behind beach	Connections inland
(122) E of Skadovsk.......	Depths of 18 ft. lie about 1 mi. offshore; dredged channel leads to small harbor W of beach.	2.5 mi. Other sand and mud areas may be present to W within bay.	Average 100 ft.	1 on 50.	Surf and drift negligible.	Sand grading to mud close offshore; soft.	Low sand hills between ponds at E; town lies close inland at W.	Roads or tracks lead inland from town.
(123) E of Khorly (Port Khorly).	Approach obstructed by extensive shoals; dredged channel leads to small harbor 0.5 mi. W of beach.	0.5 mi. interrupted by 2 channels. Other sand and mud areas may be present to E.	25 to 50 ft.	1 on 50.	Surf may be moderate in summer; drift to E.	Soft sand, probably with some mud.	Scrub covered sand and some marsh along very narrow spit.	Exit may be difficult along spit to harbor area; secondary road runs N from town.

B. Mys Kartkazak (Kartkazak Point) to Sevastopol'

(45°57'N, 33°37'E; 44°37'N, 33°31'E) (PLAN 18; FIGURE IV-89; U.S.H.O. Charts 4200, and Misc. 11,954-4; B.A. Charts 963 to 965, 2232, 2233, and 3483)

(1) Coast

From Mys Kartkazak the coast trends eastward for 5 miles, thence southwestward for 24 miles to Bakal'skaya Kosa (Bakalskaya Spit) (beach area (124)), a sandy projection which extends about 4 miles northward from the coast, terminating at Kyln Murun (U.S.H.O. Chart 4206). Bakal Bank, with a least depth of 7 feet, extends 10 miles northward. This coast is low and marshy with intermittent bluffs for most of its length. The shore is bordered by extensive shoals. Westward of Bakal'skaya Kosa the coast is steep-to, gradually rising from a height of 30 to 65 feet at Cape Kara-Burnu on the eastern side of Bukhta Yarylgachskaya (beach area (125), B.A. Chart 2232). Rocky ledges with depths of less than 3 fathoms extend off the southern entrance to the bay. Cliffs on the southern side of the bay are relatively low, about 30 feet in height, increasing to 45 feet near Akmechetskaya Bukhta, whose entrance points are about 20 feet high, rocky and reddish-yellow in appearance. The inner shores (beach area (126)) are low and shelving, fringed by a shallow bank on which are sunken rocks. The bay is about 0.6 mile wide at its entrance.

Southwestward from Akmechetskaya Bukhta for 12 miles to Mys Karamrun the cliffs are broken and irregular in outline, ranging in height from 30 to 150 feet. The shoreline consists of whitish cliffs intersected by valleys. Karadzhinskaya Bukhta, with a width of 2.5 miles, lies between Mys Karamrun and Mys Tarkhankut; the former is a high rounded bluff with a reddish summit, the latter low and rocky. At the head of the bay is a sandy beach about 600 feet wide (beach area (127)), backed by a salt lake, and the northern side is fringed by a bank with a depth of less than 3 fathoms.

From Mys Tarkhankut the coast trends eastward for 8 miles to Mys Uret, thence 4 miles northeastward (U.S.H.O. Chart Misc. 11,954-4). The former stretch is high and steep and may be approached to within 0.5 mile offshore. From Mys Uret to Ozero Donuzlav, approximately 11 miles eastward, the shore gradually lowers and the coastal hills recede inland, thence for 20 miles to Mys Yevpatoriyskiy the coast is low and sandy. Within this stretch are many small salt lakes separated from the sea by narrow strips of sand.(beach area (128)). A coastal bank extends from 1 to 2 miles offshore.

Kalamitskiy Zaliv (Kalamita Bay) (beach areas (129) and (130)) lies between the low sand dunes of Mys Yevpatoriyskiy a headland about 120 feet high, and Mys Lukull (c. Ulukol), 22 miles southeastward (B.A. Chart 2233). The northern and eastern shores of the bay as far southward as Ozero Bogayly are low and sandy with many salt lakes a short distance inland. A rocky ridge, with depth from 5 to 6 fathoms lies parallel to the coast from 3 to 3.5 miles offshore. Southward of the lake the coast becomes steep and reddish in color. The highest southern part is intersected by two river valleys, southward of which the coast slopes toward the valley of the river Al'ma which flows into the sea near Mys Lukull. The town of Yevpatoriya (Eupatoria) (FIGURE IV-90) on the northern side of the bay is situated on an arid plain. Second-class roads extend northward throughout the Crimea and southeastward to Simferopol'. A branch railroad connects with the main rail system of the peninsula just above Simferopol'. An airfield and a landing strip are located in the vicinity.

FIGURE IV-89
COASTAL SUBSECTORS 43-B and 43-C
JANIS 40

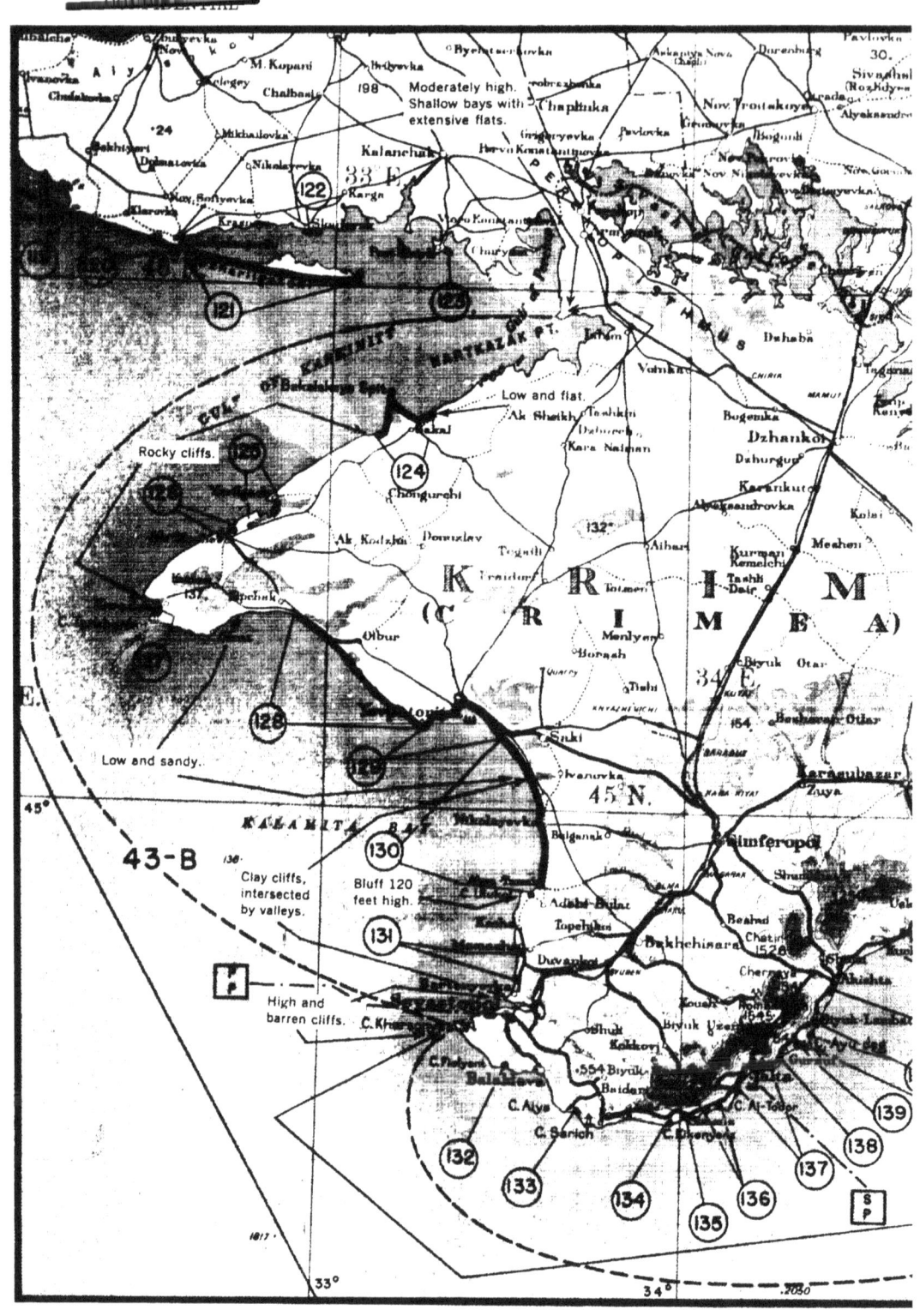

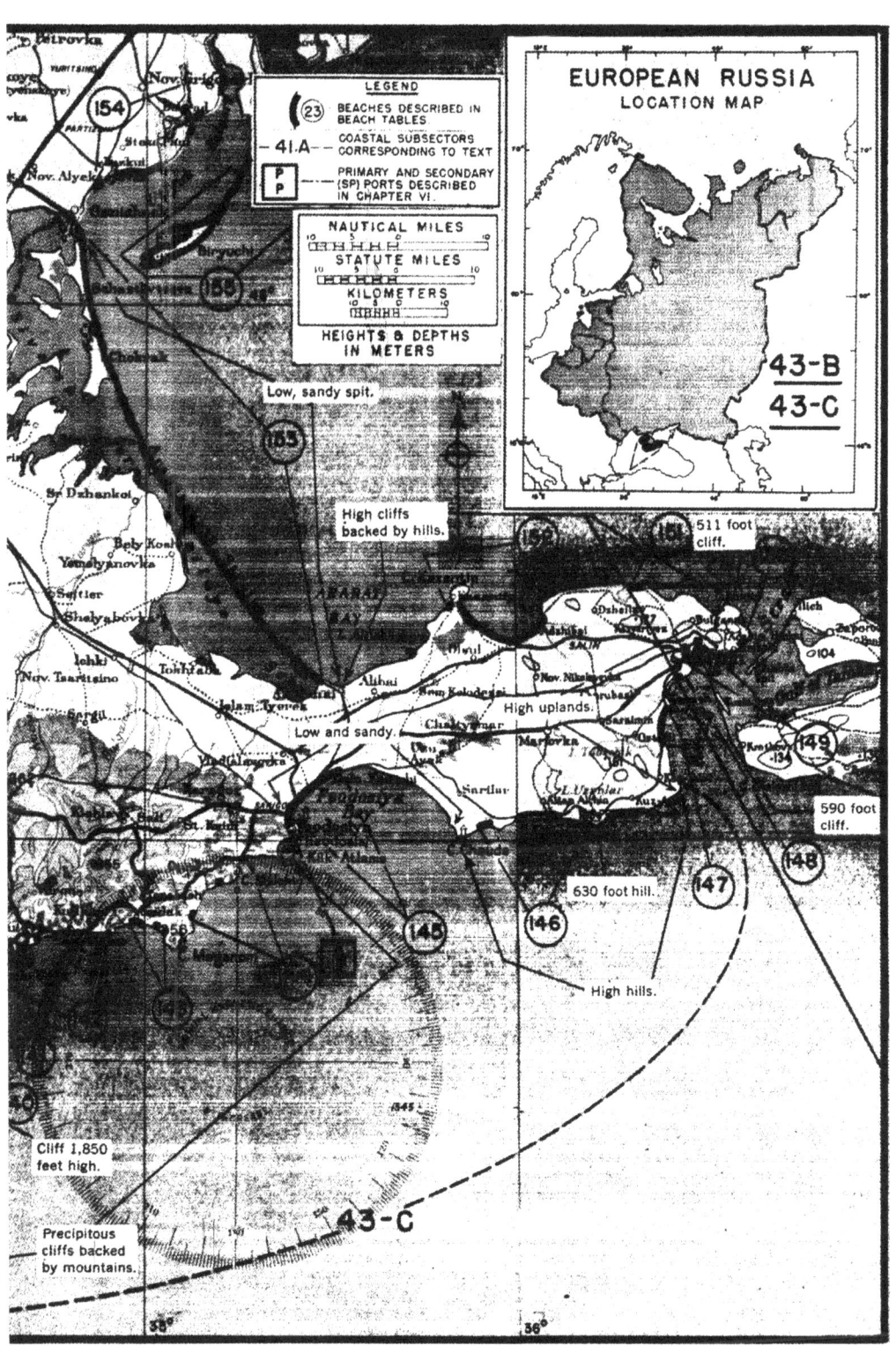

FIGURE IV-90. *Crimea, Yevpatoriya. Beach area (129).*
Looking southwestward along flat sand beach at Yevpatoriya. Prior to 1942. Approximate position 45°12′N, 33°23′E; B. A. Chart 2233.

From Mys Lukull the coast trends south-southwestward for about 3 miles to Lukull Bluff thence southward for 9.5 miles to Konstantinovskiy Mys (B.A. Charts 964 and 3483). The reddish clay cliffs along the shore are intersected by the valleys of the Kacha (Kaga) (FIGURE IV-91) and Bel'-bek rivers which flow into the sea southward of Lukull Bluff (beach area (131)). Many detached sunken rocks lie about a mile offshore between the cape and the mouth of the river Kacha.

Sevastopol' harbor (B.A. Chart 963) is entered between Konstantinovskiy Mys and Alexander Point, about 0.5 mile southward (Chapter VI). It is one of the best and safest ports in the Black Sea and is well sheltered from southward. The harbor never freezes and is accessible to vessels of the deepest draft. Inkerman ravine (FIGURE IV-92), which extends inland from the head of the harbor, is the deepest of those on the western side of Crimea; its chalk cliffs continue along both sides to the entrance and south-

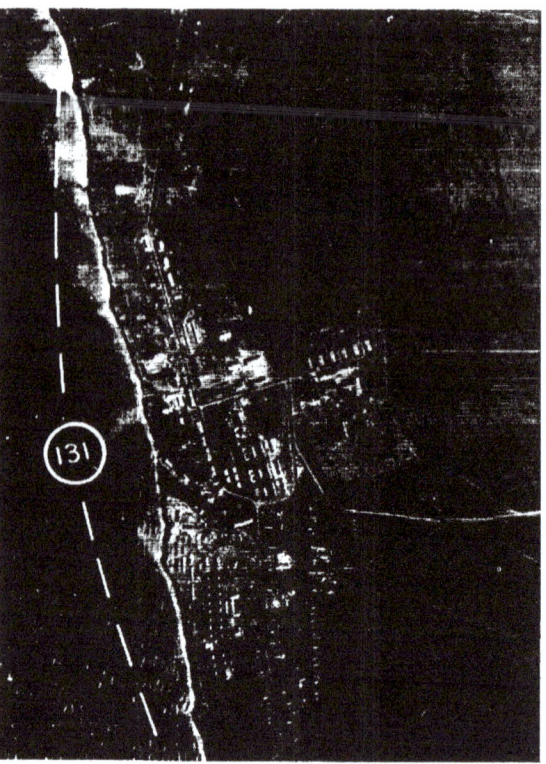

FIGURE IV-91. *Crimea, Mamashay. Beach area (131).*
Aerial view of narrow beach at north end of beach area. Note shadows cast by steep shores. Prior to 1942. Approximate position 44°44′N, 33°33′E; B. A. Chart 3433.

FIGURE IV-92. *Crimea, Sevastopol'.*
Looking eastward up Gaetne Valley, east of Sevastopol'. Prior to 1942. Approximate position 44°36′N, 33°37′E; B. A. Charts 963 and 3483.

Original

FIGURE IV-93. *Crimea, Sevastopol'*.
Panorama looking southward in approaches to South Bay and Sevastopol'. 1941. Approximate position 44°37'N, 33°31'E; B. A. Charts 963 and 3483.

FIGURE IV-94. *Crimea, Sevastopol'*.
Looking westward toward the Black Sea from one of the several inlets in the south shore of Sevastopol Bay. 1931. Approximate position 44°37'N, 33°30'E; B. A. Charts 963 and 3483.

westward to Mys Khersonesskiy (Cape Khersonyes), becoming gradually lower westward. The Chernaya river flows through this ravine into the head of the harbor. On both sides there are projecting headlands forming several indentations, the most extensive of which are on the southern side. The town of Sevastopol', with a population in 1939 of 111,946, is situated on the western bank of Yuzhnaya Bukhta (FIGURES IV-93 and IV-94). A railroad extends from the town northward across the Crimea to Melitopol' where it connects with the central system. An extensive first-class road network extends northward to Simferopol' and Feodosiya and southward along the southern and southeastern coast of the Crimea. Regular steamer communications are maintained with ports on the Black Sea and Sea of Azov. There are two landing strips and four seaplane bases in the vicinity.

The southern coast of the Crimea (B.A. Chart 3483) terminates westward in a low shelving peninsula, the extremity of which is Mys Khersonesskiy. The northern side of this peninsula, from Alexander Point to the cape, is high, rocky, and deeply indented by several bays with moderately steep and barren shores (B.A. Chart 965). Anchorage can be had at the mouths of the bays in 7 to 8 fathoms of water over mud and shell bottom. Shoal banks with less than 5 fathoms extend 600 yards offshore from the bay heads. The indentations along this stretch of coast are exposed to northerly winds.

(2) Landing beaches

The beaches of subsector 43 B are described briefly in TABLE IV-11. They lie generally along bayheads or river mouths. Except for beach areas (*128*) to (*130*) which together form a continuous beach totaling about 59 miles, the beaches are generally short, obstructed by rock, and bordered by moderate-to-steep slopes. Exits to main roads or railroads are relatively easy.

TABLE IV - 11

LANDING BEACHES OF COASTAL SUBSECTOR 43 B (PLAN 18)

Reliability POOR.

Number and location of beach area	Nearshore	Length	Width	Gradient	Surf and shore drift	Material and firmness	Terrain immediately behind beach	Connections inland
(124) Bakal'skaya Kosa (Bakalskaya Spit).	Bottom slopes *flat* and irregular; extensive shoal extends to N from end of spit. Anchorage 24 to 30 ft. E of spit with W winds.	14 mi. interrupted by 2 loading piers off Bakal.	75 to 100 ft.	1 on 25.	Surf heavy with N winds; drift toward end of spit.	Sand or sand and shell; generally firm.	Low flat land of spit; town back of SE end, lake and salt pan area behind W shore.	Minor road runs into town from near piers; track and minor road connections inland.
(125) Bay at Yarylgach.	Entrance fringed with rocky shoals; clear approach from within bay.	About 4 mi., interrupted at SE end of bay by inlet to salt lake.	25 to 100 ft.	1 on 15 to 1 on 30.	Surf negligible along N shore; moderate with W winds otherwise; drift probably outward from center.	Mainly sand; probably most firm along N end.	Town on high land back of N shore; salt lakes back much of E and S shores.	Best from town although access to town may be difficult.
(126) Bay at Chernomorskoye (Ak-Mechet.)	Entrance points fringed with rock; *mild* bottom slopes. Anchorage in about 26 ft. in center of bay.	2 pocket beaches within entrance, each 500 ft.; beach at bayhead about 3,000 ft. interrupted by pier.	Probably 15 to 50 ft., narrowest along ends of each section.	Average 1 on 20.	Surf generally negligible; drift variable.	Sand and pebbles; generally firm.	Narrow strips of low land fronting small lakes back pocket beaches and steep slopes rise from ends; town and low land with lakes back bayhead area.	Easy access into town area; main and secondary roads run inland.
(127) Bay at Karadzha.	*Gentle* bottom slopes; clear.	1.5 mi.	100 to 150 ft.	1 on 30.	Surf generally lightest near N end, heavy only with W winds; main drift probably to S.	Sand firm at water line.	Low flat land with salt pans at S end and large salt lake about 600 ft. inland along N half; town lies along inner shore of lake about 1 mi. from beach.	Exit to town best along track lying close behind S end of beach; secondary road runs inland from town.
(128)	Clear but for *mild-to-flat* bottom slopes.	About 23 miles; interrupted only by several small piers.	Probably 150 to 200 ft.	1 on 30.	Surf light to moderate; drift probably mainly to NW.	Sand; firm at water line.	Low land with numerous salt lakes; scattered villages on coast toward SE end of beach.	Main road lies directly inland of NW end of area; other tracks or roads are not known to be present.
(129) NW and NE shores of Kalamitskiy Zaliv (Kalamita Bay). (FIG. IV - 90.)	Bottom slopes *flat* and irregular; otherwise clear. Anchorage for small boats in 15 to 18 ft. off Yevpatoriya.	About 13 mi., interrupted by numerous piers fronting town and NE shore.	About 75 to 150 ft., probably narrowest along sections of town.	Average 1 on 25.	Surf light except with SW winds; drift probably weak and variable.	Firm sand with pebbles near water line; backshore soft.	Small salt lakes, some dunes, and villas along NW shore; town directly inland at center; and narrow low strip of land and salt pans bordering large lake area along NE shore.	Immediate exit to main road and railroad in town and along NE shore.

TABLE IV - 11 (Continued)

Number and location of beach area	Nearshore	Length	Width	Gradient	Surf and shore drift	Material and firmness	Terrain immediately behind beach	Connections inland
(130) E and S shore of Kalamitskiy Zaliv.	Mild bottom slopes; rocks S of river mouth near S end.	About 23 mi., continues from beach (129) interrupted by river mouths and by cliff near S end.	Average 100 ft. along N half; narrower to S.	Average 1 on 20.	Surf generally moderate; main drift to N.	Sand and pebbles; firm at water line.	Numerous small salt lakes along N half; low sandy cliffs close inland along S half; cliffed shore borders S end.	Exits generally good; best near N end directly to secondary road.
(131) (Fig. IV - 91)	Gentle bottom slopes; approach to N beach rocky; less so to S beach.	2 beaches at river mouths, each about 1 mi.; very narrow beach may connect areas.	15 to 50 ft. widest at centers.	1 on 10.	Surf moderate; drift probably varies.	Sand and pebbles; with some rock.	Steep narrow river valleys with settlements about 1 mi. inland; cliffs between beaches.	Exit up valleys to main road to S.

C. Sevastopol' to Mys Takil'

(44°37′N, 33°31′E; 45°06′N, 36°28′E) (PLAN 18; FIGURE IV-89; B.A. Charts 2210, 2221, 2233, 2340, and 3483)

(1) Coast

The southern coast of the Crimea from Mys Khersonesskiy for about 135 miles east-northeastward to Kerch Strait (Kerchenskiy Proliv) is mountainous, consisting generally of gently descending mountain slopes, or terraces, and is sheltered from northerly winds by the Khrebet Yayla (B.A. Chart 3483). This range consists of several ridges made up of large limestone masses and attains an elevation of over 4,500 feet near Yalta. Most conspicuous in this coastal subsector are the promontories which rise in heights from 526 feet at Mys Feolent (Cape Fiolyent) to 1,850 feet at Mys Ayu-Dag (cape). Throughout this part of the coast exceptionally steep precipices rise from the sea, with many bays and smaller indentations between, intersected by brook basins which dry in summer (beach areas (132) to (136); TABLE IV-12; FIGURES IV-95 to IV-102). Before the war the mountain slopes were inhabited by a Tatar population who built their towns in the oriental style (Chapter X, 102, E). This coastline represents the so-called Russian Riviera, with its modern structures and beautifully designed parks. Approaches from seaward are unobstructed and general depths of 5 fathoms lie close to the shore. The current of the Black Sea sets westward

FIGURE IV-95. *Crimea, Balaklava.*
Looking northeastward from Cape Balaklava along the Black Sea coast. Prior to 1942. Approximate position 44°29′N, 33°36′E; B. A. Charts 2340 and 3483.

FIGURE IV-96. *Crimea, South Coast.*
Looking southeastward to church on coast road south of Baydary. Prior to 1942. Approximate position 44°24′N, 33°48′E; B. A. Chart 3483.

FIGURE IV-97. *Crimea, South Coast.*
Mys Aytodor (top) and rugged terrain inland (bottom). Prior to 1942. Approximate position 44°26'N 34°07'E; B. A. Chart 3483.

FIGURE IV-98. *Crimea, Balaklava.*
Looking southward toward harbor mouth on the Black Sea. Compare Cape Balaklava, left background, with FIGURE IV-95. No date. Approximate position 44°30'N, 33°36'E; B. A. Charts 2340 and 3483.

FIGURE IV-99. *Crimea, Simeiz.*
Looking westward across resort town. Steep Khrebet Yayla at left. Approximate position 44°24'N, 34°E; B. A. Chart 3483.

FIGURE IV-100. *Crimea, Simeiz. Beach area (135).*
Looking eastward showing irregular coast and pocket beaches of area fronting Simeiz. For approximate location refer to FIGURE IV-99.

FIGURE IV-101. *Crimea, South Coast. Beach area (136).*
Looking northeastward toward Alupka and typical pocket beach at west end of area. No date. Approximate position 44°24′N, 34°02′E; B. A. Chart 3483.

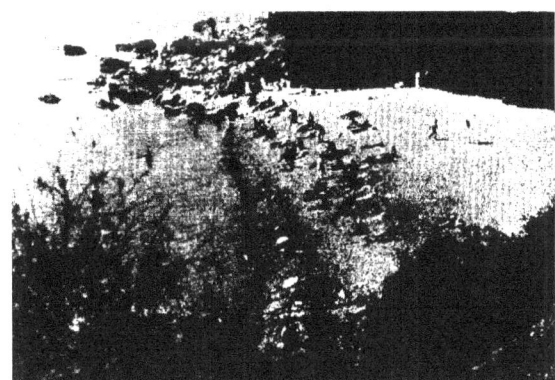

FIGURE IV-102. *Crimea, South Coast. Beach area (136).*
Looking westward across beach similar to that shown in FIGURE IV-101, at east end of area. No date. Approximate position 44°26′N, 34°06′E; B. A. Chart 3483.

and is especially strong off the headlands, attaining velocities of from 0.5 to 2 knots. A primary road parallels the coast from Sevastopol' to Feodosiya, with roads leading over the mountains to connect this road with the main highway and Simferopol', farther inland.

The most important of the several ports and anchorages on the southern coast of the Crimea is Yalta, at the western end of Yaltinskaya Bukhta (beach area (137); FIGURES IV-103 and IV-104; B.A. Chart 2210). The well-sheltered, ice-free harbor has a least depth of 10 feet in the northern and northeastern part (Chapter VI). The population of the town was 28,000 in 1930. A primary road connects with the Sevastopol' - Simferopol' highway, but there are no railroad connections. The eastern slopes of Mount Myegabi slope down to the western side of the bay and terminate in a sandy beach a short distance south of the town.

FIGURE IV-103. *Crimea, Yalta. Beach area (137).*
Looking northward along beach area toward Yalta. Note steep gradient and coarse composition of beach. No date. Approximate position 44°29′N, 34°10′E; B. A. Charts 2210 and 3483.

FIGURE IV-104. *Crimea, Yalta.*
Coastal terrain at foot of Khrebet Yayla. Prior to 1942. Approximate position 44°31′N, 34°15′E; B. A. Charts 2210 and 3483.

The coast curves northeastward to form a wide bight between Nikitin point, on Yalta Bay, and Mys Ayu-Dag. In the northeastern corner of the bight lies Gurzuf (Urzuf) road, with a village of the same name scattered along the rocky slope within its head. Southward of the village there is a low shingle beach (beach area (*138*)), and on its eastern side there is a small rocky point within which a high cliff rises to an old Genoese fort on its summit (Figures IV-105 to IV-110). Gurzuf has a seaplane station. There is partially sheltered anchorage in a small bay at the northeastern end of the bight between Adalar rocks, which lie about 0.3 mile offshore, and Cape Ayu-Dag, 2 miles eastward (beach area (*139*)).

From Mys Ayu-Dag the coast trends north-northeastward for about 7 miles to Ahishta (beach area (*140*)). Chatyr Dag, (Chatir-Dag), about 11.5 miles north-northwest of Mys Ayu-Dag, is the highest mountain in the Crimea, rising to 4,998 feet. Ahishta, a minor port with a population in 1930 of 4,800, is situated in the foothills of Chatyr-Dag, between two wide valleys (beach area (*141*); Figure IV-111). It is located on the main coastal highway and is also connected overland by a primary road to Simferopol'. There is regular steamship communication with other Black Sea ports.

The coast curves northeastward from Ahishta to Feodosiya Bay (B.A. Chart 2233). Rugged mountains rise abruptly from the shore, broken by a number of ravines. There are low sandy beaches at the mouths of these ravines and between the headlands of bights and coves which indent the coast (beach areas (*142*) to (*144*)).

Feodosiya Bay (B.A. Chart 2221), 17 miles in width between Mys Ill'i and Mys Chauda, the western and eastern entrance points, is the largest body of water indenting the southern and eastern Crimean coast. The northwestern shore of the Bay is low and sandy (beach area (*145*)), but the northeastern shore is bluff. Except near the town of Feodosiya, in the western corner of the Bay, the coastal area is barren and sparsely inhabited. The bay affords good anchorage anywhere, in depths from 5 to 12 fathoms, over soft mud. The town of Feodosiya, with a population in 1930 of 29,600, is situated on the low shore at the head of the bay and on the slopes of Khrebet Teze-Oba. Most of the harbor is dredged to 24 feet (Chapter VI). The

Figure IV-105. *Crimea, Gurzuf. Beach area (138).*
Looking southwestward along beach area south of Gurzuf. Note rocks near shore and road embankment limiting beach. 1911 or earlier. Approximate position 44°32'N, 34°16'E; B. A. Chart 3483.

FIGURE IV-106. *Crimea, Gurzuf. Beach areas (138) and (139).*
(Top) Looking northeastward from hillside southwest of Gurzuf toward Mys Ayu-Dag and across beach areas shown in FIGURES IV-107 to 110. Beach areas (138) and (139) are divided by town and promontory at (a). Note rocks, Belyye Kamni Adalar, (b). (Bottom) Gurzuf and boat harbor. Prior to 1942. Approximate position 44°32'N, 34°16'E; B. A. Chart 3483.

town has rail connections with Kerch' and the system extending to the mainland. First-class roads extend to Kerch', Simferopol', and the coastal highway. Steamer communications are maintained with other Black Sea ports.

From Mys Chauda eastward (beach area (146)) to Mys Takil' the coast is hilly and considerably lower, rising to 630 feet at Opuk. Shoals with a least depth of 12 feet extend southward from Mys Kyz-Aul for 1.3 miles. Mys Takil', a high, rounded bluff, is fringed by a rocky bank which extends 1 mile southeastward. The 5-fathom curve

FIGURE IV-107. *Crimea, Gurzuf. Beach area (139).*
Looking northeastward from Gurzuf across southwest end of beach area toward interruption in beach and Mys Ayu-Dag. Prior to 1936. Compare FIGURES IV-106 and IV-110. Approximate position 44°32'N, 34°17'E; B. A. Chart 3483.

lies about 1 mile offshore along this section of coast.

(2) Landing beaches

Small pebble and cobble pocket beaches between steep-cliffed slopes predominate in subsector 43 C (beach areas (132) to (146); TABLE IV-12). These beaches are relatively numerous and front a heavily populated resort area. Road exits are generally close by, although exit is hindered by the irregular steep slopes. The two beaches at the east end of the subsector, beach areas (145) and (146), lie between steep sections of the coast, but front low salt lake or marsh areas similar to those in subsector 43 A.

FIGURE IV-108. *Crimea, Gurzuf. Beach area (139)*.
Looking southwestward at interruption in beach shown in FIGURE IV-107. Note bathing pier and steep bank behind beach. 1936. Compare FIGURE IV-109. Approximate position 44°33'N, 34°18'E; B. A. Chart 3483.

FIGURE IV-109. *Crimea, Gurzuf. Beach area (139)*.
Looking southwestward from east end of beach area across section immediately northeast of FIGURE IV-108. Note road close inland in right center and pier in foreground. 1936.

FIGURE IV-110. *Crimea, Gurzuf. Beach area (139).*
Looking eastward toward east end of beach area. Note pier, right center; road on slope back of beach; and automobile. Compare FIGURES IV-106, IV-107, and IV-109. 1934. For approximate location refer to FIGURE IV-108.

FIGURE IV-111. *Crimea, Ahishta. Beach area (141).*
Looking southwestward from Alushta (Ahishta) across beach area. 1911 or earlier. Approximate position 44°40′N, 34°25′E; B. A. Chart 3483.

TABLE IV - 12

LANDING BEACHES OF COASTAL SUBSECTOR 43 C

Reliability POOR. (PLAN 18)

Number and location of beach area	Nearshore	Length	Width	Gradient	Surf and shore drift	Material and firmness	Terrain immediately behind beach	Connections inland
(132) E of Mys Feolent (Cape Fiolyent).	Moderate to gentle bottom slopes; rocks close off E end of beach.	About 2,000 ft.	Probably 15 ft.	1 on 10.	Surf generally negligible; drift probably to W.	Pebbles, sand, and some rock; firm.	Steep bluffed slopes leading to buildings of sanatorium; cliffs rise to 680 feet close inland.	Exit up slopes difficult; track ends inland from buildings.
(133) NW of Mys Sarych (Cape Sarich).	Moderate to steep bottom slopes; obstructed by rocks.	2,000 ft.	15 to 25 ft.	Average 1 on 15.	Surf generally only light; drift probably to W.	Pebbles, and some rock; firm.	Fishing huts lie immediately behind beach and are backed by high tree-covered slopes.	Tracks to main road at coast to W are probably available but exit is difficult.
(134) NE of Mys Kekeneiz (Cape Kikenyenz).	Probably steep bottom slopes and rocks close to shore.	1,500 ft., interrupted by small stream.	25 ft.	1 on 20.	Light surf.	Mainly sand.	Steep slopes.	No connections with main road about 1 mi. inland are known.
(135) Simeiz (Simenz). (FIG. IV - 100.)	Bottom slopes probably steep; anchorage reported in 18 ft. E of rocks off village, details not known.	At least 2 beaches between rocky points, each 500 to 1,000 ft.	50 ft.	1 on 20.	Surf generally light to moderate.	Sand with pebbles or small cobbles near water line.	Heavily wooded moderate slopes with buildings of resort and town.	Main coastal road is accessible in town.
(136) Alupka to Mys Aytodor. (FIGS. IV - 101 and IV - 102.)	Probably moderate to steep bottom slopes; direct approach probably clear.	Probably 5 short pocket beaches, between rocky points, average length 1,000 ft.	25 to 50 ft. at center of each beach, narrows to 10 ft. at ends.	1 on 15.	Surf light to moderate; drift varies but may be mainly to W.	Mainly pebbles or cobbles; firm.	Rocky partly tree-covered slopes, or more gentle slopes with vineyards, encircle beaches; bath houses or pavilion may lie directly on beach.	Main road lies between 60 and 100 ft. above beach.
(137) S and E of Yalta. (FIG. IV - 103.)	Steep bottom slopes; direct approach usually clear except off E end.	Total about 4 mi. on either side of harbor area; each section interrupted by rocky points.	25 to 75 ft., S sections probably widest.	1 on 5.	Surf negligible during summer; heavy during fall or winter with SE winds; drift weak.	Pebbles and cobbles; firm.	Wooded or vineyard- and garden-covered slopes generally; part of town directly inland at N end of S section.	Main road generally within 1,000 ft. inland along S but locally as much as 250 ft. above shore; lies about 1 mi. inland along E section and as much as 700 ft. above shore.
(138) S of Gurzuf. (FIGS. IV - 105 and IV - 106.)	Moderate bottom slopes with rocks nearshore.	About 1.5 mi. extending S from small pier fronting town.	15 to 25 ft.	1 on 20.	Surf generally light or negligible; drift weak, probably mainly to N.	Pebbles with scattered rock; firm.	Stone road embankment 5 to 10 ft. high limits most of beach; inland are tree- and vineyard-covered slopes or town buildings.	Direct to road and to main road connection in town.

TABLE IV - 12 (Continued)

Number and location of beach area	Nearshore	Length	Width	Gradient	Surf and shore drift	Material and firmness	Terrain immediately behind beach	Connections inland
(139) NE of Gurzuf. (Figs. IV - 106 to IV - 110.)	*Moderate* bottom slopes; rocks off break in beach and along center of each section.	Total about 2 mi., broken by cliff.	Average 50 ft. N of interruption; generally narrower toward E end.	Average 1 on 15.	Surf generally light, breaks close to shore; main drift to W.	Sand to W of interruption; pebbles predominate toward E end.	Steep slopes except near E end, partly wooded and covered with gardens and vineyards; steps lead to buildings of summer camp.	Exit by road W to Gurzuf available from camp area or direct to road near E end.
(140) N of Mys Ayu-Dag...	*Steep* bottom slopes; rocks off point N of beach limit. Details unknown.	About 2.5 mi., broken by steep shore.	25 ft. average.	1 on 15.	Moderate surf; drift to S.	Sand and pebbles; firm.	Steep, rather barren slopes at S end; villages, gardens and vineyards along more moderate slopes to N.	Exit to main road from S village; otherwise by tracks to road within 1.5 mi. of shore.
(141) Alushta (Ahishta). (Fig. IV - 111.)	*Gentle* bottom slopes; approach clear.	About 2 mi., crossed by 2 small streams and interrupted by pier.	25 to 50 ft.	1 on 20.	Surf heavy in winter; drift probably mainly to S.	Sand and pebbles; foreshore firm.	Small buildings stand on beach near S end; relatively flat open valley inland with town along N end.	Main coastal road lies within 1 mile; easily accessible.
(142) Kuokuk-Uzen' and E.	Details not known; bottom slopes *mild* to *flat*; rocky shoal off W beach.	Several beaches at ravine mouths, average about 3,000 ft.	15 to 50 ft., W area probably widest.	1 on 15.	Moderate surf, lightest in summer; drift mainly to SW.	Sand and pebbles; firm.	Wooded narrow steep sloped ravines; villages close inland of W beach.	Access to main road through villages or up ravine slopes relatively easy.
(143) Sudak and E.	Generally clear with *flat* bottom slopes.	Several beaches between rocky points; W section 1.5 mi., interrupted by river and piers; E sections average 3,000 ft.	W beach 50 to 75 ft., E beaches narrower.	Average 1 on 25.	Surf light or moderate; drift varies.	Mainly sand, pebbles along water line; foreshore firm.	Houses and coast guard station back W beach with wide flat valley and town inland; E beaches backed by wooded moderate slopes.	Main road easily accessible from W beach.
(144)	Details not known; bottom slopes probably *mild* to *flat*; rocky shoal off NE beach, with 12-ft. channel leading to pier in bay.	3 small beaches, average 2,000 ft., other areas may be present.	25 ft.	Probably 1 on 15.	Surf light or moderate; drift varies.	Sand and pebbles; firm.	Small stream valleys between steep slopes; villages close inland of NE beach.	Access from NE beach through village to main coastal road.
(145) NE of Feodosiya	*Flat* bottom slopes; clear approach.	8.5 mi.	25 to 100 ft., widest at SW end and along center.	1 on 25 average.	Surf generally negligible or light; drift probably to SW.	Mainly sand; foreshore firm.	R.R. close inland at SW end, road embankment bordering low wet land, lake, and finally low bluffs increasing in height to E.	Road or R.R. readily available from SW half of beach.
(146) E of Mys Chauda...	*Flat* bottom slopes: foul ground reported for 1 mi. off W beach.	3 beaches each 1.5 to 2 mi. long.	25 ft.	1 on 20.	Surf generally light; main drift to W.	Sand, relatively soft.	Marsh and salt lake areas between steep or bluffed shores.	Only trail from W beach; track and section of main road directly accessible from E beaches.

FIGURE IV-112
COASTAL SUBSECTOR 43-D
JANIS 40

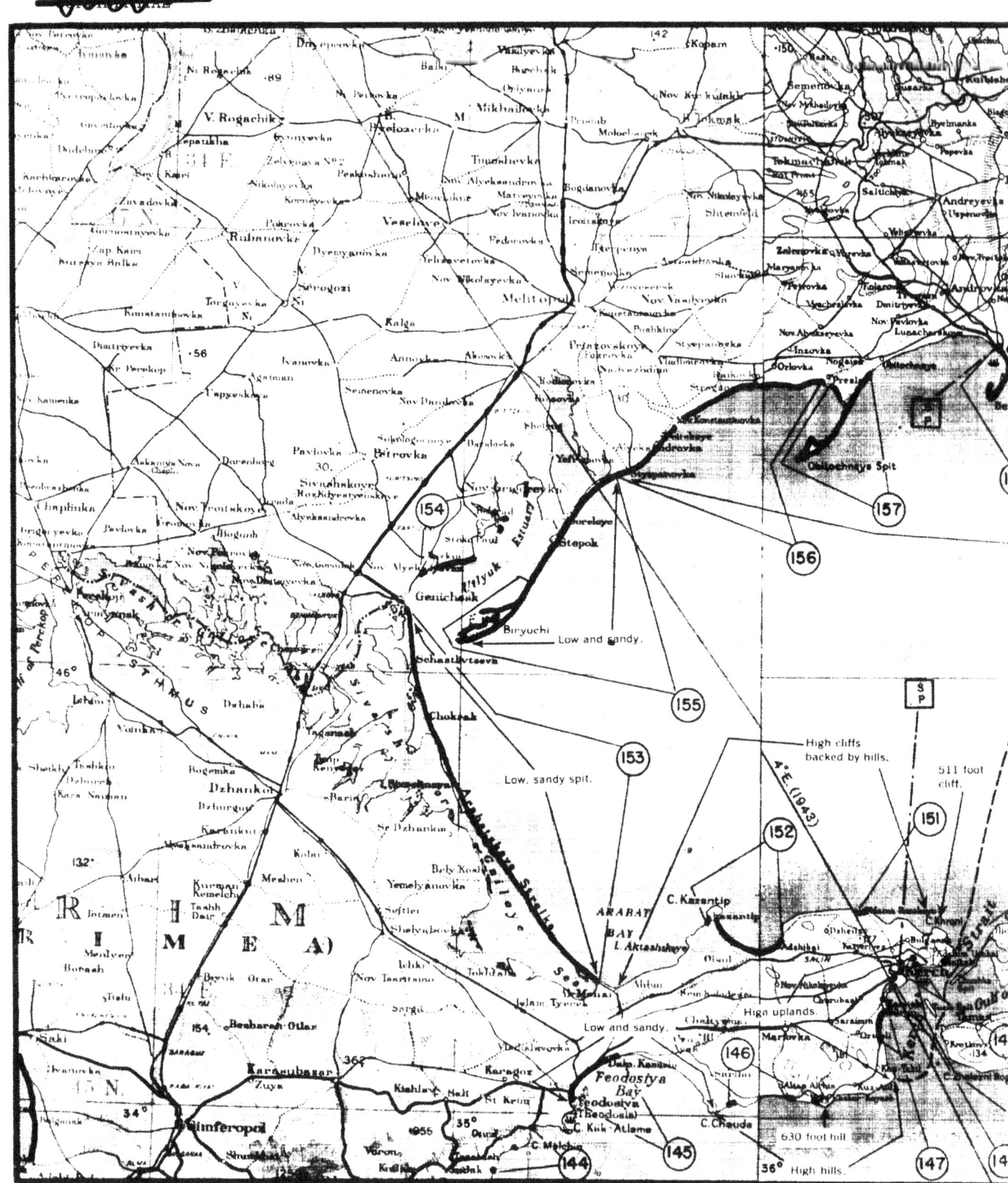

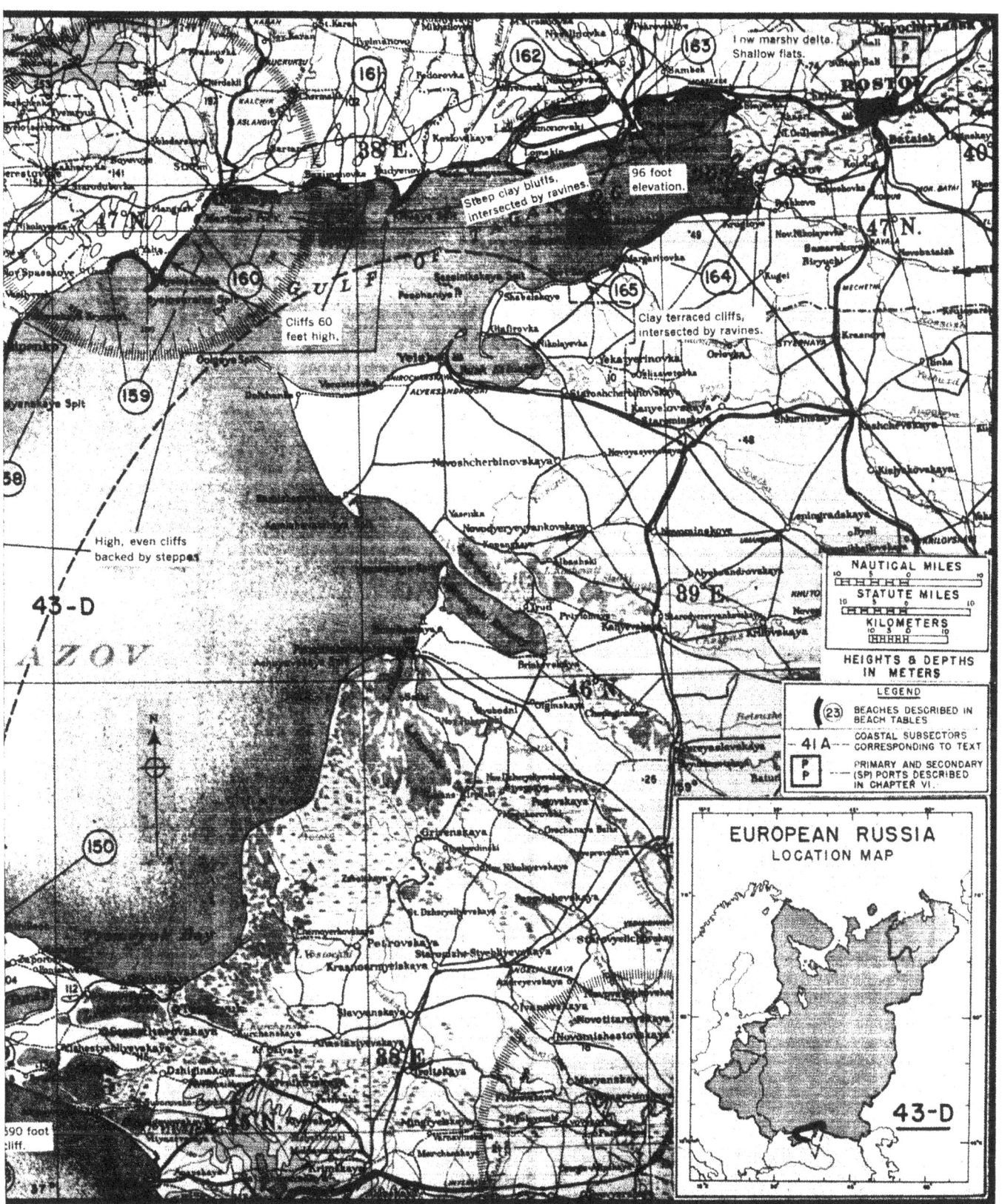

D. Mys Takil' to Port-Katon

(45°06′N, 36°28′E; 46°53′N, 38°45′E) (PLANS 18 and 19; FIGURE IV 119; U.S.H.O. Chart 4215; B.A. Charts 2205, 2214, 2233, 2234, and 3389)

(1) Coast

Kerch Strait (Kerchenskiy Proliv), at the eastern end of the Crimea, connects the Sea of Azov with the Black Sea (B.A. Charts 2205 and 2233). The strait varies in width from 2.5 to 8 miles and is encumbered by extensive shallow banks and shoals, through which a narrow channel has been dredged. In 1940 the channel was available for vessels drawing not more than 23 feet. Along the western side of the strait from Mys Takil' to Mys Khroni (beach areas (147) to (150); TABLE IV-13) the coast consists of high uplands rising in places to hills which terminate in bluffs and cliffs along the shore. In the lowlying areas between the hills are marshes and lakes. Gora Khronya, a ridge rising to a conspicuous peak 590 feet high, lies near the northern entrance of the strait.

The Kerchenskaya Bukhta, on the northwestern side of the strait, is about 3 miles wide at its entrance between Cape Ak Burnu and Mys Zmyeinyy. The southern side of the bay is steep and precipitous in places. The western side is low and sandy (beach area (149)), increasing in elevation northward at Gora Mitridat. The northern part is low and fronted by a flat with depths of less than 1 fathom extending as far as 400 yards offshore. Eastward, at Mys Karantinnyy the shore becomes high and rocky. The harbor, formed by three breakwaters, has depths from 8 to 22 feet (Chapter VI). The town of Kerch', with a population in 1939 of 101,471, lies at the head of the bay, on the slopes of Mitridat Hill. It is the industrial center of the Crimea and the transshipping point for trade between ports in the Black Sea and Sea of Azov. The harbor is connected to the general railway system, and a primary road extends southwestward to Feodosiya. During the season of navigation steamers ply between the ports in the Black Sea and Sea of Azov. The town has two seaplane stations and four landing strips.

The northern coast of Kerch Peninsula from Mys Khroni to the southeastern end of Arabatskaya Strelka (Arabat Spit) about 50 miles westward, is high and backed by hills attaining elevations of from 330 to 500 feet (B.A. Chart 2234). Khronya and Temir Oba hills, with heights of 590 and 511 feet, are conspicuous. The coast is indented by several small bays with steep clifflike shores sloping toward the sea (beach areas (151) and (152)). Anchorage is afforded in deep water to within a mile from shore. Arabatskiy Zaliv (Arabat Bay), the largest of these bays, is about 20 miles wide at its entrance between Mys Kazantip and the southeastern end of Arabatskaya Strelka. The eastern side is high and rocky while the western side, formed by the southern part of the spit, is low and sandy. Partially sheltered anchorage can be obtained in a depth of 3 fathoms over mud and shoal bottom about 1 mile offshore in the bight at the head of the bay.

Arabatskaya Strelka is low and sandy and from 0.3 to 4.5 miles wide. It extends in a north-northwesterly direction for about 60 miles to Proliv Tonkiy, dividing Sivash sounds from the Sea of Azov. The southern half of the spit is barren and has only a few widely separated hamlets. The northern part is characterized by several villages and clumps of tall trees. The whole of the eastern side (beach area (153)), which is almost a straight line, is fringed by a flat with depths of 20 feet one mile offshore. From a position about 18 miles northwestward of Arabat fort a narrow shoal, with a least depth of 10 feet, extends 7.5 miles northward.

The Sivash sounds are divided into two branches, one of which extends westward to the isthmus of Perekop and the other southeastward in the direction of Feodosiya (B.A. Chart 2214). It is connected with the Sea of Azov by Proliv Tonkiy which is 2 miles long. The sounds have very shallow water and the shores, which are constantly changing in outline due to the varying water level, are composed of ruddy, salt mud. In summer a great portion of the shallow water area becomes dry. A railroad line from the mainland to the Crimea leads across the Sivash lagoon on an elevated embankment.

Utlyukskiy Liman (Utlyuk Estuary) lies between the mainland and Fedotova Spit and Ostrov Biryuchiy (Biryuchi) (B.A. Chart 2234). It is 8.5 miles wide at the entrance between the northern extremity of Arabatskaya Strelka and Ostrov Biryuchiy. The central part of the estuary is divided from the southern part by two sandy shoals extending from the mainland and Ostrov Biryuchiy. A narrow channel, with a depth of 19 feet has been cut between the flats. The northern part of the estuary is shallow. A shallow salt lake approximately 10 miles long, connected with the sea by a narrow channel, lies off the western shore of the estuary (beach area (154)). Good anchorage can be obtained anywhere in the southern part in depths of 19 feet. The town of Genichesk, with a population of 14,000 in 1938 is situated on the western shore of the estuary on the northern side of the strait (U.S.H.O. Chart 4215). The harbor can be used only by small craft. The wharves are connected to the general railway system.

Kosa Fedotova (beach area (155)), extends about 23 miles southwestward from Fedotova Point, the southern extremity of the highland at the head of the estuary (FIGURE IV-114; B.A. Chart 2234). It is divided about midway into two parts by a narrow silted-up strait forming Ostrov Biryuchiy on the southwestern part (FIGURE IV-118). The island is flat and low, covered with grass and scrub growth. The northern part of the spit is narrow and covered with coarse grass and some scattered bushes. A group of shoals, with depths from 18 to 20 feet lie between positions about 11.5 miles eastward and 20 miles southeastward of the southern end of Ostrov Biryuchiy.

From Fedotova Point, the northern shore of the Sea of Azov trends east-northeastward for about 170 miles to the head of the Taganrogskiy Zaliv (Gulf of Taganrog). The coast consists mainly of cliffs of even elevation on the tops of which barren plains or "steppes" extend inland. Several sandspits, bordered by extensive flats, project in a south-southwesterly direction from the general line of the coast. Owing to the action of the sea the configuration of the ends of these low spits is subject to constant change. Obitochnyy, Berdyanskiy and Byelosaria bays, entered westward of the spits, afford good shelter from easterly winds.

Zaliv Obitochnyy (beach area (156)) lies between Fedotova Point and the southwestern extremity of Obitochnaya Kosa (spit), about 30 miles east-northeastward. For about 9 miles northeastward of Fedotova Point the coast is composed of a narrow sandy strip separating Ozero Molochnoye from the sea. The lake, approximately 16 miles long and 2.5 to 4.5 miles wide, is salt and shallow, with depths ranging from 1 to 7 feet. There is no exit to the sea. The village of Stepanovka is located on the rising ground at the end of this sandy strip. Farther northeastward the coast becomes bluff and of even elevation. The town of Bot'yevo, with a population in 1937 of 10,000, lies

Original

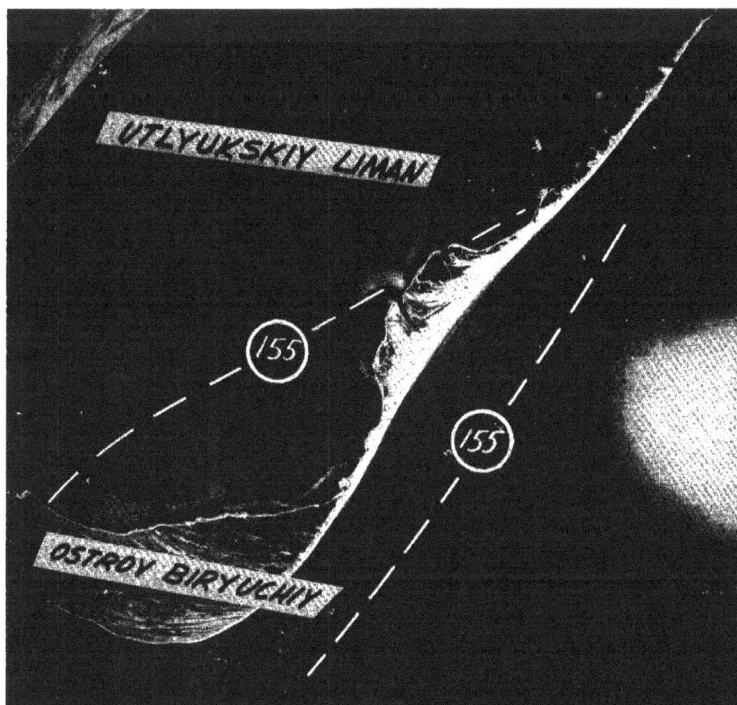

FIGURE IV-113. *Ukrainian SSR, Utlyukskiy Liman. Beach area (155).* Oblique aerial view northward of Ostrov Biryuchiy and barrier northward toward Kosa Fedotova. Area lies southwest of FIGURE IV-114. July 1943. Approximate position 46°10'N, 35°10'E; B. A. Chart 2234.

FIGURE IV-114. *Ukrainian SSR, Utlyukskiy Liman. Beach area (155).* Oblique aerial view northward of Kosa Fedotova and barrier northward, forming beach area. Compare FIGURE IV-113. July 1943. Approximate position 46°20'N, 35°20' E; B. A. Chart 2234.

about 2 miles inland in the valley of the river Korsak, which flows into the sea 7 miles northeastward from Novo-Konstantinovka. The river dries in the summer. Near the village of Preslav, 5 miles northward of Obitochnaya Kosa (spit), the coast suddenly decreases in elevation. On the high ground within the root of the spit there is a row of six moundlike hills which are visible for quite a distance at sea. The northeastern part is very narrow. The spit (beach area (157)) is fringed by a flat and numerous small patches with depths from 10 to 17 feet extending 2 miles from each side and 6.5 miles from its extremity.

Berdyanskiy Zaliv is 27 miles wide between Obitochnaya Kosa (spit) and Byerdyansk Point. The coast consists of flat-topped cliffs. About 9.5 miles northwestward of Byerdyansk Point the cliff is intersected by a gully through which flows a small river. Byerdyanskaya spit (beach area (158)), at the eastern entrance, is similar in configuration to Obitochnaya Kosa (spit). The narrow central portion is formed of washed-up sand about 1 foot in elevation. The southern extremity is fringed by a bank with depths of less than 3 fathoms, extending 1.5 miles offshore.

Berdyanskiy Reyd (U.S.H.O. Chart 4215), comprising the eastern part of the bay, is unobstructed and affords sheltered anchorage in 18 feet over excellent holding ground. The town of Osipenko, with a population in 1939 of 51,664, is situated on the level ground a short distance from the bold tableland in the northeastern part of the bay. It lies on the main rail line and is connected by secondary roads to the central road network. Steamship communication is maintained with ports on the Black Sea and Sea of Azov (Chapter VI). There are a landing strip and a seaplane station at the town.

Byelosaria Bay (B.A. Chart 2234), the easternmost of the bays which indent this stretch of coast, is 26 miles wide at its entrance between Berdyanskaya Kosa (spit) and Belosarayska Kosa (Byelosaraika Spit). A short distance eastward of the tableland within the head of the Berdyanskaya Kosa (spit) is the broad valley of the river Berda, which forms a shallow lagoon before entering the sea through a narrow channel. The village of Petrovskaya Krepost' (Petrovskaya Kryepost) lies on the northern bank of the river. Between this village and Byelosaria Point the coast is backed by bare, reddish-colored cliffs, intersected by three wide valleys. A low, sandy spit (beach area (159)) extends 5 miles southward from the high land on the point. An extension of the bank which encumbers the whole eastern part of the bay continues 1.5 miles southwestward from the southern end of the spit.

Taganrogskiy Zaliv (Gulf of Taganrog; B.A. Chart 3389), the eastern part of the Sea of Azov, extends from Belosarayskaya Kosa (Byelosaraika Spit) to the Don river delta about 80 miles eastward. The gulf is approximately 15.5 miles wide at its entrance between Belosarayskaya Kosa (Byelosaraika Spit) and Kosa Dolgaga. Within the northern side of the gulf there is a level, uniform, and in places, salty steppe, terminating at the coast in steep clay cliffs which reach elevations of 180 feet. They are precipitous in places, but generally are broken up into terraces by landslips. There are isolated small hills and mounds, and the cliffs are intersected by streams which form deep ravines. The shore consists of a narrow beach of sand and shells. Several low, sandy spits, fringed by shallow flats, extend southward from the general line of the coast. The southern shore consists of terraced clay cliffs of even elevation, intersected by ravines. The spits which extend from this side are more extensively fringed by flats than those to the northward. Ice usually appears in the gulf in December and remains solid until the end of February or the middle of March.

From the high land within the root of Belosarayska Kosa (Byelosaraika Spit) the coast trends northeastward for 7.5 miles to the mouth of the Balka Zintseva valley. This stretch consists of a steep, level-topped cliff, intersected about midway by the deep and narrow Balka Samarina. From the mouth of the Zintseva the coast rises sharply for about 3 miles to the Kal'mius (Kalmius) river valley, thence it trends eastward to the extremity of Kosa Lyapina. Between the mouths of these rivers the coast is fronted by a beach of fine sand fringed by a bank with depths of 6 feet, extending 0.5 mile offshore. Kosa Lyapina terminates in two low islands with a shallow flat extending some distance into the gulf.

The town of Mariupol' stands partly on a hill on the western bank of the river Kal'mius and partly on the low coast westward of its mouth (beach area (160)). It is a large industrial town with a population in 1939, of 222,000. The harbor (B.A. Chart 3389) is connected to the general railway system and by a primary road to the central road network. Air facilities consist of two landing strips and a seaplane base. Steamer communication is maintained with Black Sea and Sea of Azov ports. The port of Mariupol', about 2.5 miles southeast of the city, consists of the Zintseva and Kal'mius valley harbors with general depths from 11 to 24 feet (Chapter VI). The roadstead has good anchoring ground but is unprotected from southwesterly winds.

From Kosa Lyapina the coast trends eastward for about 18 miles to Krivaya Kosa (spit). The shore, to the village of Shirokoye 5.5 miles eastward, consists of a narrow sandy beach fringed by a shallow flat. Between the village and the Balka Samsonova the coast is a continuous cliff which recedes inland back of the lowland near Krivaya Kosa (spit) (beach area (161)). The spit extends about 4 miles southward from the coast and is fringed by a shallow bank.

The coast between Krivaya Kosa (spit) and Beglitskaya Kosa, 14 miles eastward, is intersected at the midpoint by a ravine, on the eastern slope of which lies the village of Veselo-Voznesenskaya (Veselo-Voznyesenskaya). Farther eastward, near the root of the latter spit, the coast is intersected by the wide valley of the Mius river, which flows into a shallow estuary narrowed by two sandy spits at its mouth. Beglitskaya Kosa extends about 1.5 miles southeastward from the coast and is fronted by a shallow bank.

East of Beglitskaya Spit, for about 12 miles to Pyetrushin Point, steep cliffs about 60 feet high approach the sea. Along the cliffs there are numerous villages and farms. Two small spits extend southward from the cliff. Mys Taganrog, about 4 miles east-northeastward of Pyetrushin, is a conspicuous bluff 96 feet high. This whole stretch of coast (beach area (162)) is bordered by a flat with depths of 2 fathoms extending to 6 miles offshore.

Original

The town of Taganrog is situated on the flat summit of the point; the port consists of a harbor at the southeastern end of the town and a roadstead which occupies the central and eastern portions of Taganrogskiy Zaliv. The harbor, composed of three basins and a quay, has depths of 6 to 14 feet (Chapter VI). The roadstead is comparatively open but the holding ground is good. The town of Taganrog, with a population in 1939 of 188,808, is an important administrative and industrial center. The harbor and town are connected with the general railway system and by second-class road to the central road network. During the summer, steamship communication is maintained with ports on the Sea of Azov. Air facilities consist of four landing strips and a seaplane base.

Between Mys Taganrog and Kurichiy Rozhok, 5 miles northeastward, lies a shallow bay. Between the head of the bay and the delta of the river Don, 11 miles eastward, the coast (beach area (163)) is bluff and of even elevation, intersected by deep ravines.

The delta of the river Don, which forms the head of Taganrogskiy Zaliv, commences near the village of Nizhne-Gnilovskaya, about 17 miles from the head of the gulf and about 3 miles below Rostov where Donets, the most northerly branch, divides from the main river (B.A. Chart 2234). A few miles farther downstream the river Kalancha branches off northward; thence the Rukav Staryy Don, the remainder of the main stream, continues westward, emptying into the gulf. Near the gulf all branches divide to enter the gulf in about 24 mouths, all of which frequently change direction and vary in depth. After gales from seaward new mouths are sometimes formed. The approach to Rostov-on-Don is by way of the Rostov approach channel which leads to the Peschanoye mouth, thence through the Rukav Staryy Don. The channel had been dredged to 12 feet (in 1934); depths in the river vary from 12 to 60 feet. The whole of the head of the gulf is fringed by a very shallow flat and numerous islands which are almost awash. The banks rise gradually farther upstream to a height of 6 feet. Within about 4 miles of the head of the gulf the islands are completely covered by dense masses of reeds, 7 to 8 feet in height. The southern side of the delta, from the village of Kagalnik to the town of Azov, about 5 miles eastward, rises steeply to high land which recedes southward a short distance inland.

The port of Azov, which lies on the southern bank of the Staryy Don about 8 miles above Peschanoye mouth, is accessible to vessels not exceeding 12-foot draft. The town of Azov, with a population in 1935 of 25,000, is situated on rising ground southward of the port. It is connected to the general railway system and by a secondary road to Rostov-on-Don. Azov has two landing strips and a seaplane station.

The port of Rostov-on-Don is situated on the river Don about 27 miles from Peschanoye mouth (Chapter VI). The river is navigable as far as Pavlovsk, about 450 miles upstream. The port has a depth of about 12 feet alongside its quays and piers. Owing to this and the probability of the approach channel silting, the greater part of all exports from Rostov-on-Don are transshipped in Bol'shoy Taganrogskiy Reyd. Rostov-on-Don, the largest town on

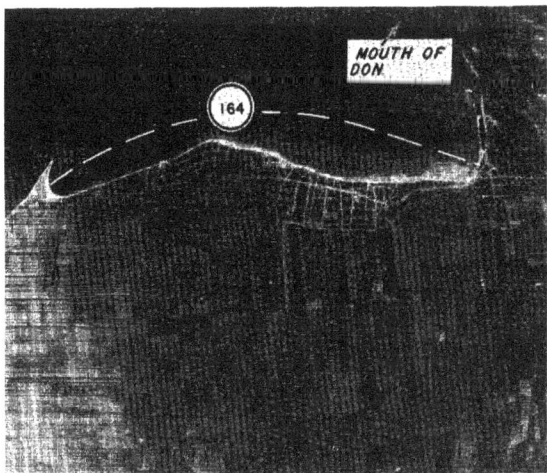

FIGURE IV-115. *Rostov area. Beach area (164).*
Oblique aerial view northward toward beach area and mouth of river Don. June 1943. Approximate position 47°01'N, 39°10'E; B. A. Chart 3389.

the southern coast of USSR, is a large industrial and administrative center. In 1938 the population numbered 800,000. The town is connected to the general railway system and by primary roads with the interior. Regular steamer communication is maintained with ports in the Sea of Azov and Black Sea. An airfield with complete facilities and two landing strips are located at Rostov-on-Don.

From the head of the gulf the southern shore trends westward for 19 miles to Mys Chimburskiy. Along the shore (beach area (164); FIGURE IV-115; B.A. Chart 3389) are clay slopes of even elevation. A low sandy spit lies off the point, fronted by a flat with depths of less than 12 feet extending 6 miles northwestward. Ochakovskaya Kosa, 11 miles eastward from the point, is low and sandy; fringed by a shoal with depths of less than 6 feet. Westward from Mys Chimburskiy (beach area (165)) the high clay slopes are intersected by three gullies. The large village of Port-Katon is situated at the mouth of the Balka Kruglaya.

(2) Landing beaches

The most common type of beach in subsector 43 D lies along a narrow spit. The entire western shore of the Sea of Azov is composed of such beaches (beach areas (153) and (155)), and they are present at regular intervals along the north shore (beach areas (157), (158), and (159)). Between the spits are narrow beaches backed by low bluffs or cliffs. Exits from beaches are usually fair and generally limited to roads leading from the small ports lying at the heads of the bays formed within the long spits. Bottom slopes over the area are flat. Navigation through Kerch Strait and into most of the Sea of Azov harbors is limited to dredged channels.

The beaches of subsector 43 D are described briefly in TABLE IV-13.

TABLE IV - 13

LANDING BEACHES OF COASTAL SUBSECTOR 43 D (PLANS 18 and 19)
Reliability FAIR.

Number and location of beach area	Nearshore	Length	Width	Gradient	Surf and shore drift	Material and firmness	Terrain immediately behind beach	Connections inland
(147)	Gentle slopes; generally clear but for projecting piles near center.	About 7 mi., N end along spit; interrupted N of center by high cape.	15 to 25 ft. along S half, 75 to 100 ft. along N half.	Average 1 on 20.	Surf light; drift to N.	Sand; generally firm except along spit.	Road embankment and salt lake at S end; low bank N to beach interruption; sandy plain with marsh and meadow land terminating in narrow spit at N end.	Secondary road directly inland except at N end; access generally over low embankment or bank; road connects with main road to N.
(148) Bay at Kamysh-Burun.	Very flat slopes; dredged channel through strait (23.5 ft.) lies about 2 mi. off S end. Sunken rocks likely off bayhead.	Totals about 2 mi., interrupted near center by low bluff and along S section by harbor which may still be under construction.	Average 25 ft.	1 on 25.	Surf generally light; drift probably weak and mainly to N.	Sand; S section probably soft.	Town areas located above low bank back entire area.	Main road and R.R. connections are readily available.
(149) Bay at Kerch'	Mild-to-flat bottom slopes; dredged channels lead to harbor areas.	Total about 2.5 mi., interrupted by piers along S section, by harbor area at center.	15 to 25 ft.	1 on 25 ft.	Light surf; main drift to N.	Sand; generally soft.	Factories and other buildings line W shore; NE shore more open and hilly.	Road and R.R. connections available in harbor area.
(150) NE of Yenikal	Mild-to-flat bottom slopes; dredged channel through strait (23.5 ft.) lies 1 mi. off S end; rocks are present nearshore.	About 2 mi., interrupted by piers.	Average 100 ft.	1 on 30.	Surf light or negligible; drift probably mainly to SW.	Sand; firm only near water line.	Low sandy plain, may be partly marshy; fishing huts and canneries along shore, and town of Yenikal beyond SW end.	Exit best from SW end into town; secondary roads run W to Kerch'.
(151)	Details not known. Bottom slopes probably moderate; shoal extends 3 mi. off point and rock lies nearshore SW of point.	Total 3 mi. along narrow spit and around bayhead to W; interrupted by steep cliff at tip of point.	Average 50 ft.	1 on 20.	Surf moderate to heavy on E side of spit; generally light in bay.	Pebbles and sand; firm.	Narrow strip of low sandy land with salt lake behind bayhead; steep slopes dominate end of beach.	Trail from inner end of spit on E side and from W end of bayhead.
(152) SE and SW of Mys Kazantip.	Mild-to-flat bottom slopes. Anchorage off SE end in 30 ft. and in 15 to 20 ft. off NW end of bayhead beach.	Total about 13 mi. along bayhead and narrow neck to W; interrupted at W entrance to bay by rocky point.	15 to 75 ft. narrowest along SE shore of bay, widest along narrow neck.	Average 1 on 20.	Surf lightest off SE end of bayhead and off beach W of bay; drift varies.	Sand; generally firm.	Low bluffs along SE shore of bay; sandy plain and salt lake along W shore.	Secondary road or tracks generally accessible; R.R. runs close inland along center of bayhead.
(153) Arabatskaya Strelka.	Details not known; bottom slopes probably flat. Anchorage off SE end in 25 ft.	65 mi. limited to N by narrow strait, to S by high land.	Probably 75 to 150 ft.	1 on 30.	Surf heaviest along SE half; main drift to NW.	Sand; firm at water line.	Soft sand of narrow spit; inner shore is somewhat marshy. Scattered villages with clumps of trees especially along NW half.	Lateral movement possible along poor road or track.

Original

TABLE IV-13 (Continued)

Number and location of beach area	Nearshore	Length	Width	Gradient	Surf and shore drift	Material and firmness	Terrain immediately behind beach	Connections inland
(154) W shore of Ulyukskiy Liman.	Flat bottom slopes and offshore bars.	Total about 15 mi., interrupted by lake inlets and by bluffs; may be more or less continuous than shown.	15 to 50 ft., widest at lake inlets.	1 on 50 to 1 on 30.	Surf generally negligible, moderate with S or SE winds along SW sections of beach; breaks in wide belt; drift to NE and N.	Sand; soft along lake inlets.	Low bluff with cultivated fields inland or low swampy land bordering lakes.	Exit by trail and secondary road.
(155) Ostrov Biryuchiy (Biryuchi Island) and shore to NE. (Figs. IV-113 and IV-114.)	Mild bottom slopes; shoals off inner shore, outer shore more clear.	About 55 mi., beach on inner shore may not be as continuous as shown.	Probably 100 to 200 ft., probably widest along center of spit.	1 on 30 average.	Moderate-to-heavy surf on outer shore; varies on inner shore.	Sand; generally soft.	Very narrow spit or barrier fronting lake; island at end of spit is composed of grass covered old beach ridges; town and cultivated land lie between spit and lake barrier.	Lateral movement along track over spit might be hindered by soft sand; best exit between spit and lake barrier.
(156)	Bottom slopes flat; other details not known. Anchorage except with S winds.	About 40 mi., continues from beach (155) on W, bounded by partly marshy stream mouth on E.	15 to 50 ft., widest at stream on ravine mouths.	Average 1 on 20.	Surf light except with S winds; drift mainly to W.	Sand; firm except near stream mouths.	Bank probably about 20 ft. high generally with level cultivated ground inland; bank broken at numerous stream mouths and many villages lie close to shore.	Best up valleys to villages; tracks or secondary roads offer means of access inland.
(157) Obitochnaya Kosa	Shallow water with sand and shell bottom; depths of 18 ft. lie 3.5 mi. offshore of inner side of spit.	About 34 mi., along both sides of spit; inner shore may not be as continuous as shown.	100 to 200 ft., along spit, probably narrow to about 25 ft. to NE.	1 on 30 average.	Surf moderate along outer shore; drift to S.	Sand relatively soft.	Narrow sandy spit or barrier fronting lakes; wider sandy area banks NW end.	Best exit from village back of NW end.
(158) Berdyanskaya Kosa	Very shallow water with shoals along inner shore, slightly steeper slopes along outer shore. Anchorage in 15 to 21 ft. with NW to NE winds.	About 25 mi. along both sides of spit, may be interrupted along inner shore.	75 to 150 ft. along spit, narrows to 15 to 25 ft. along NW and NE ends.	Average 1 on 30.	Moderate surf on outer shore with NE winds, on inner shore with SW winds; drift to S.	Sand, relatively soft.	Low sand spit or narrow barrier fronting lakes; harbor area lies to the NW, low cliffs to the NE.	Best exit into harbor area to NW.
(159) Belosarayskaya Kosa	18 ft. depths lie 2,000 ft. off outer shore locally, more generally 2 to 5 mi. offshore.	About 23 mi. along both sides of spit and around bay to W.	15 to 200 ft. widest along spit.	Average 1 on 30.	Moderate surf with NE or SW winds; drift to SW and SE.	Mainly sand; most firm along W end of area.	Low sand and partly marshy spit along E; town and low cliffs along W.	Exit by track to village near NE end or along bay shore to town of Yalta.
(160) Mariupol'	Very shallow bank of 6 ft. depth extends nearly 1 mi. locally; dredged channels lead to harbors.	About 11 mi., interrupted by 2 harbors.	25 to 50 ft., may be wider locally toward E end.	1 on 50.	Moderate surf with NE winds; drift may vary but is mainly to W and S.	Sand, firm only near water line.	W sections lie in front of town and between harbor structures; narrow sandy plain backed by hills toward E end.	Exit to road and R.R. in Mariupol' best from W sections.
(161) Krivaya Kosa and W.	Shallow water, best approach to outer shore	About 22 mi. along Krivaya Kosa and	Averages 75 ft.	Average 1 on 30.	Surf generally light or negligible W of	Sand; firm only at water line.	Low sandy plains, partly marshy, rising to low	Best exits from village near E end of area

44. PRINCIPAL SOURCES

A. Evaluation

The source material available for the preparation of the coastal study was adequate. USSR and German topographic maps were good, while hydrographic charts and coastal descriptions were only satisfactory. German military geography studies, while thorough, approached the subject matter from the standpoint of inland troop movements, thus devoting only a small portion of the text to the coastal areas. Photographs from captured material were good, although limited to small local areas and not lending themselves readily to reproduction.

Material for beach studies was inadequate, mainly because of the scarcity of aerial photographs. Those which were available covered only a portion of Sector 43 and were so greatly distorted and of so small a scale that they were of relatively little value. Coastal pilots and hydrographic charts, although complete in coastal coverage, furnished little or no pertinent data on the beaches of certain areas, such as the northern portions of subsectors 42 A and 42 B. Source material on landing beaches found in technical and travel literature was very helpful, particularly for Sector 41. Less material was available for Sectors 42 and 43, and this was generally of value in describing only small local areas. Ground photographs of Sector 42 were most plentiful. They were of considerable value in the descriptions wherever available, but again, however, covered only relatively small areas. Intelligence documents, reports, and dispatches generally yielded no pertinent coast or beach information.

B. List of references—Coasts

1. Germany, Generalstab der Luftwaffe.
   DIE KUSTENGEBIETE DER BARENTS-SEE. Berlin. 1943.
2. ———
   LUFTGEOGRAPHISCHES EINZELHEFT MITTEL- U. OSTRUSSLAND. Section on Leningrad region, Berlin. 1942.
3. ———
   LUFTGEOGRAPHISCHES EINZELHEFT DER RUSSISCHEN SCHWARZMEER- UND KAUKASUSLÄNDER. Sections B1, B2, and B3, Berlin. 1941.
4. Great Britain, Admiralty, Hydrographic Department.
   ARCTIC PILOT, VOL. 1. 4th ed., pp. 1-472, London. 1933.
5. ———
   BALTIC PILOT, VOL. 1. pp. 304-388, London. 1939.
6. ———
   BALTIC PILOT, VOL. 3. pp. 40-138, London. 1937.
7. ———
   THE BLACK SEA PILOT. 9th ed., pp. 173-341, London. 1942.
8. ———
   SUPPLEMENT NO. 8—1944 RELATING TO THE ARCTIC PILOT, VOL. I. London. 29 May 1944.
9. Taracouzio, T. A.
   SOVIETS IN THE ARCTIC. pp. 1-28, New York. 1938.
10. Woods, E. G.
    THE BALTIC REGION. pp. 355-379, New York. 1932.

MAPS AND CHARTS

11. Germany, Generalstab des Heeres.
    ABTEILUNG FUR KRIEGSKARTEN UND VERMESSUNGSWESEN. II, Weltkarte, Topographic maps, scale 1:1,000,000, 1941-44.
12. ———
    MILITÄRGEOGRAPHISCHEN ANGABEN ÜBER DEN EUROPÄISCHEN RUSSLAND. Mappe B, Die Baltischen Länder, 1941; Mappe C, Gebiet Leningrad, 1941; Mappe D, Karelien und Kola, 1941; Mappe F, Ukraine, 1941; Mappe M, Gebiete-Wologda-Arkhangel'sk, 1941; Mappe N, Nord-Ost-Russland, 1942; Berlin.
13. U.S. Coast and Geodetic Survey.
    OPERATIONAL AIRFIELD MAPS. Washington, D. C. 1945. (Confidential.)

14. U.S. Army Map Service.
    TOPOGRAPHIC MAPS. Series G.S.G.S. 4363, scale 1:100,000, 1943; series G.S.G.S. 4312, scale 1:500,000, 1943; series G.S.G.S. 2758, scale 1:1,000,000, 1945; series G.S.G.S. 4464, scale 1:2,000,000, 1943; series G.S.G.S. 2957, scale 1:4,000,000, 1944; series 5307, scale 1:1,500,000 (Russian), 1943.
15. U.S. Navy Department, Hydrographic Office.
    H.O. CHARTS. Various scales and dates; reproductions of British Admiralty Charts, various scales and dates. Pertinent chart numbers listed in sector and subsector headings.
16. USSR, General Staff of the Red Army.
    MAPS. Scale 1:500,000, photographic copies. 1941.
17. USSR, Council of People's Commissars, Principal Administration of Geodesy and Cartography.
    MAPS. Scale 1:1,000, photographic copies. 1938-1939.

C. List of references—Landing beaches

1. Davies, Ellen C.
    A WAYFARER IN ESTONIA, LATVIA, AND LITHUANIA. 273 pp., New York. 1937.
2. Edelberg, Max, editor.
    PICTURESQUE ESTONIA. 102 pp., Copenhagen. 1937.
3. Granö, J. G., editor.
    ESTONIA. Tallinn. 1922.
4. Great Britain, Admiralty, Hydrographic Department.
    ARCTIC PILOT, VOL. 1. 4th ed. London. 1933.
5. ———
    BALTIC PILOT, VOL. 1. London. 1939.
6. ———
    BALTIC PILOT, VOL. 3. London. 1937.
7. ———
    THE BLACK SEA PILOT. 9th ed. London. 1942.
8. Greiner, T.
    DIE FRISCHE NEHRUNG, Geographischer Anzeiger, vol. 36, no. 3. 1935.
9. Gronie, O. T.
    CONTRIBUTIONS TO THE QUATERNARY GEOLOGY OF NOVAYA ZEMLYA, Report, scientific results of Norwegian Expedition to Novaya Zemlya, 1921, no. 21. 1924.
10. Holtedahl, O.
    NOVAYA ZEMLYA, A RUSSIAN ARCTIC LAND, Geog. Rev., vol. 12, no. 4, pp. 521-531. 1922.
11. Homer, T.
    EAST CARELIA AND KOLA LAPMARK, Bull. de la Société Géographique de Finlande, vol. 42, no. 3, pp. 1-264. Helsingfors. 1921.
12. International Geological Congress, 17th Session.
    THE NOVAYA ZEMLYA EXCURSION, PARTS 1 AND 2. Leningrad. 1937.
13. Jackson, F. G.
    THE GREAT FROZEN LAND. 288 pp. London. 1895.
14. Kihlman, A. O.
    BERICHT EINER NATURWISSENSCHAFTLICHEN REISE DURCH RUSSISCH LAPPLAND IM JAHRE 1889, Bull. de la Société Géographique de Finlande, vol. 3, no. 6. Helsingfors. 1890.
15. Kihlman, A. O., and Palmeri, J. A.
    DIE EXPEDITION NACH DER HALBINSEL KOLA IM JAHRE 1887, Bull. de la Société Géographique de Finlande, vol. 3, no. 5. Helsingfors. 1890.
16. Leiviskä, I., and Levamachi, L., editors.
    GUIDE TO FINLAND. Helsinki. 1930.
17. Philippson, W.
    LANDESKUNDE DES EUROPÄISCHEN RUSSLANDS NEBST FINNLANDES. Leipzig. 1908.
18. Pullertts, A., editor.
    ESTONIA, POPULATION, CULTURAL AND ECONOMIC LIFE. 207 pp. Tallinn. 1937.
19. Rae, Edward.
    THE WHITE SEA PENINSULA. 314 pp. London. 1881.
20. Ramsay, Wilhelm.
    ÜBER DIE GEOLOGISCHE ENTWICKLUNG DER HALBINSEL KOLA IN DER QUATERNÄRZEIT, Bull. de la Société Géographique de Finlande, vol. 16, no. 1. Helsingfors. 1898.
21. Ramsay, Wilhelm, and Poppius, B.
    BERICHT ÜBER EINE REISE NACH DER HALBINSEL KANIN IM SOMMER 1903, Bull. de la Societe Géographique de Finlande, vol. 21, no. 6. Helsingfors. 1903.
22. Rudnitsky, Stephen.
    UKRAINE. THE LAND AND ITS PEOPLE. 340 pp. New York. 1918.
23. Shoulejkin, W.
    HYDRODYNAMICS OF THE TIDES IN A SMALL SEA COMMUNICATING WITH THE OCEAN (WHITE SEA), Beitrage Zur Geophysik, vol. 15, no. 3. Leipzig. 1926.
24. Tammekann, A.
    DIE OBERFLACHENGESTALTUNG DES NORDOSTESTLANDISCHEN KUSTEN TAFELLANDES. Tartu (Dorpat) ulikool. Acta et Commentationes, Series A, vol. 10. 1926.
25. Trevor, B. A.
    ICE-BOUND ON KOLGUEV. Westminster. 1895.
26. U.S. Headquarters AAF, Directorate of Weather.
    SUMMARY OF THE STATE OF THE ICE IN ARCTIC SEAS DURING THE YEARS 1935-1938, vol. 5. 1942. (Restricted).
27. U.S. Navy Department, Hydrographic Office.
    BALTIC PILOT, VOL. 1. H.O. no. 142. 1930.
28. ———
    BALTIC PILOT, VOL. 3. H.O. no. 143. 1934.
29. ———
    BLACK SEA PILOT. H.O. no. 155. 1926.
30. ———
    SUPPLEMENT TO H.O. 155. 1943.

MAPS AND CHARTS

31. Germany, Oberkommando der Kriegsmarine.
    HYDROGRAPHIC CHARTS. Various scales and dates.
32. Great Britain, Admiralty, Hydrographic Department.
    HYDROGRAPHIC CHARTS. Various scales and dates.
33. Great Britain, General Staff, Geographical Section.
    TOPOGRAPHIC MAPS. Series 2758, scale 1:1,000,000. 1942-1945.
34. ———
    TOPOGRAPHIC MAPS. Series 4072, scale 1:500,000. 1942.
35. U.S. Navy Department, Hydrographic Office.
    HYDROGRAPHIC CHARTS. Various scales and dates.
36. USSR, General Staff, Red Army.
    TOPOGRAPHIC MAPS. Scale 1:500,000. 1932-1941.
37. ———
    TOPOGRAPHIC MAPS. Scale 1:100,000. 1936-1941.
38. Other sources.
    In addition to the sources cited above, aerial and ground photographs, and intelligence dispatches were used.

LEGEND FOR FIGURES IV-110 TO IV-118
COASTAL TERRAIN
JANIS 40

LEGEND FOR FIGURES IV - 116 TO I
COASTAL TERRAIN

The following symbols, placed inland of the coastline, indicate features of coastal topography for a distanc going conditions for cross-country movement within large areas and the general distribution of soils accor of soil units is highly generalized.

Terrain Type Symbol	Trafficability	Soil
Steep terrain. 1.	Movement stopped except locally by steep terrain.	Permanently frozen substrata (tundra), poor drainage. Mixed shallow, deep loamy and clayey soils. Well drained over consolidated rocks.
Forests on hilly terrain. 2.	Movement stopped except locally by forests or hilly terrain.	Sandy, gravelly soils over boulder sands and boulder loams or stratified sand. Partly over permanently frozen substrata, with numerous marshes and swamps. A mixture of well and poorly drained soils.
Level to rolling terrain. 3.	Movement stopped except locally by forests on level to rolling terrain.	Sandy soils over deep sands and silts. Gravelly soils over boulder sands and loams, with numerous marshes, swamps and permanently frozen substrata. A mixture of well drained and poorly drained soils.
Swamps and marshes. 4.	Movement stopped except locally by swamps and marshes.	Areas dominated by poorly drained soils with marshes and swamps.
Frozen substrata. 5.	Dominantly poor going. Movement stopped for 8 weeks—May to June; poor—July to October; snow hinders—October to May.	Soils with permanently frozen substrata or tundra.
Poorly drained. 6.	Dominantly poor going. Movement stopped for 10 weeks—early March to July; going poor—July to November; snow hinders—December to April.	Areas dominated by poorly drained silty and clayey soils with numerous marshes and swamps, salt marshes and salty soils. Some lesser areas composed of sandy, gravelly and alluvial soils that are subject to flooding.
Well drained on hilly terrain. 7.	Well drained areas and dominantly fair going among numerous obstructions on hilly terrain. Poor going for 3 weeks—early March to April; snow hinders locally—November to April.	Mixed deep loamy and clayey soils. Silty soils over deep silts, sandy or loamy soils over boulder loams or stratified sand and gravel, with some numerous marshes and swamps.
Level to rolling terrain among numerous wet land obstructions. 8.	Well drained to poorly drained, but dominantly good going among numerous wet land obstructions. Movement stopped for 6 weeks—late March to early May; snow hinders—November to April.	Alluvial soils subject to flooding. Sandy, gravelly and stony soils partly over permanently frozen substrata, with numerous marshes and swamps.
Level, rolling terrain through nontrafficable forests. 9.	Well drained and dominantly good going on level to rolling terrain among numerous nontrafficable forests. Going poor for 2 to 3 weeks—March and April; snow hinders—November to April.	Sandy, loamy, clayey soils, over stratified sandy, gravelly material and silts.
Level to rolling terrain. 10.	Good going on level to rolling terrain with few corrections. Areas dominated by well drained soils over unconsolidated materials.	Deep loamy and clayey soils predominating in these areas. Sandy soils over deep sands or stratified sand and silts on and near coast.

Relative reliability: Kaninskaya Zemlya to Gulf of Baidaratzhaya, VERY POOR; West Coast of Kaninskaya Zemlya to N

V - 118

e of about fifty statute miles. The three maps are designed to show dominant
ding to properties of major importance to military problems. Trafficability

Vegetation	Coasts
Scattered tree growth at hill bases. Limited growth higher.	Steep, rocky, cliffy coasts backed by rocky mountains. Great nearshore depths.
Forests, mostly coniferous in the north. Observation very poor. Concealment excellent.	Rugged and rocky, fronted by rocks, shoals, and many islets.
Moderately forested with pine, fir, and some broadleaf. Forest islands conspicuous bordering the tundra area. Observation restricted. Concealment fair.	Generally steep shores with occasional rocky cliffs. Unsatisfactory beaches fronted with rocks and shoals.
Generally covered with reeds, rushes, and swamp grass. Some wooded swamps in the north with heavy underbrush.	Mud or spongy beach areas backed by low marshes or marshy valleys.
Limited to Arctic vegetation. Moss, grass, bushes, and stunted trees covered with lichens. Observation excellent. No concealment.	Long sandy beaches fronted by shoal water and backed by dunes and sand hills, with occasional cliffy areas fronted by rocks. Murman Coast is steep, rounded granite hills with beaches at bay heads and great nearshore depths.
Reed and grass covered swamps. Low bushes.	Low marshy deltas fringed by shallow flats.
Limited to meadows, plains, and grassland. Extensive cultivation.	Cliffs reaching 180 feet in height at abrupt termination of steppeland on northern shore of Azov Sea. High cliffs of uneven elevation in the Crimea.
Heavily wooded locally. Extensive meadows and cultivated localities. Observation good. Concealment good.	Good beach areas, with fair to good approaches and backed by occasional dunes and sandhills.
Wooded meadows, scrub fir, and oak.	Steep clay cliffs along southern shore of Gulf of Finland, east of Paldiski Samland Peninsula high and wooded. Elsewhere, shores are low and rocky with occasional low hills and cliffs.
Limited to scattered bushes in north. Scattered bushes and tree groves on Baltic. Extensive grassland with isolated tree groups on Black Sea. Observation excellent. Concealment very limited.	Sandy beach areas in North. Dune areas on Baltic. Cliffs of even elevation backed by flat steppeland on Black Sea. Broad coastal plain between Dniester and Danube mouths. Low sandy coasts and spits in the Crimea.

orway, POOR; Baltic Area, fair to good; Black Sea Area, GOOD.

EUROPEAN USSR
NORTH COASTAL SECTOR
COASTAL TERRAIN

The following symbols are placed inland of the coastline for a distance of approximately fifty statute miles. Refer to the key chart for further description in trafficability, soils, vegetation, and coasts.

TERRAIN TYPES

1. Steep terrain
2. Forests on hilly terrain
3. Level to rolling terrain
4. Swamps and marshes
5. Frozen substrata. Tundra
6. Poorly drained
7. Well drained on hilly terrain
8. Level to rolling terrain among numerous wet land obstructions
10. Level to rolling terrain

High steep mountains of solid rock, standing snow and much fog. No soil and untrafficable.

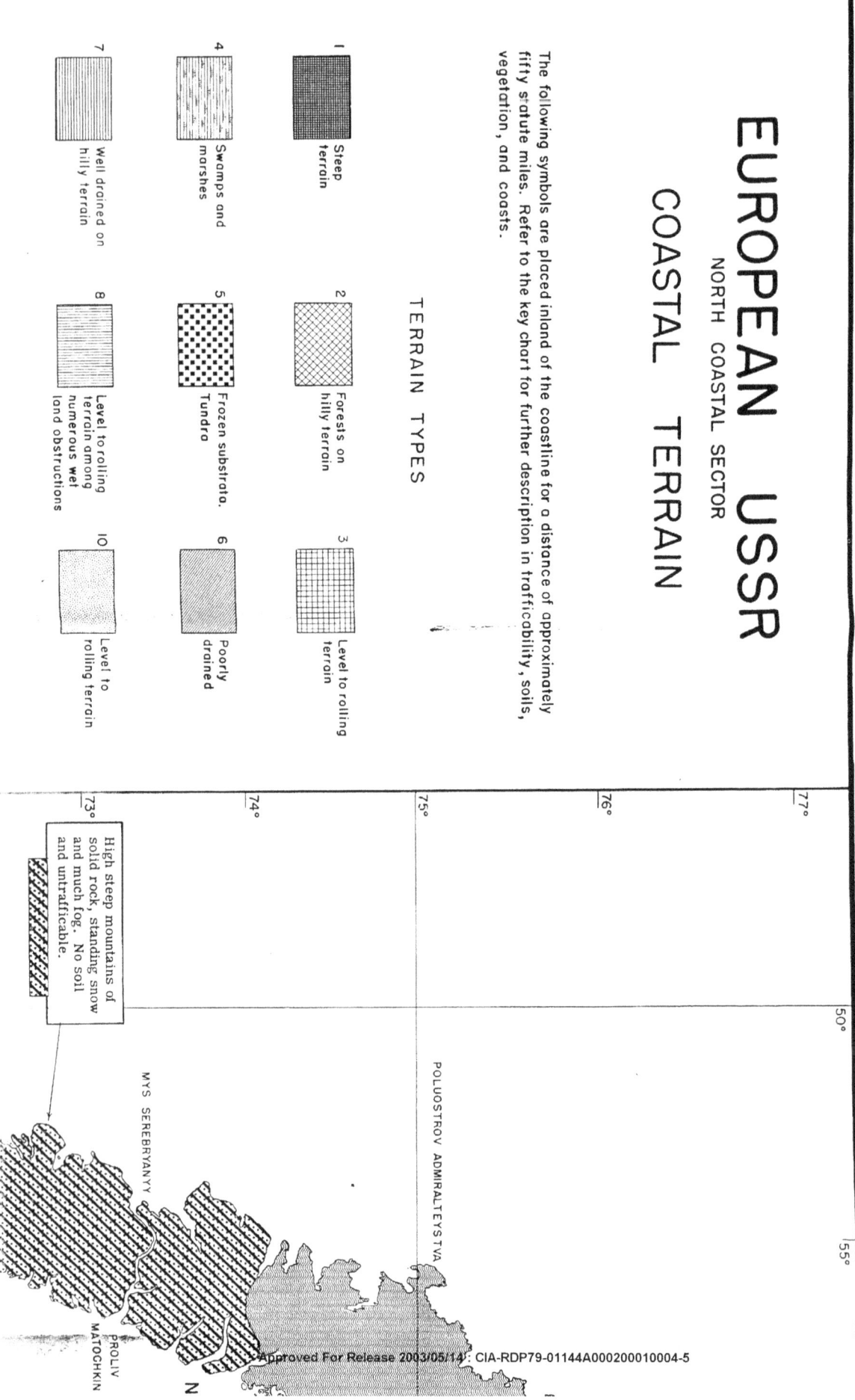

MYS SEREBRYANYY
POLUOSTROV ADMIRALTEYSTVA
PROLIV MATOCHKIN

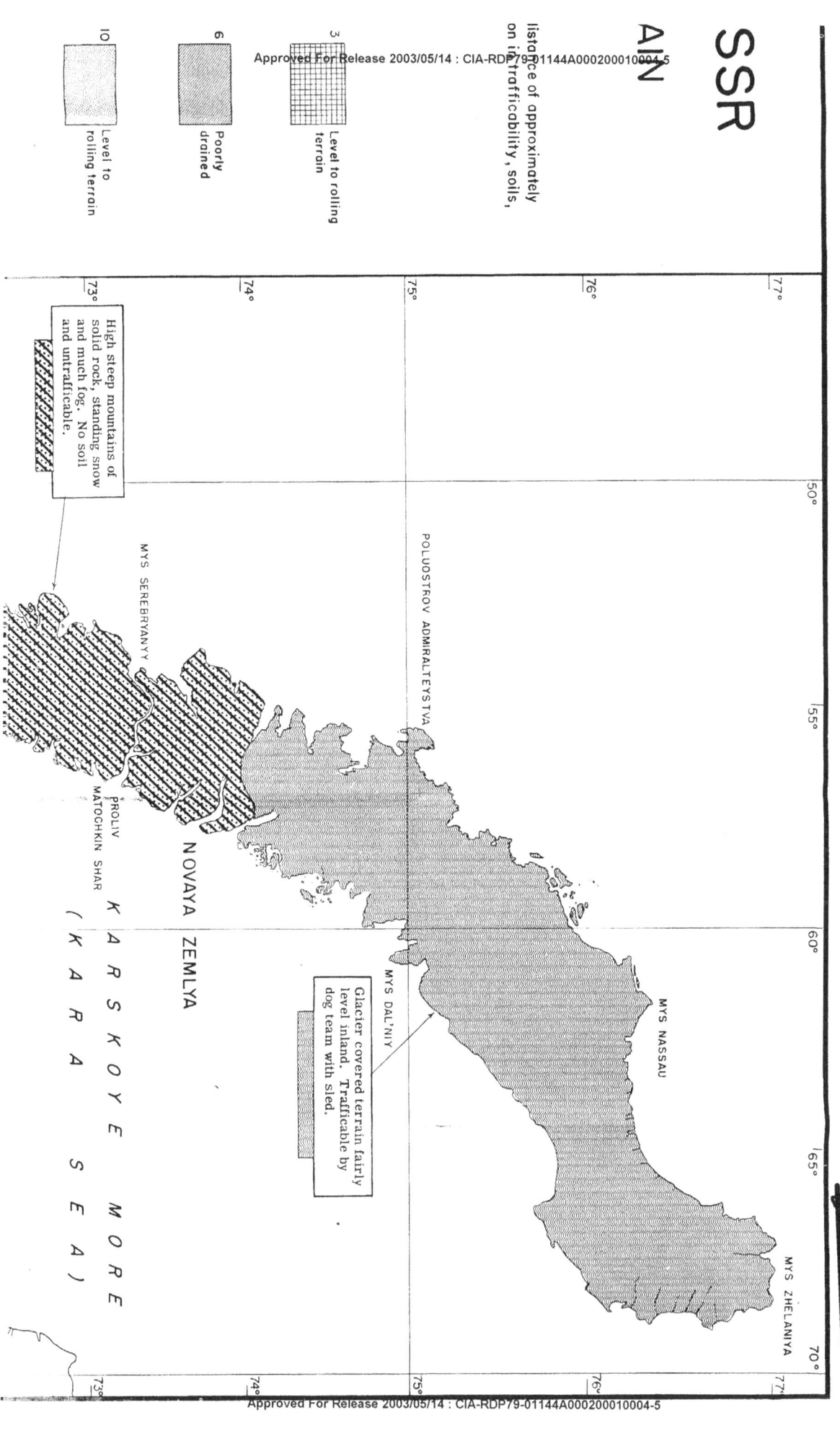

FIGURE IV-116
COASTAL TERRAIN OF NORTH COASTAL SECTOR
JANIS 40

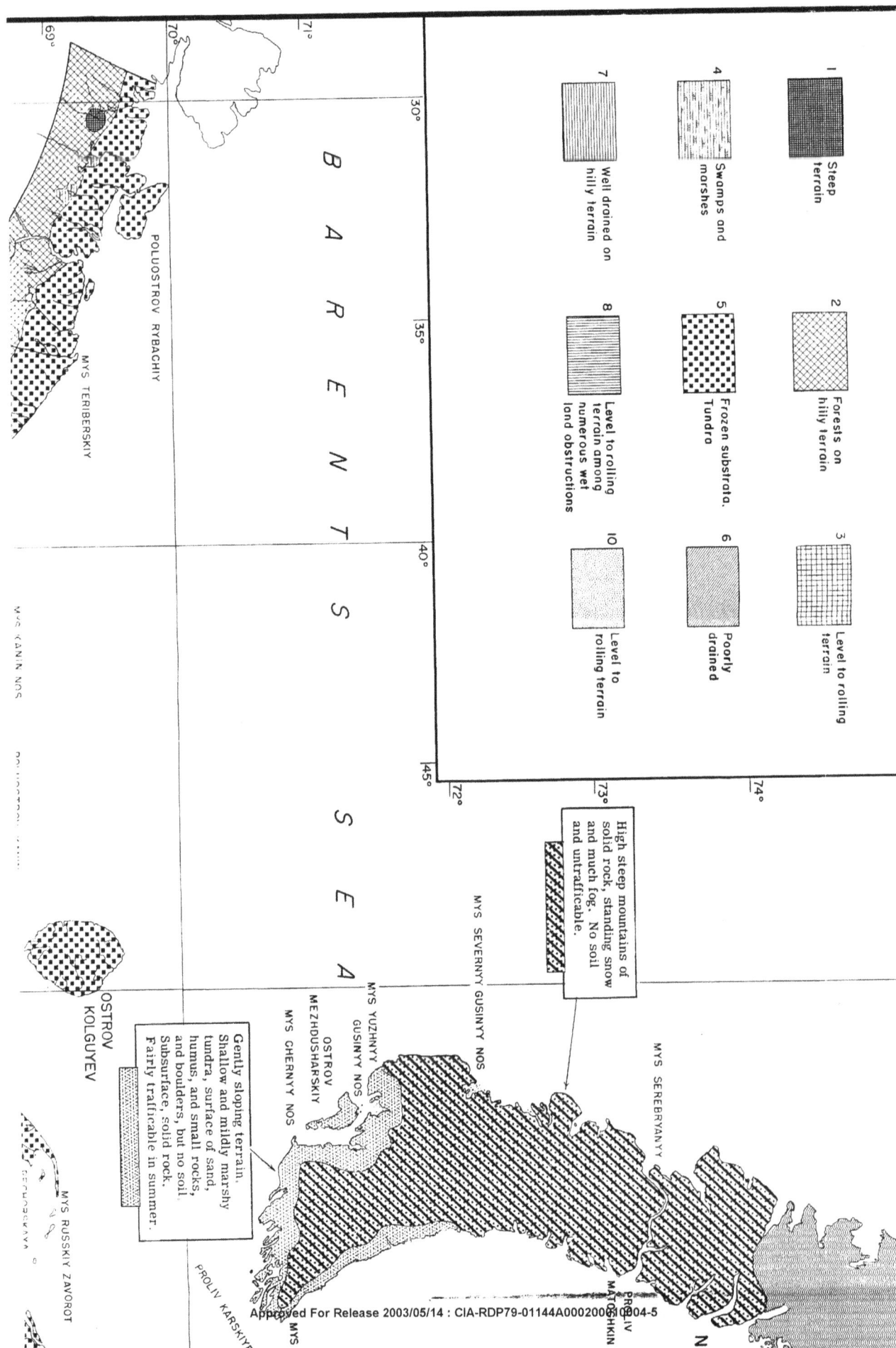

Legend

▦	Level to rolling terrain
▨	Poorly drained
░	Level to rolling terrain

Map Labels

BARENTS SEA

- MYS KANIN NOS
- POLUOSTROV KANIN
- OSTROV KOLGUYEV
- MYS PECHORSKAYA
- MYS RUSSKIY ZAVOROT
- PEChORSKAYA GUBA
- PROLIV KARSKIYE VOROTA
- OSTROV VAYGACH
- KARSKAYA GUBA
- BAYDARATSKAYA GUBA
- MYS MEN'SHIKOVA
- MYS CHERNYY NOS
- OSTROV MEZHDUSHARSKIY
- MYS YUZHNYY GUSINYY NOS
- MYS SEVERNYY GUSINYY NOS
- MYS SEREBRYANYY
- PROLIV MATOCHKIN SHAR
- NOVAYA ZEMLYA
- MYS DAL'NIY
- KARSKOYE MORE (KARA SEA)

Terrain Descriptions

[Novaya Zemlya northern region]: High steep mountains of solid rock, standing snow and much fog. No soil and untrafficable.

[Coastal region]: Gently sloping terrain. Shallow and mildly marshy tundra, surface of sand, humus, and small rocks, and boulders, but no soil. Subsurface, solid rock. Fairly trafficable in summer.

[Eastern region near Mys Dal'niy]: Glacier covered terrain fairly level inland. Trafficable by dog team with sled.

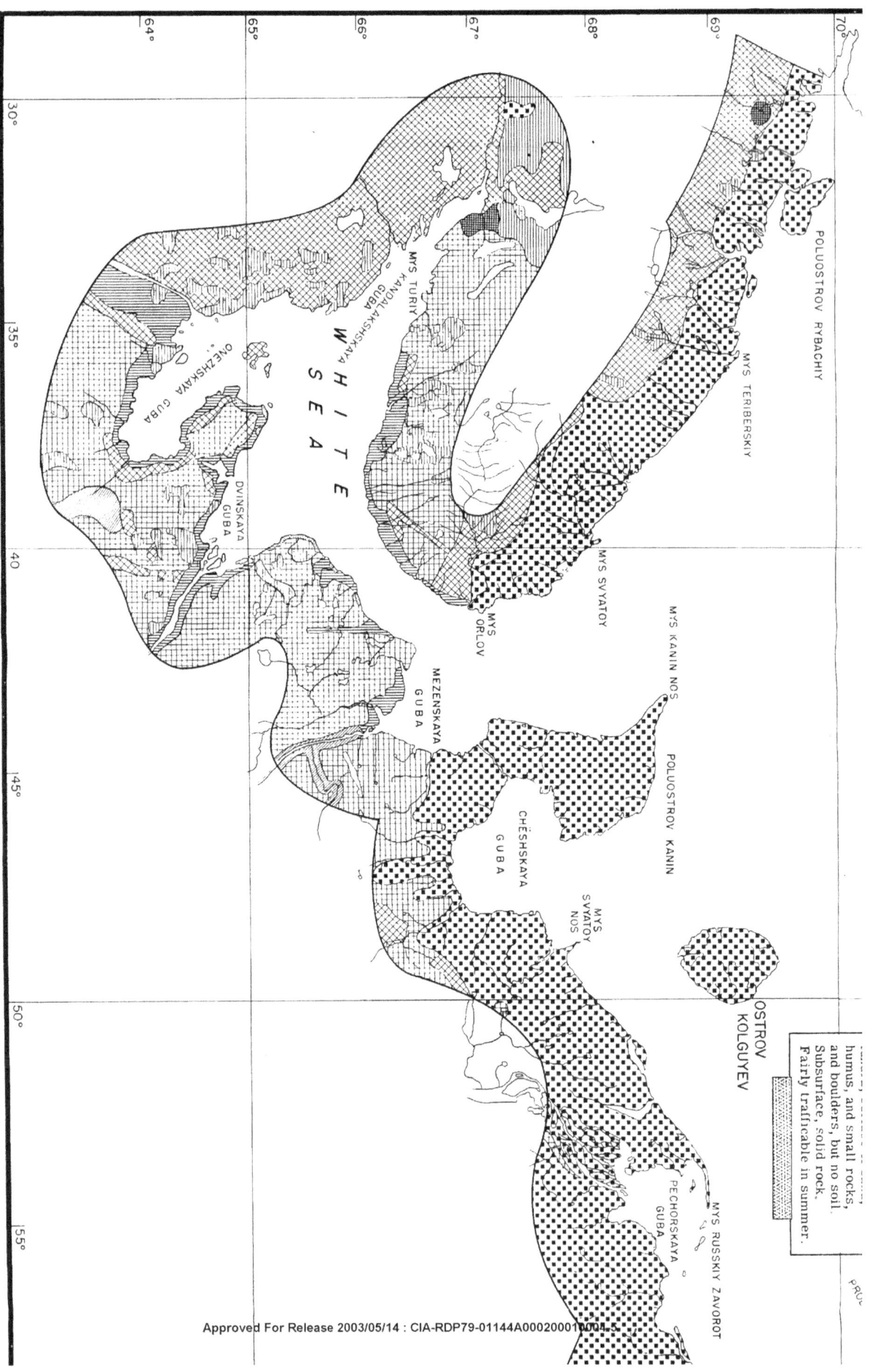

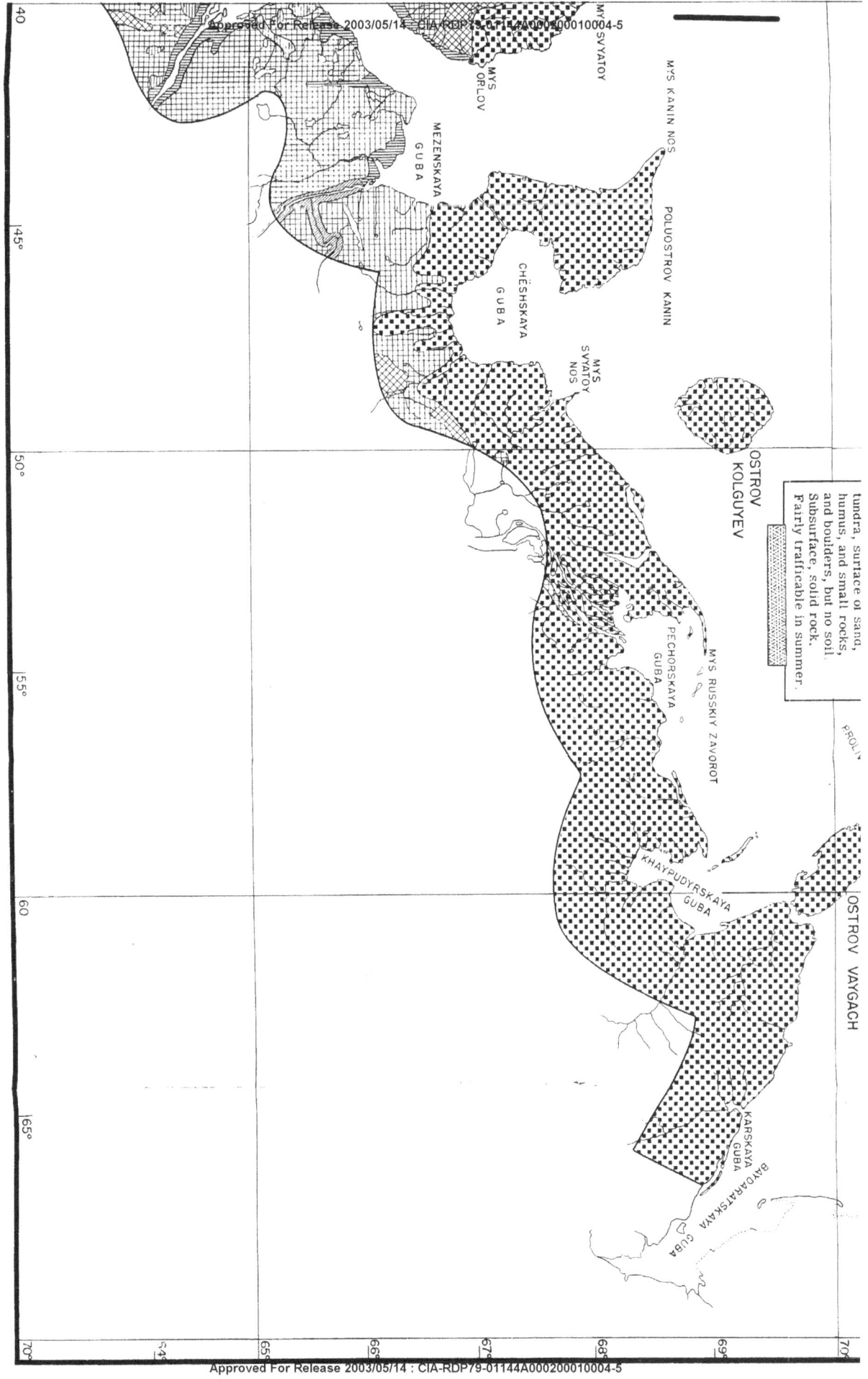

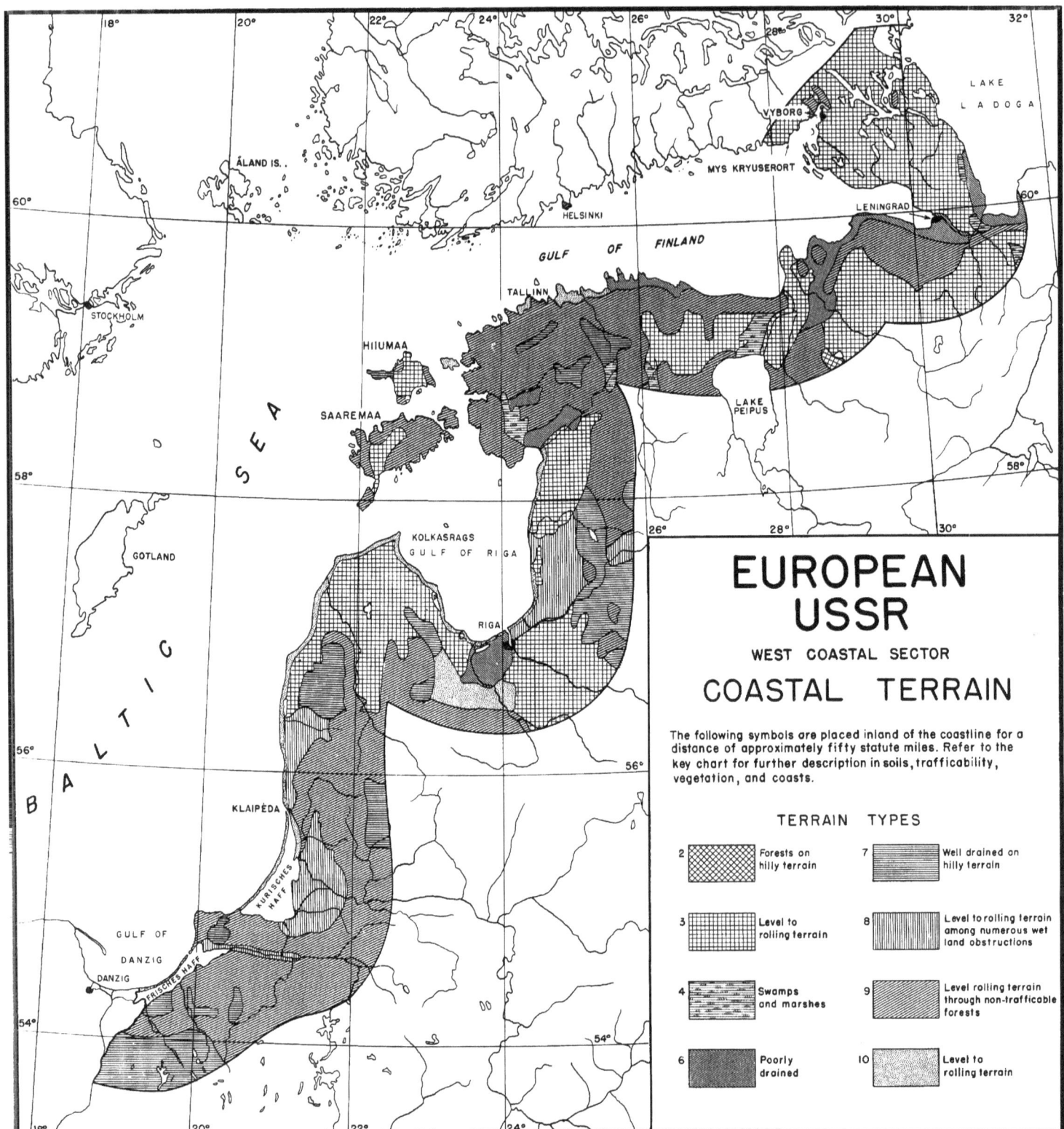

FIGURE IV-117
COASTAL TERRAIN OF WEST COASTAL SECTOR
JANIS 40

EUROPEAN USSR
SOUTH COASTAL SECTOR
COASTAL TERRAIN

The following symbols are placed inland of the coastline for a distance of approximately fifty sta[tute miles. See] chart for further description in trafficability, soils, and coasts.

TERRAIN TYPES

- 1 Steep terrain
- 6 Poorly drained
- 7 Well drained on hilly terrain
- 8 Level to rolling terrain among numerous wet land obstruct[ions]

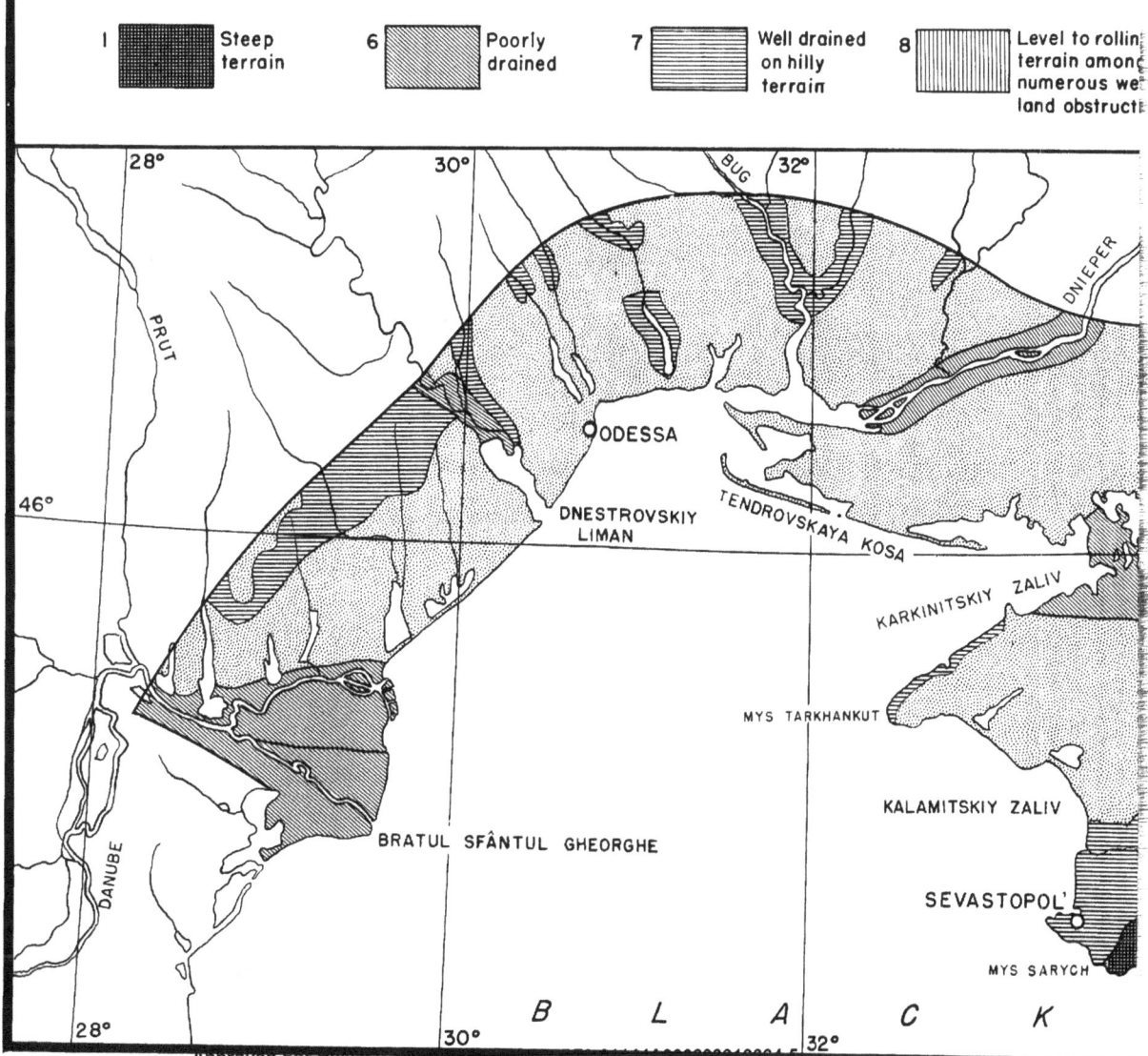

FIGURE IV-118
COASTAL TERRAIN OF SOUTH COASTAL SECTOR
JANIS 40

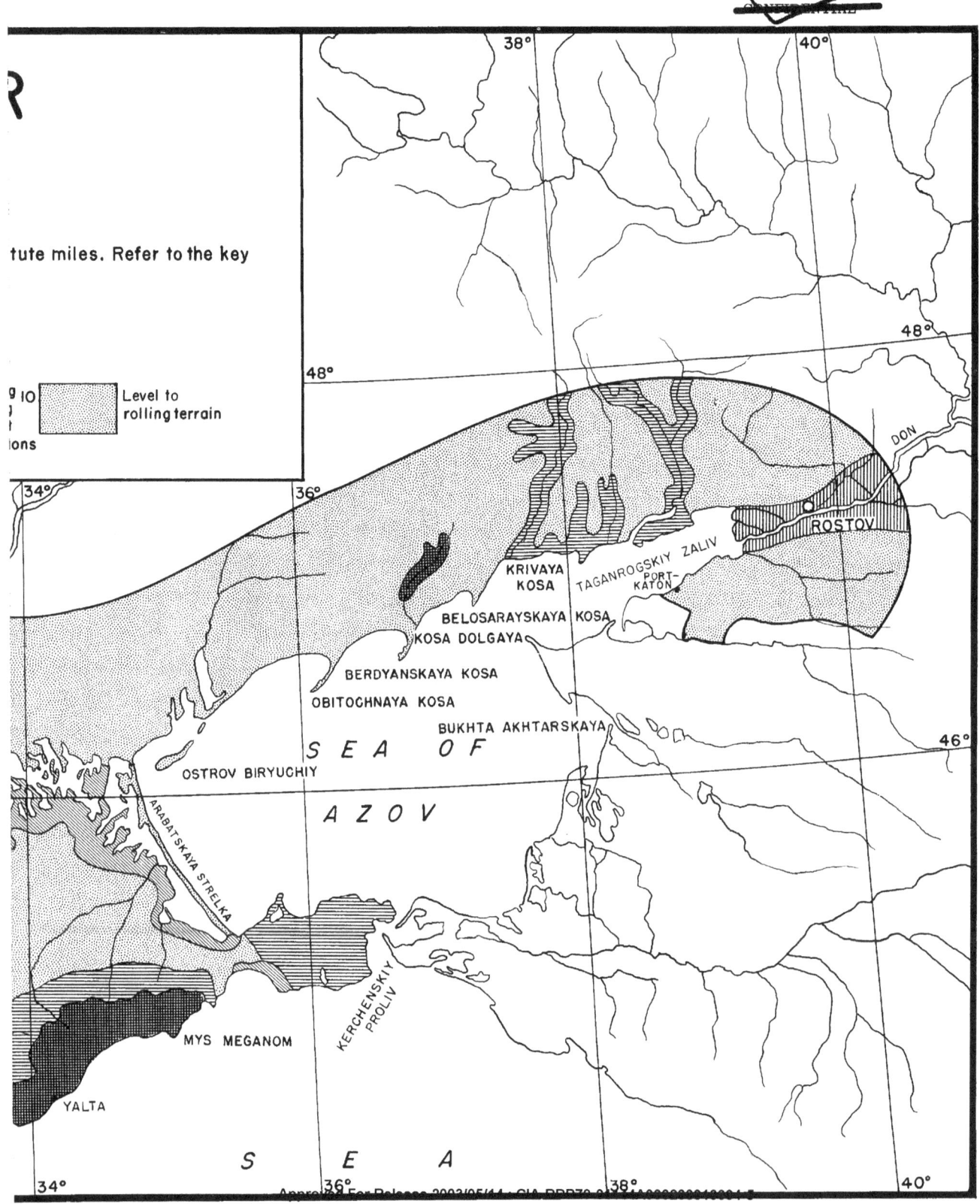

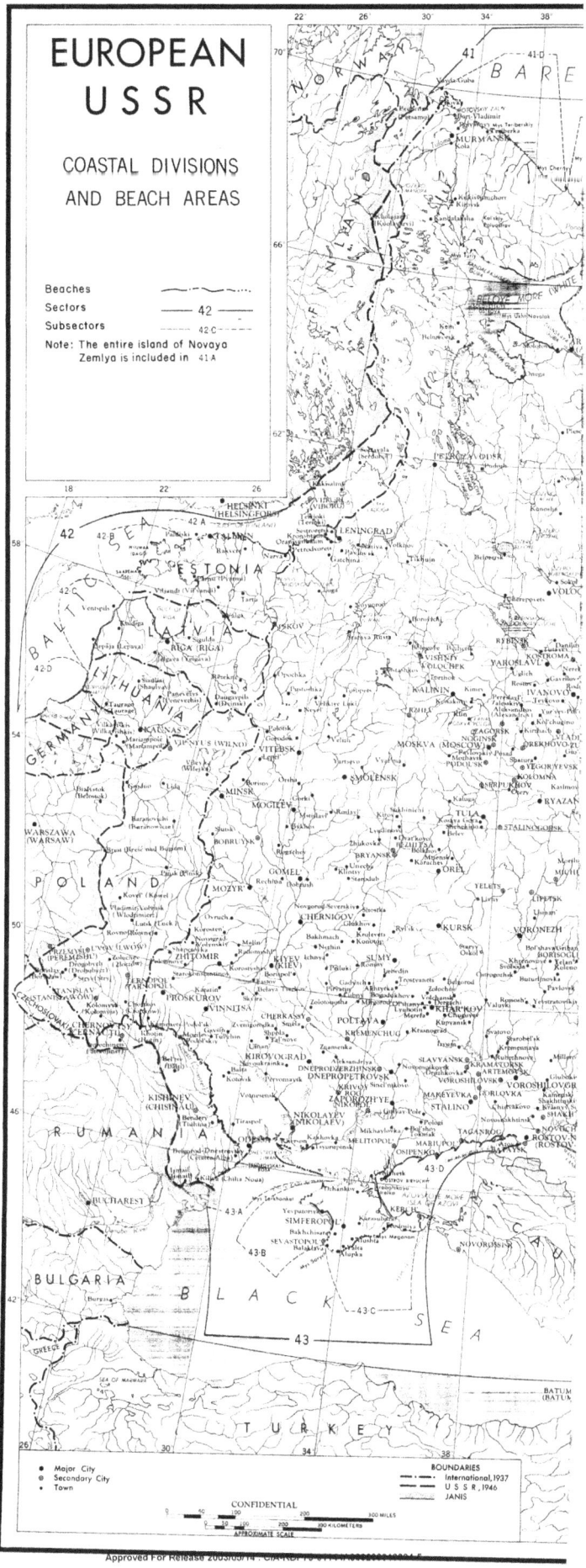

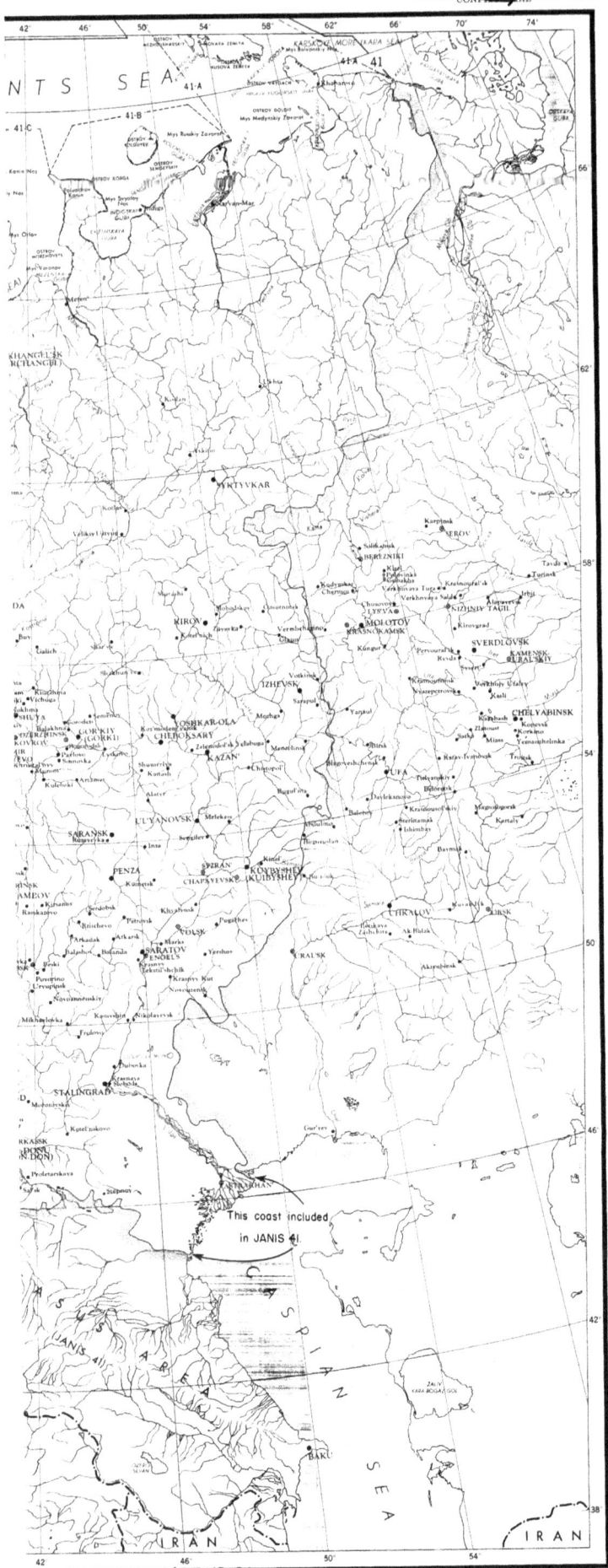

FIGURE IV-119
COASTAL DIVISIONS AND BEACH AREAS
JANIS 40

Department of State

Department of the Army

Department of the Navy

Department of the Air Force

Published by

THE CENTRAL INTELLIGENCE AGENCY

WASHINGTON, D.C.

~~Confidential~~

www.ingramcontent.com/pod-product-compliance
Lightning Source LLC
Chambersburg PA
CBHW080344170426
43194CB00014B/2679